W9-CTK-288

STUDIES IN

THOUGHT AND LANGUAGE

Edited by
J. L. COWAN

Collaborating Authors	J. L. COWAN
	RULON WELLS
	PAUL ZIFF
	ZENO VENDLER
	GEORGE MANDLER
	CHARLES OSGOOD

THE UNIVERSITY OF ARIZONA PRESS

TUCSON   ARIZONA

Note: The research reported in "The Myth of Mentalism in Linguistics," by J. L. Cowan, was largely supported by the Office of Education, U.S. Department of Health, Education and Welfare, under Contract No. OEC-4-7-068228-2872, and is therefore in the public domain.

THE UNIVERSITY OF ARIZONA PRESS

S.B.N. 8165-0189-0
L.C. No. 75-89620

Contents

Introduction

Interaction among the fields of philosophy, psychology and linguistics has intensified steadily in recent years with results in each bearing strikingly on those in each of the others. In a sense such interaction is hardly surprising. While there have been grammarians virtually since time began, it is only rather recently as such things go that either psychology or a relatively full blown linguistics has been pursued separately from the general study of "philosophy." What distinguishes the present interaction is thus perhaps not so much its novelty in a broad historical perspective as its contrast with the immediate past from which it has developed. This recent period, as opposed to both the present and the more distant past, was characterized by a relative isolation of the three fields. Perhaps a more accurate image would be that of the present feverish tangle as preceded by and the outcome of a minuet in which brief episodes of somewhat artificial and stylized interaction were but preludes to much more prolonged periods of distinct and definite separation.

Philosophy's present concern with language traces its lineage back on the one side to that concern with logic and the foundations of mathematics which developed in the late 19th and early 20th centuries, to Frege, Russell and the "logical" element in a logical positivism. This concern flows on the other side from Moore through the "linguistic analysis" or "ordinary language philosophy" of Ryle and Austin. Wittgenstein, of course, like a proper colossus, stands astride both traditions. The early indifference and even opposition of "ordinary language analysis" to sciences such as psychology and linguistics arose from several sources varying from the relatively more accidental, such as the organization of curricula at Oxford and Cambridge, to the relatively more principled, such as opposition to the "scientism" of positivism both in itself and as the official or "house" philosophy of the sciences themselves.

In no case, however, was this opposition really deeply grounded. The line from Wittgenstein's musings over depth grammar and Austin's reading of grammar books to a study such as that by Vendler in the present volume is a direct one, and it is hardly surprising that Osgood in the work here reported finds valuable suggestions in Ryle. Positivism, on the other hand, was early and loud in its avowals of affection for the sciences. Unfortunately this love, like too many others, was at first of a somewhat Procrustean variety, more interested in fitting its object or victim into a rigid bed of logical, epistemological, and metaphysical presuppositions than in accommodating itself and its furniture to the somewhat different physiogonomy the latter happened actually to possess. But this attitude too, while principled to some extent, was not sufficently so to prevent, on the part of philosophers at any rate, efforts at accommodation which began early and have continued up to and including the present volume.

The active and aggressive *non*-concern of psychologists with language had its roots in the introspectionist-structuralist origins of psychology as a separate science. Language was viewed by the pioneers in psychology as a mere outer garment of the essential thought within, a conception remnants of which are still atavistically present in the concept of encoding. The behavioristic revolution should perhaps have rectified this situation immediately. Much that is linguistic is palpably behavior and much behavior is palpably linguistic. But in part because in science, as in philosophy and for that matter in politics, revolutions are often concerned initially at least more to change the treatment of problems dealt with by predecessors than to select new problems; in part because of the behaviorists' distrust of the vast component of ordinary language they considered "mentalistic"; and in part just because psychologists quite reasonably preferred to begin with simpler things, the non-concern continued.

It was thus not until about 1950 that psychologists in seriousness and in numbers began to take up problems of language. This movement resulted in its turn in part from the feeling of psychologists that their science had matured enough to turn to the more difficult challenges language posed. In part it resulted from their being assured by taxonomic linguists that the latter had produced a very paradigm of completely successful positivistic-behavioristic science. These events thus produced on the part of psychologists exactly the right circumstances, exactly the right set, for the generative-transformation revolution in linguistics itself to burst upon them with the maximum possible effect.

Within the science of linguistics as formed by Bloomfield and his followers the dominant ideology was to shun psychology at all costs. This development occurred, ironically enough, at the very time when psychology itself was ceasing to be that sort of thing the linguists wanted to avoid. It was in good part the rejection of this constraining attitude, along with virtually everything else they thought of as offered by their immediate predecessors, that the new transformational-generative revolutionaries in linguistics reacted or over-reacted by positively insisting on their psychologism.

The contact of both psychology and linguistics with philosophy during this earlier period was brief but, for the former two at least, traumatic in the extreme. Both psychologists and linguists adopted in large numbers in the 1930s the earliest and most extreme forms of positivism-operationalism. Again with not-so-subtle irony, an essential part of this philosophy they then adopted was a distrust, and indeed a wholehearted rejection, of "philosophy." As a result of this distrust and rejection being passed along to most students of both fields as a normal part of their selection and training, both psychology and linguistics entered their present era of difficulties encumbered by rigid and outmoded philosophical positions long since abandoned by philosophers themselves—including even the survivors among those who had originally purveyed them to the psychologists and linguists. This encumbrance has in turn been too largely shared even by the rebels in both fields who, while they thought they were rejecting their inheritance wholesale, were inevitably condemned to operate without ever realizing it largely within the basic and archaic conceptual structure handed down to them by their teachers. Among the most tragic fruits of this embrace by science of a philosophy which rejects "philosophy" has been this relative lack of preparedness, even of those scientists who would rebel against that philosophy, most effectively so to do. The ultimate consequence has been rather more confusion than is absolutely necessary in a world in which even absolutely necessary confusion seems more than adequately abundant.

All this is prologue. Whatever its sources in the past, the present finds the three fields intimately intertwined. Much of the most exciting work in each has the most direct relevance for each of the others. The rapid development of important results in the area where the three fields impact on one another made inevitable the topic for this interdisciplinary presentation. It was our aim in choosing "Thought and Language" as the framework for the 1968 University of Arizona Department of Philosophy Symposium to illustrate and in so far as possible to advance this interaction. The results have abundantly fulfilled our expectations.

Each of the studies in this volume was conceived in independence of the others. The author was in each case given complete freedom to deal with the general topic in whatever manner seemed most appropriate to him in the light of his ongoing research. The material of his fellow contributors was first available to each author, with the exception of Professor Wells, on its oral presentation on the campus of the University of Arizona on February 23 and 24, 1968, to an audience consisting of students and faculty representing a variety of fields and a number of institutions. Professor Wells was prevented by illness from attending the conference but was kind enough to allow us to include his paper none the less.

Each of the other authors then had the opportunity to revise his paper in the light of the remaining papers and of the discussions which followed the formal presentations. While each availed himself of this opportunity, he was limited by pressures from the University of Arizona Press and your editor, both of whom felt that the importance of the material made it deserving of prompt publication. We have thus been able to secure in the studies here presented an excellent sample both of the diversity of approaches to our topic obtaining in 1968 and of interrelationships which are natural rather than forced.

I have placed first my own study, "The Myth of Mentalism in Linguistics," not because I think it the best, but rather for qualities which make it in some ways less satisfactory than the others. It ranges rather widely, perhaps raising more questions than it resolves. But it does have the virtue of bringing to the fore in a way that is clear, if only because over-simplified, some of the basic issues confronted by all the contributors and weaving as unifying threads through all the studies in the volume.

These core issues are those involved in the following question: what do the results emerging from the study of language imply about thought, the thinker, the methods which must or should be employed in the effort to understand thought and the thinker, and the form, significance and implications of the results of such efforts? Each of the studies in this volume may be thought of as a series of changes rung on this basic question. Each is, in effect, a different attempt to interpret it and on its interpretation to sketch a series of answers.

On the basis of the interpretation of the question I have chosen I suggest that the very real, solid and substantial results of generative or transformational linguistics have come to us clothed in a complex set of metaphors so firmly connected and so well integrated as fully to deserve to be called a "myth," and that the greater part of the challenges apparently flung by the new linguistics at traditional linguistics, at psychology and at philosophy spring not from the linguistic reality but rather from the mentalistic myth in which that reality has been conveyed to us.

Rulon Wells, in "Comprehension and Expression" reaches a somewhat similar conclusion by a rather different route. He argues that while the relation of thinking and speaking concerns psychology and linguistics, it concerns philosophy as well; that a sharp and fundamental distinction should be drawn between philosophy and science; and that when this distinction is correctly understood both some apparent problems of recent psychology and some apparent advances of recent linguistics may be seen to be apparent only. The empirical sciences use but do not study the a priori, he contends, while philosophy deals (among other things) both with the distinction between the a priori and the factual and with the criteria of the a priori. The greater part of Professor Wells' paper is accordingly devoted to a careful examination of the ways in and extent to which thought and speech might be identified or distinguished as an empirical or as an a priori matter, and, in particular, of the sorts of grounds on which identifications or distinctions of the latter sort might rest.

In "Understanding" Paul Ziff rings a further change on our question and to his version gives an affirmative answer as opposed to the relatively negative responses Wells and I were forced to give to our renderings of it. He asks, what is it to understand what is said? What is the difference then and there between two persons, one of whom understands something said while the other does not, although both have heard? The difference is not, he argues with vigor and grace, one of overt behavior actual or potential, of ability to make inferences, nor of ability to provide paraphrases. It must therefore be, he concludes, a matter of data processing of some sort, presumably involving both analysis and synthesis.

Zeno Vendler in "Say What You Think," develops still a fourth alternative and, like Ziff, is able to advance a relatively affirmative set of answers to his construction of our question. He begins by attempting to provide what J. L. Austin himself despaired of: grammatical criteria for classifying illocutionary verbs and for distinguishing them from thought verbs, or verbs of propositional attitude. He next utilizes the same machinery for making a parallel classification of verbs of the latter class. This parallel classification gives him the wherewithal to consider both the common objects of the two types of verbs and the differences in that of which they are the objects, a set of lenses through which to focus on knowledge and belief, propositions and facts, minds and bodies, thought and language.

In "Words, Lists and Categories: An Experimental View of Organized Memory" George Mandler presents both theoretical reasoning and experimental results bearing on word memory. This study has a special kind of value in broadening our address to the basic question of the book because Mandler is dealing with words in non-syntactic contexts. His work is thus a bridge between psychological studies of non-linguistic materials and those of language full blown in its normal habitats. From this position he is then able to illustrate the continuity which can obtain between recent work in specifically linguistic studies and that in behavioral studies of other kinds. To cite only one example, Mandler argues cogently that the atomistic chaining hypothesis is inadequate to explain serial learning and sequential behavior generally. But from this it follows as a corallary that well-known attempts (such as that by Chomsky) to demonstrate the inadequacy of this hypothesis for syntactic contexts do not, even in so far as successful, demonstrate differences between linguistic behavior and behavior of the other kinds, nor do they demonstrate any basic flaw in the accepted techniques of behavioral studies. If Mandler's contention is correct, such proofs will at most illustrate further limitations on one specific type of widely employed functional hypothesis.

Finally, Charles Osgood sends his construction of our question through the wringer of a sustained program of psychological research. His study, "Interpersonal Verbs and Interpersonal Behavior," is essentially a summary and interpretation of some four years of research aimed at the specification of a theoretically principled and empirically rigorous procedure for discovering the semantic features of word forms. This attempt to develop explicit procedures and to validate them, where linguists and philosphers have generally been content with intuition supplemented by vaguely programmatic promises, cannot but be extremely instructive, in its partial successes and perhaps even more so in its partial failures, to all concerned with the semantics of natural languages. As a sort of a bonus or icing on the cake, those also concerned with the history and philosophy of science will find themselves presented at the same time with a valuable narrative of science in process related by an unusually perceptive protagonist.

The chief overall impression given by the studies as a group is of how very much exciting work remains to be done if we are to attain an adequate comprehension of thought and language in their inter-relations. This is a point stressed by each author without exception. We have not by any means finished off once and for all our topic "Thought and Language." What these studies have accomplished, taken as a whole in their complex, interweaving complementation, is to indicate with increased clarity and depth where we are in this field, what more needs to be done, and how we might best go about doing it.

J. L. Cowan

Notes on the Contributors

JOSEPH L. COWAN edited this collection as Professor and Head of the Department of Philosophy at the University of Arizona. He received his B.A., M.A. and Ph. D. degrees from the University of Chicago. His publications include *Pleasure and Pain: A Study in Philosophical Psychology,* 1968; and articles, discussions and reviews on logical theory, the logic and methodology of the behavioral sciences and philosophical psychology in journals such as the *Philosophical Review, Mind, and Analysis.*

RULON WELLS' publications reflect the unusual breadth of his background in linguistics, logic and philosophy. His articles appear in such diverse journals as the *International Journal of American Linguistics, Language, Word, The Journal of Philosophy* and *The Review of Metaphysics.* He has had chapters in *Readings in Linguistics* (M. Joos, ed.), *Philosophy in Mid-Century* (R. Klibansky, ed.), *Aspects of Style* (T. A. Sebeck, ed.), *Structure of Language and Its Mathematical Aspects* (R. Jacobson, ed.), *Language and Philosophy* (S. Hook, ed.), *Studies in the Philosophy of Charles Sanders Peirce* (E. C. Moore and R. S. Robin, eds.) and *Perspectives on Peirce* (R. J. Bernstein, ed.). And he has edited with R. Brumbaugh *The Plato Manuscripts: A New Index.* Before joining the faculty of Yale University as Professor of Linguistics and Philosophy, Professor Wells taught Bengali and Japanese at the University of Pennsylvania. He has held Guggenheim, More, and American Council of Learned Societies fellowships. He graduated from the University of Utah and received his doctorate from Harvard.

PAUL ZIFF, Professor of Philosophy at the University of Illinois at Chicago Circle, after studying art at Columbia University and at the Master Institute of Arts in New York, functioned as a practicing artist for several years partially subsidized by the Solomon Guggenheim Foundation of Nonobjective Art and exhibited at several New York galleries. Returning at length to the academic life, he first took a Bachelor of Fine Arts degree at Cornell University and then entered the Sage School of Philosophy from which he received the Ph. D. He has taught at the University of Michigan, Harvard, Princeton, the University of Pennsylvania, and the University of Wisconsin, as well as at Chicago Circle. He served as a Research Assistant in the Rockefeller Foundation-sponsored project in language and symbolism at the University of Michigan and has held Rockefeller and Guggenheim fellowships. He has also served as consulting editor of *Foundations of Language* and as a consultant for Systems Development Corporation. His publications include *Semantic Analysis,* 1960; *J. M. Hanson,* 1962; *Philosophic Turnings,* 1966; and articles, discussions and reviews on aesthetics, philosophical psychology, and philosophy of language in *The Philosophical Review, Mind, Analysis* and others.

ZENO VENDLER'S career has included work as research associate for the University of Pennsylvania Department of Linguistics National Science Foundation Project in Linquistic Transformations, and teaching at Cornell University, Brooklyn College, the University of California at Berkeley, and the University of Calgary. He obtained the M.A. at Szeged, Hungary, the S.T.L. at Masstricht, Netherlands, and the Ph.D. at Harvard. His publications include *Linguistics in Philosophy,* 1967; *Adjectives and Nominalizations,* 1967; and articles, discussions and reviews on topics pertaining to linguistics and philosophy of language in journals such as *Mind, The Philosophical Review, Journal of Philosophy,* and *Foundations of Language.*

GEORGE MANDLER taught at Harvard University and the University of Toronto before becoming Professor and Chairman of the Department of Psychology and Director of the Center for Human Information Processing at the University of California, San Diego. A graduate of New York University, he received his M.A. and Ph.D. degrees from Yale. He has held research fellowships at Harvard, Yale, and the Center for Advanced Study in the Behavioral Sciences. At the time of this symposium he was editorial consultant for *Psychological Review, Canadian Journal of Psychology, Journal of Personality, Journal of Abnormal and Social Psychology, Journal of Nervous and Mental Diseases, Journal of Verbal Learning and Verbal behavior, Psychonomic Science, Journal of Experimental Child Psychology,* and *Science;* Editor of the *Perspectives in Psychology* series; and Advisory

Editor to John Wiley and Sons. His publications include *The Language of Psychology*, with W. Kessen, 1959; *Thinking: From Association to Gestalt*, with Jean Mandler, 1964; numerous chapters; and even more numerous articles and reviews in the psychological journals.

CHARLES E. OSGOOD contributes to this collection from the vantage point of Professor of Psychology and Research Professor in Communications at the University of Illinois. He graduated from Dartmouth College and received a Yale University Ph.D. He served as Director of the Institute of Communications Research at the University of Illinois for many years, and in 1965 was appointed Professor in the Center for Advanced Study at Illinois. Professor Osgood has been president of the American Psychological Association and has received that Association's Award for Distinguished Contribution to the Science of Psychology for his research into the nature and measurement of meaning. He has been a Fellow with the Social Science Research Council, a Guggenheim Fellow, and a Fellow at the Center for Advanced Study in the Behavioral Sciences. He has served as a consultant to the Air Force, the Navy, and the Arms Control and Disarmament Agency. His publications include *Method and Theory in Experimental Psychology*, 1953; *The Measurement of Meaning*, with Suci and Tannenbaum, 1957; *An Alternative to War or Surrender*, 1962; *Perspectives in Foreign Policy*, 1966; and numerous articles on psycholinguistics and the psychology of international relations.

1

The Myth of Mentalism in Linguistics

J. L. Cowan

> If you wish to learn from the theoretical physicist anything about the methods which he uses, I would give you the following piece of advice: Don't listen to his words, examine his achievements. For to the discoverer in that field, the constructions of his imagination appear so necessary and so natural that he is apt to treat them not as the creations of his thoughts but as given realities.
>
> *A. Einstein*

> As physics goes so goes linguistics.
>
> *J. L. Cowan*

Much of the excitement generated by the MIT school of linguistics has arisen from the explicit and repeated challenges apparently flung by the various members of that school in the faces of so many of the rest of us. The methods and results of the structural linguistics dominant on the continent, the British Firthian and neo-Firthian schools, and perhaps above all the taxonomic approach of pre-MIT American linguistics have all been subjected to these challenges. Nor have even such ancillary disciplines as psychology and philosophy been spared. Psychologists have repeatedly been castigated for the sterility which must inevitably result from their ignorance of the very latest, and indeed often still-unpublished, conclusions of the new linguistics. The great bulk of the apparatus of method and theory, especially in the area of learning, so painfully wrought by psychologists over the century or so prior to the publication of Chomsky's *Syntactic Structures* in 1957, and still dominating the field has thus now been called into question. The very empiricism which as a general epistemological position and as an absolutely essential element in the understanding of science has been accepted by the vast majority of Anglo-American philosophers and scientists—not, I hope, as dogma, but certainly as eminently well secured philosophically—has itself been held refuted by these new results as the challenging title of Chomosky's *Cartesian Linguistics* (1966) itself indicates.

Now the thesis of this study is fairly simple and quite straightforward. I shall argue that the very real, solid and substantial results of generative or transformational linguistics have come to us clothed in a complex set of metaphors so firmly interconnected and so well integrated as fully to deserve to be called a "myth," to be called, in fact, from its most central or core metaphors, "the myth of mentalism." I shall further contend that the greater part of the challenges of the new linguistics spring not from the actuality but from the appearance, not from linguistic reality, but from the mentalistic myth in which that reality has been conveyed to us.

Noam Chomsky initiates his *Aspects of the Theory of Syntax* with statements such as the following:

Linguistic theory is concerned primarily with an ideal speaker-listener, in a completely homogenous speech-community, who knows its language perfectly and is unaffected by such grammatically irrelevant conditions as memory limitations, distractions, shifts of attention and interest, and errors (random or characteristic) in applying his knowledge of the language in actual performance . . . . To study actual linguistic performance, we must consider the interaction of a variety of factors, of which the underlying competence of the speaker-hearer is only one. In this respect, study of language is no different from empirical investigation of other complex phenomena. We thus make a fundamental distinction between *competence* (the speaker-hearer's knowledge of his language) and *performance* (the actual use of language in concrete situations) . . . . The problem for the linguist, as well as for the child learning the language, is to determine from the data of performance the underlying system of rules that has been mastered by the speaker-hearer and that he puts to use in actual performance. Hence, in the technical sense, linguistic theory is mentalistic, since it is concerned with discovering a mental reality underlying actual behavior. Observed use of language or hypothesized dispositions to respond, habits, and so on, may provide evidence as to the nature of this mental reality, but surely cannot constitute the actual subject matter of linguistics, if this is to be a serious discipline. (1965, pp. 3-4)

That we are dealing here with a set of metaphors seems undeniable. One might be tempted to say that the validity of modern linguistics does not rest on the truth of Platonism, but even this would be misleading since even Plato's "Platonism" consists largely in the deployment of much the same metaphors equally metaphorically to comprehend much the same range of facts. There is, for example, no such ideal speaker-listener or speech community, and the much ado of recent linguistics, whatever it may be about, is most certainly not about nothing.

Now the metaphors which compose this myth of mentalism are, like most metaphors, not without their positive values. They present in a powerfully compressed and tightly organized fashion a whole mass of sloppy and initially confused facts. They have certainly played a great part in the brilliance of style, tone and direction which has characterized the MIT school. In spite of certain misleading consequences which I shall point out, the myth may even have had some heuristic value.

It is therefore with some reluctance that I turn to the tedious, pedestrian—even Philistine—task of unpacking some of these metaphors, of revealing for inspection some of the grubby facts which the beautiful myth of mentalism has served to clothe and thus to hide, of twitching the gorgeous mantle of linguistic fancy from the knobby knees of linguistic fact. It is my hope that the sacrifice of aesthetic values incurred in this painful process will be compensated for by the gain in understanding.

ENDS

Let us begin at, or at least with, the end. What is the purpose of the professional output of the linguist? For the sake of specificity, let us take the example of a grammar of English. As is usually done in such discussions, I will have syntax uppermost in mind, but my remarks will also be applicable with slight changes to phonology, to semantics, and to the broader theory in which a grammar containing these three components might have its place.

What is the purpose of such a grammar? As soon as this question is explicitly raised, the answer becomes obvious. Grammars have no purposes at all. They are not the sorts of things that could have purposes. They simply sit there on the pages of notebooks or professional journals or monographs or texts, not, certainly, content with their lot, but just as certainly not projecting directions of movement or maintenance for the future. Nor does linguistics as an institution have purposes, let alone a purpose. It is people who have purposes and both people and purposes in the plural at that. There are many different purposes which may go into the making of a grammar, and many different purposes for which a grammar, once made, may be employed.

One might, for example, want a grammar to be a scientific instrument of the greatest power and accuracy, capable of saving the appearances, of handling one or another body of data down to the finest detail. On the other hand, one might be interested primarily in a grammar as a pedagogic instrument to be used in instructing one or another group of learners of the language in question. One might be concerned, on the one hand, with the constructibility of one's grammar, aiming for something which could be arrived at in a fairly or quite mechanical way from a body of data, of one or another kind. Or one might, on the other hand, be more concerned with the fairly or quite mechanical application, or operation, of the grammar. One might be concerned with one's grammar simply as the most efficient instrument for dealing with one particular language only or even just with some part of one particular language. Or one might be concerned to observe certain general constraints such as might be imposed by taking into account such factors as supposed linguistic universals. One might be content with a synchronic grammar, or one might want to build in parameters of evolutionary change. One might want a grammar for descriptive purposes of one sort or another or again for one sort or another of prescriptive purposes. For in spite of current fads in linguistics there are no stronger reasons against prescription with respect to language than there are against prescription with respect to the movement of vehicular traffic, and probably at least as strong reasons for. Since this brief sample can be added to indefinitely, since each item is itself indefinitely subdivisible, and since an indefinite number of combinations of items and sub-items is possible, such grammatical aims are quite literally innumerable.

It is, moreover, equally obvious that the grammar most suitable for obtaining one of these ends will often not be that most suitable for attaining another. Why should we suppose, for example, that the grammar which is scientifically most precise in one or another sense will also be the instrument pedagogically most effective in one or another sense? Why should we suppose that the most efficient grammar for improving the English of Headstart pre-kindergarteners in Detroit will also be the most efficient for teaching English to Turkish businessmen with no previous exposure to the language? Why should we suppose, indeed, that the most efficient instrument for businessmen in Ankara will also be the most efficient for those in Gaziantep?

Consider only the question of generative grammar. Surely one of the great contributions of the MIT school has been the increased application to linguistics of the conceptions of rigor and precision developed by modern logic and mathematics. The operation of a truly generative grammar is to be mechanical or effective in the technical sense of logic. As Chomsky puts it, such a grammar "does not rely on the intelligence of the understanding reader . . ." (1965, p. 4) But as these terms are being used in the technical sense of logic, we have already here a sort of metaphor with respect to their ordinary acceptations. Valuable as rigor and precision and even effective or mechanical operations are in some respects and for some purposes, they are by no means a be-all or an end-all. The fact that a comparatively stupid and unimaginative computer might be programmed to operate a grammar does not necessarily help you or me to do so. Thus a college freshman, for example, might very well find more helpful an instrument which required for its application an intelligence he could muster, than he would find one which, while it did not require even this modicum of intelligence to apply, required far more intelligence than he could bring to bear in the time available to master it in the first place.

A good analogy here is logic itself. If the time of students in an introductory course in logic is taken up with presentation of the propositional calculus and a reasonably complete version of quantificational logic, the brighter among them will attain some facility in formal manipulations. But almost none of them will be able to do as good a job of the analysis of ordinary, non-formalized arguments as they would have had they been given instead a simpler and in some ways inherently less complete and adequate formal machinery, but more practice in applying it.

Very, very few are the scientific theories which more than approximate the logician's ideal of explicitness, rigor, precision and full logical articulation. Most such theories are far closer to violins and oboes in the skill required of their operators than they are like good computer programs. Even mathematics in some of its most creative episodes has fallen far short of the modern ideals of rigor, and the fact that most of the probings and many of the proofs which led to our most significant mathematical results leave much to the intelligence, insight and intuition of their readers make them defective in some respects, but at the same time more effective in others.

All this being the case it would seem inevitably to follow that there is and can be no such thing as *the* (only) correct grammar even of the English of some limited linguistic group at some specific time. And as this is so, I should like to steal a bit from Carnap on logical syntax and propose for syntax in general, and even more broadly for all linguistics, a *Principle of Tolerance:* It is not the business of linguists to set up prohibitions but to arrive at linguistic descriptions which may quite legitimately be at least as diverse and various in their characteristics as they are in their potential applications. There are no morals in linguistics.

Now what I have been saying thus far seems rather obvious to me. I hope it is equally obvious to my readers since I have refrained on the assumption that it was obvious from more than beginning to move to its support the mountain of evidence available for that task. It has been necessary to mention it, however, since it has not by any means always been uppermost in the minds of all linguists and commentators. Thus we find Katz in "Mentalism in Linguistics" telling us that "the aim of theory construction in linguistics is taken to be . . ." (1964, p. 128); Katz and Postal in *An Integrated Theory of Linguistic Descriptions* telling us that "a linguistic description of a natural language is an attempt to reveal . . ." (1964, p. 1); Chomsky in *Syntactic Structures* asserting that "Syntax is the study of the principles and processes by which sentences are constructed in particular languages. Syntactic investigation has as its goal the construction of a grammar that can be viewed as a device of some sort for producing the sentences of the language under analysis," (1957, p. 11) and in *Aspects of the Theory of Syntax,* "A grammar of the language purports to be . . ." (1965, p. 4) If my principle is accepted, then, a fair number of statements like these which actually read *"The* purpose, aim or goal of syntax, grammar, linguistic theory and so on is . . ." will have to be understood as meaning *"A* or *one* legitimate purpose, aim or goal is . . ."

I should like to suggest, moreover, that it is the very prevalence of the mentalistic myth which has for these linguists obscured the obvious. The Bloomfieldian approach, while in its over-restrictive conception of scientific theories being to some extent anti-tolerance, was basically pro-tolerance in its emphasis on the artificiality in the non-pejorative sense, that is, the artifactness, of linguistic results. When, however, one envisages grammar as somehow written on the soul or inscribed in the brain of the speaker-hearer and conceives of description as some kind of exact duplication of the object described, it is more difficult to retain the balance tolerance requires.

In the remainder of this paper I shall treat exclusively of grammars considered as scientific theories since it is only with this limitation that mentalism in linguistics has any plausibility whatsoever. It has been necessary to supply the foregoing considerations, however, because they are both intrinsically important and frequently ignored in recent discussions and because they bring out clearly the narrowness of even the greatest possible domain of mentalism in linguistics.

DATA

If, then, the linguist's output is to be considered a scientific theory as opposed, say, to a piece of pure logic or mathematics, it must be connected with, must be a means of organizing, some kind or kinds of observable data. Presumably, if our scientific theory is to be in the field of linguistics at all, these data should have something to do with language; but this still leaves a very great deal of leeway. We might, for example, limit ourselves to actual stretches of discourse—utterances spoken or written. There is and can be nothing inherently wrong with such a procedure nor with the grammars which might result from choosing it. The subscribers to the mentalistic myth will of course say that these data of performance result not from the operation of linguistic factors alone, but from these plus innumerable others which are linguistically irrelevant. But this response indicates only a difference in a choice of ranges of data and types of theory to employ in handling these data. We are perfectly free to follow such prescriptions or to reject them. Even in linguistics considered as scientific theorizing there are no morals.

But just as there is no a priori reason why we should not limit ourselves to such data, so there is no a priori reason why we should. We may also utilize, in particular, as linguists almost universally do when possible, judgments on the part of those who have learned the language as to what is or is not a grammatically acceptable sample of it. As these are the two chief types of data actually used and discussed by linguists, I shall confine myself to them, merely pointing out in passing that just as there can be no a priori ground for excluding either of these, so there can be none for excluding data of still further kinds.

A number of points must be remarked about even these two kinds of data, however. It must first be noted that there is nothing mentalistic, not to say spiritualistic, about data of the second kind, judgments of grammaticalness, any more than there is about those of the first kind. One factor leading to the failure to see this is that these judgments are often said to be "intuitive"—to express the "linguistic intuition" of their subjects. So they are and do. In one perfectly good sense of the terms 'intuition' and 'intuitive,' such statements simply mean that the judgments are not derived from any consciously articulated linguistic theory or grammar. In spite of the fact that MIT, in accord with its myth, uses the term 'performance' as a technical term for data of the first kind only, for actual samples of discourse, actually such judgments are also performances in just as good a sense of the term. They are perfectly legitimate pieces of behavior in their own right and as such are perfectly unexceptionable pieces of data for behavioral theory.

This is an extremely important point. Just as failure to grasp it led some earlier linguists to hold too low an opinion of judgmental data in theory if not in practice, so failure to grasp it has led the new linguists, in theory if not in practice, to hold too high an opinion of them. Thus Chomsky is extremely misleading, for example, in speaking of a "lower" level of success achieved by a theory which accommodates utterance data correctly and a "higher" level of success if judgmental data are also accommodated. Neither kind of data is higher or lower than the other. Neither is deeper or more superficial. Neither explains the other. Judgments of grammaticalness are not the competence which, together with other factors, produces discourse. This might be the case if we spoke by selecting from a number of possibilities offered those sentences we judge grammatical, but in general this does not seem to be the way we do proceed. Both judgments and utterances may rather be regarded, in a sense still to be explored, as different manifestations or results of competence—or, for that matter, of incompetence. Both of these kinds of data are thus, while different in kind, on the same basic level, and both are perfectly good hard data.

THEORY

A linguistic theory, then, may be regarded as a device for systematizing enormous amounts of such data, actual or potential. A generative grammar, together with a lexicon, will enable us indefinitely to produce sentences all of which will hopefully be grammatical in the sense of being consonant with the data themselves. The grammar will provide a test of grammatical sentence-hood for any proferred object. And for each grammatical sentence it will provide one or more structural descriptions which will indicate important relations between sentences and between their elements. Finally, the broader linguistic theory in which such a grammar is embedded may, in a sense still to be explored, explain or justify the grammar itself or proper parts of it.

What, then, is the cash value of speaking of such a theory as about the "competence" of an "ideal speaker-hearer?" What is actually meant by this, basically, is that linguistic theories, like other scientific theories, may with perfect propriety be regarded as having some life of their own and not merely as the slaves, let alone the creatures, of their data. Such a theory may be considered about an ideal because the language as defined by it need not, and almost inevitably will not, correspond exactly with the language as defined by the actual data. If a theory does a good job on the whole and for the most part we will not worry about a few deviations here and there. We will not be bothered by these particularly where we have or hope to have a supplementary theory or set of theories to account for them.

This is the real burden of the competence-performance distinction. Chomsky says in the quote on page 12, "To study actual linguistic performance, we must consider the interaction of a variety of factors, of which the underlying competence of the speaker-hearer is only one. In this respect, the study of language is no different from empirical investigation of other complex phenomena." (1965, p. 4) He clearly does not mean to imply by this that he has discovered a strange entity called 'competence' which works in just the way his generative grammar does in the better, purer world which is its home, but which here below is corrupted and bedeviled and turned from its mark by brute matter, necessity and chance. The fact is that we have theories, some of them rather rough and ready, some fairly complex and sophisticated like the Freudian, which we can and do use *together* with our grammar to account more or less for the actual data.

A paradigm here is mechanics, in which we might account for a movement in terms of the interaction of, say, inertial and gravitational forces. We should certainly be aware, however, that the actual movement is actually a simple smooth parabola. This in turn is "composed" of horizontal and vertical elements, not in the sense that these independently exist and are somehow even more real than their "resultant," but simply in that they are distinct elements in our equations. In employing the phrase "complex phenomena" as Chomsky does, we are not saying anything about the phenomena simply in and of and unto themselves, but merely referring to the fact that our treatment of them is accomplished through a complex theory or even a complex of theories.

"Competence" is thus not an antecedent datum which justifies one conception of grammar over others, but is rather a consequence of adopting one such conception instead of others. This choice obviously cannot therefore be justified in terms of a competence-performance distinction. The choice will rather be justified only in so far as the total complex of theories successfully copes with the actual data of performance, and it will even then be justified no further than alternative analyses which do the same job equally well.

We must recognize, then, that since neither of these two kinds of data is actually, as the myth would have it, based on, or the direct outcome of the other, conflicts or incompatibilities between them might emerge. It might very well develop that a sort of thing judged grammatical is a sort of thing never actually said, or, conversely, that a sort of thing consistently said and inexplicable by our ancillary theories as a deviation is consistently judged to be grammatically unacceptable. In actuality, as opposed to myth, we have no guarantee whatsoever against this sort of occurrence. Once the myth is abandoned, however, this sort of thing, while requiring more complexity in our theories, need bother us no more than discrepancies within each type of data, such as judgments which vary somewhat from subject to subject or from time to time.

The myth bemuses even further. To an extent the "speaker-hearer competence" metaphor conceals the full force of the "ideal" metaphor. Chomsky has noted that the characterizations of the data actually employed in linguistic practice, present as well as past, are rather rough and ready. Eliciting a judgment of grammaticalness or of ambiguity, for example, is usually not merely a matter of presenting a sentence in isolation. Instead it is common to provide a context—to tell little stories as ordinary language philosophers do. It might even be suggested, in fact, that an ungrammatical sentence is simply one such that no one has yet thought of a suitable context in which it might be employed.

Be that as it may, however, different operations of elicitation may clearly produce quite different sets of data. Chomsky of course is well aware of this but points out quite correctly that while more precise operational specifications of data elicitation may be necessary at some point in the development of linguistics, the present problem is rather a lack of theories adequate to handle the superabundance of unquestionably adequate data already available. Uninhibited by the myth, one could go even further than this and suggest that not only is it practically unnecessary further to develop operational specifications in the present absence of solid theory, but that it would be theoretically unwise to do so. One may expect that, in linguistics as in other sciences, the best procedure will be to develop data and theory reciprocally, to have the theory fit the data more or less, true, but also at least to some extent to define the data in accord with the developed theory.

Here again Chomsky's practice is superior to his description of it. His sharp distinction between grammaticalness and acceptability is clearly somewhat circular insofar as grammaticalness is defined by acceptability. What actually happens, of course, is that the linguist formulates rules based on some acceptable instances and then insists that other examples generated by these rules, but not acceptable, must be so on grounds other than grammatical ones. This slight circularity, which is obscured by the myth that grammatical rules are inscribed on the soul, would be better recognized as such. It is not, however, necessarily a vicious circularity, but, to judge from the example of other sciences which have practiced this sort of thing, may be most virtuous.

There is one further area in which what is and what is not actually contained in the "ideal" and "competence" metaphors should be spelled out. One may expect that in linguistics, as in other sciences, theories will not always be mere shorthand summaries or representations of given data as was thought, or wished, by early positivists such as Mach. One fairly trivial reason for this is that such theories will generally employ universal variables. More significant is the fact that there is no essential reason for requiring theoretical terms to be explicitly definable in terms of observable data. It is true that some kind of observational tests must be obtainable for a theory if it is to be an empirical theory at all, but it is certainly not necessary that either the theory itself or all the concepts in it be somehow reducible to any collection, even infinite, of such data. These matters have been discussed at such great length in recent years and are now so well understood and accepted by even the most empirically minded philosophers that I shall not dwell upon them further here.

What it is necessary to do here, however, is to point out that this freedom from referential function in any direct or simple sense on the part of such theoretical terms is indeed just that, a freedom from referential function. The fact that such terms do not simply denote sets of empirical observables, pieces of behavior, for example, does not mean that they must therefore denote some *other* theory-independent entity, whether a supposedly intrinsically non-empirical-non-observable entity like unconscious mental states or a simply not-yet-intelligibly-observable-in-these-terms entity like brain states. To suppose that such terms must have such a reference is to accept again that primitive, Neanderthal theory of meaning as theory-independent reference on which the errors of the early positivists, behaviorists, *et al.* were themselves exactly based. To work essentially and well in a perfectly good empirical theory, neither the expression 'psi function' nor the expression 'grammatical transformation' need designate an independently specifiable kind of entity—a bit spooky and inaccessible perhaps, but an entity still.

Linguists, I must add, are by no means alone in misleading others, if not themselves, in these respects. A psychological theory such as operant conditioning, which directly and relatively simply connects events outside the organism with behavior, is called in a quite proper technical sense an "empty organism" theory. Thus when we find it necessary to complicate the simple connection between externals and behavior we may perhaps be said, in the technical sense, no longer to have an empty organism theory. But it is essential to realize that this technical sense is by no means the ordinary sense.

The emptiest organism of empty organism theory was already filled with blood and bone and nervous tissue. We do not by modifying our psychological theories fill it any fuller. To complicate a theory is not to populate an organism.

These, then, I should like to suggest, are the main and multifarious points meant and not meant literally by the mentalistic metaphor. Perhaps the central fact about which we should now be clear is this: There is nothing whatsoever in linguistic practice which should lead us to believe that the internal structure and operation of a grammar is in any way identical with or a duplication of the internal structure or operation of a mind or a brain. A grammar represents, ideally, the output of the speaker-hearer-judge. Whether or not it also represents that which actually puts out that output is quite another question, and a question linguistics itself gives us no means even of formulating in intelligibly adequate detail, still less of answering. The new linguists iterate and reiterate that they are trying to represent the knowledge of the speaker-hearer, what he knows. This is perfectly true. But it does not mean that they are representing what is inside his head. What the speaker-hearer knows is the language. To say that linguists are representing what the speaker-hearer knows is therefore no more than a picturesque way of saying that they are representing the language. One might as well say that astronomy is mentalistic since it represents what the ideal star-gazer knows, or, to take a somewhat more precise analogy, that mechanics is mentalistic since what the physicist is trying to represent is what we all learn when we learn to walk.

PERFORMANCE

Now that Chomsky is himself far more in control of and far less controlled by his metaphors than are many others is quite clear. Thus he tells us clearly and well in *Aspects* that:

To avoid what has been a continuing misunderstanding, it is perhaps worthwhile to reiterate that a generative grammar is not a model for a speaker or a hearer. It attempts to characterize in the most neutral possible terms the knowledge of the language that provides the basis for actual use of language by a speaker-hearer. When we speak of a grammar as generating a sentence with a certain structural description, we mean simply that the grammar assigns this structural description to the sentence. When we say that a sentence has a certain derivation with respect to a particular generative grammar, we say nothing about how the speaker or hearer might proceed, in some practical or efficient way, to construct such a derivation. These questions belong to the theory of language use—the theory of performance. No doubt, a reasonable model of language use will incorporate, as a basic component, the generative grammar that expresses the speaker-hearer's knowledge of the language; but this generative grammar does not, in itself, prescribe the character or functioning of the perceptual model or model of speech production. (1965, p. 9)

What Chomsky is asserting here would seem to be in fundamental agreement with Bloomfield's own position as expressed in statements such as the following:

We can describe the peculiarity of these plurals [*knives, mouths,* and *houses*] by saying that the final [f, θ, s] of the underlying singular is replaced by [v, ð, z] before the bound form is added. The word 'before' in this statement means that the alternant of the bound form is the one appropriate to the substituted sound, thus, the plural of knife adds not [-s], but [-z]: 'first' the [-f] is replaced by [-v], and 'then' the appropriate alternant [-z] is added. The terms 'before', 'after', 'first', 'then', and so on, in such statements, tell the *descriptive order*. The actual sequence of constituents, and their structural order . . . are a part of the language, but the descriptive order of the grammatical features is a fiction and results simply from our method of describing the forms; it goes without saying, for instance, that the speaker who says *knives,* does not 'first' replace [f] by [v] and 'then' add [-z], but merely utters a form (*knives*) which in certain features differs from a certain other form (namely, *knife*). (1933, p. 213)

But that this position, apparently shared by Chomsky and Bloomfield, is not universally understood or accepted, is clear from the fact, for example, that Katz in his "Mentalism in Linguistics" bitterly criticizes exactly this quotation from Bloomfield, and provides himself such statements as the following:

To explain how speakers are able to communicate in their language, the mentalist hypothesizes that, underlying the speaker's ability to communicate, there is a highly complex mechanism which is essentially the same as that underlying the linguistic ability of other speakers. He thus views the process of linguistic communication as one in which such mechanisms operate to encode and decode verbal messages. (1964, p. 128)

This "encoding-decoding" bit, by the way, leads me to characterize this as the "secret agent" theory of language. Katz continues:

The aim of theory construction in linguistics is taken to be the formulation of a theory that reveals the structure of this mechanism and explains the facts of linguistic communication by showing them to be behavioral consequences of the operation of a mechanism with just the structure that the formulated theory attributes to it. (1964, p. 128)

Outlining a description of speech production and recognition which exactly parallels the structure of a generative grammar Katz then informs us that:

Within the framework of the above model of linguistic communication, every aspect of the mentalistic theory involves psychological reality. The linguistic description and the procedures of sentence production and recognition must correspond to independent mechanisms in the brain. Componential distinctions between the syntactic, phonological and semantic components must rest on relevant differences between three neural sub-mechanisms of the mechanism which stores the linguistic description. The rules of each component must have their psychological reality in the input-output operations of the computing machinery of this mechanism. The ordering rules within a component must, contrary to the claims of Bloomfield and many others, have its psychological reality in those features of this computing machinery which group such input-output operations and make the performance of operations in one group a precondition for those in another to be performed. (1964, p. 133)

It is therefore clear that in unpacking Chomsky's metaphors as I have been attempting to do, one is working against not only potential, but also quite actual, misunderstandings. A generative grammar is not, *per se*, a model of the mind, a model of thinking or even a model of speaking. It is perfectly true that insofar as such a grammar is linguistically adequate it will, as Chomsky notes, be reasonable to "incorporate it into" any such model proposed. If it is the production of more or less English sentences in which we are interested, then it will be reasonable to consider the best available characterization of English sentences. But it is essential to realize that such "incorporation" is needed only as a characterization of output and not as a characterization of outputter. It tells us what a "language production device" has to come up with, but not how it has to go about or does in fact go about doing it.

ACQUISITION

Chomsky is, of course, as the last quotation from him indicates, aware that this point has been misunderstood. He has even suggested that the term 'generative' as characterizing grammars of the sort in which he is interested might be abandoned in an effort to avoid such misunderstandings. I should like to suggest that it is not this particular term which is at fault but the whole series of metaphors which compose the mentalistic myth in which generative grammars have been enshrouded and the mists of which I have been endeavoring in this paper to penetrate. The value of the contribution to understanding which the abandonment of this mythology would make is perhaps indicated above all by the fact that while, as should now be quite pellucidly clear, it is very difficult to tell what in Chomsky is intended literally and what metaphorically, on turning from the question of performance to that of acquisition even Chomsky himself would seem to have been misled by his own myth. The same confusions of grammar with performatory model and knowing how with knowing that and still other and new confusions affect Chomsky's remarks about the "innateness" of language capacities and "Cartesian Linguistics." Chomsky's use of terms such as 'innate-ideas,' 'rationalism,' 'empiricism,' 'induction,' and 'behaviorism' is, briefly, as idiosyncratic, as metaphorical, as is his use of the key terms already considered above. In the central senses usually given to these terms Chomsky is himself not a believer in innate ideas, but is an empiricist, an inductivist, and even a behaviorist. Let us begin with behaviorism.

BEHAVIORISM

The term 'behaviorism' had already from the time of its inception and thus well before the generative grammarians came along, been applied in a manner sufficiently imprecise as quite effectively to function as a source of confusion of things in themselves quite distinct. Chomsky and his followers are thus, even if guilty as charged, by no means the sole or original culprits in this regard. One sense of 'behaviorism' which might be clarified out of this historical confusion is that criticized above as based on a primitive conception of meaning. Behaviorists in this sense, believing that terms to be meaningful must designate entities of some sort, and wishing to escape "mental" entities, were compelled to adopt the view that psychological terms necessarily designate, function as names for, chunks of behavior.

In this sense of the term Chomsky is clearly not a behaviorist. It is, in fact, at least partly to signalize his rejection of just this sort of doctrine, his recognition that theoretical terms in linguistics need not designate pieces of behavior, that he has employed the term 'mentalism.' Now this usage is, as argued above, misleading. The behaviorism-mentalism dichotomy is valid only if the theory of meaning behind it is correct. Thus to reject "behaviorism" in this sense on the very good grounds Chomsky does—the grounds that not all psychological or linguistic terms do designate behaviors—is, as I have already indicated, to embrace "mentalism" only in a most unusually etherial sense of that term. It is true nevertheless that from behaviorism in this sense Chomsky, and generative grammarians generally, are free of all taint.

But this is, after all, a definitely old fashioned and distinctly outmoded sense of 'behaviorism.' The doctrine which most contemporary psychologists who consider themselves behaviorists designate by that term is quite a different one. It is, moreover, a doctrine to which Chomsky himself has given an excellent formulation, which he has explicitly recognized his holding in common with the most radical of the behaviorists such as B. F. Skinner, and to which he has, in fact, avowed an inability to conceive any alternative.

Putting it differently, anyone who sets himself the problem of analyzing the causation of behavior will (in the absence of independent neurophysiological evidence) concern himself with the only data available, namely the record of inputs to the organism and the organism's present response, and will try to describe the functions specifying the response in terms of the history of inputs. This is nothing more than the definition of his problem. There are no possible grounds for argument here, if one accepts the problem as legitimate, though

Skinner has often advanced and defended this definition of a problem as if it were a thesis which other investigators reject. (1959, p. 27)

The only change one might suggest here might be in the phrase "inputs to the organism." As Chomsky himself later points out, the problem of determining just what aspects of the environment do in fact constitute inputs or stimuli is itself one of the key problems the investigator must solve. It might thus be better to frame the program somewhat more neutrally as simply one of finding functions connecting features of the organism's past and present environment with its behavior. With this slight modification, however, Chomsky's statement could hardly be improved upon as a formulation of the program of behaviorism in the currently most generally accepted sense of that term. I would tend to agree with Chomsky that any alternative to this program is, in a sense, inconceivable. But it does not follow from this that those who, like Skinner, have argued for it were therefore wasting their time in so doing. It is also in a sense inconceivable that one could trisect an angle with straight edge and compass. But the number of people who have tried makes proof of its inconceivability very helpful indeed. The number of Cartesian linguists who have thought they could provide some alternative to the behavioristic program is likewise sufficient to make proof of the inconceivability of such alternatives helpful as well.

The "behaviorism" Chomsky rejects, then, and the "mentalism" to which he opposes it must both be seen as simply subdomains within behaviorism in this broader and more basic sense. The above quotation continues:

The differences that arise between those who affirm and those who deny the importance of the specific 'contribution of the organism' to learning and performance concern the particular character and complexity of this function, and the kinds of observation and research necessary for arriving at a precise specification of it. If the contribution of the organism is complex, the only hope of predicting behavior even in a gross way will be through a very indirect program of research that begins by studying the detailed character of the behavior itself and the particular capacities of the organism involved. (1959, p. 27)

Here the phrase "importance of the specific contribution of the organism" may, as Chomsky's use of scare quotes indicates, mislead. Sticks and stones do not behave at all well in Skinner boxes. The "contribution of the organism" is in every case essential, and it is difficult to get more importance than that. What Chomsky's "mentalism" amounts to in this context, then, is simply the hypothesis that the functions connecting verbal behavior with environmental factors will in most cases be complex, may differ from any involving solely non-verbal or at least non-human behavior, and, presuming that 'organism' means organism rather than species, may even vary significantly from individual to individual.

Even this is not sufficiently precise. Those, and there would seem to be many, who think that, in the review from which these quotations have been taken or elsewhere, Chomsky has shown a Skinnerian type of conceptual framework of stimulus, response, reinforcement and the rest to be somehow inadequate in principle to cope with verbal behavior, have been grossly unfair to Chomsky as well as to Skinner. Such people have simply not read Chomsky carefully enough to do justice to the care, precision, rigor and avoidance of hyperbolic claims his actual argument displays.

What Chomsky has pointed out, and correctly so, is the vast extent of our ignorance of the variables and functions actually involved in verbal behavior: "...how little is really known about this remarkably complex phenomenon."(1959, p. 28) His entire case against Skinner consists of pointing out that this factual ignorance is not alleviated in the slightest simply by the introduction into it of a new conceptual structure. The only thing which could remedy this ignorance is actual empirical studies which neither Skinner nor anyone else has yet sufficiently provided. In this sense, then, Skinner's *Verbal Behavior* does nothing to explain verbal behavior, and may even, insofar as it masks our actual ignorance in an elaborate display of apparently scientific terminology, obstruct understanding.

Even this is probably not being quite fair. We do not know very much about the factors and functions involved in verbal behavior. Skinner does not provide us with this knowledge. In this sense his key concepts are indeed empty. We can talk of stimuli and responses and contigencies of reinforcement, but in the realm of verbal behavior by human beings, as opposed to that of bar pressing behavior by rats, we do not yet have enough knowledge to tell us to what specifically these terms are to be applied. In this sense Chomsky is quite correct in calling Skinner's employment of these terms "metaphorical" and at best merely equivalent to our ordinary terminology. Yet there is another sense in which the two terminologies are not equivalent. The real advantage of the Skinnerian formulations is just exactly that their nakedness is so very obvious; that, unlike our ordinary formulations, they make it so very clear that and what we do not know. They succeed in this way because their form, as opposed to that of our ordinary locutions, makes so very easy their contrast with other situations, such as bar pressing by rats, in which we do have a fairly good knowledge of what is going on.

We can be sure in any event that the knowledge of verbal behavior we lack is not going to be supplied simply by the adoption of a "mentalistic" vocabularly anymore than simply by the adoption of a "non-mentalistic" one, and that the Skinnerian terminology at least frees us from certain temptations inherent in "mentalistic" alternatives. One example, only. In this same review Chomsky points out that one might readily form an hypothesis as to how the development of the gaping response of a nestling thrush developed through differential reinforcement but that there is good evidence that these responses actually develop simply through genetically determined maturation. Stressing that the development of a child's imitating new words is in many respects parallel to that of the thrush's behavior, Chomsky suggests that it, too, could conceivably be largely simply a matter of maturation. "To the extent that this is true," Chomsky concludes, "an account of the development and causation that fails to consider the structure of the organism will provide no understanding of the real processes involved." (1959, pp. 43-44)

But to say that the development either of gaping or of imitative behavior is a product simply of maturation is not to say anything at all about the structure of bird or child except in the completely trivial sense that the structure is such as to mature in this way. The study which would lead to such a conclusion is not an anatomical but rather a behavioral one. To make such statements about the development of behavior through maturation is rather to relate the behavior to a set of environmental conditions of which its development is or is not a function—exactly the sort of question Chomsky characterized in the above quotation as the only kind conceivable.

The "behaviorism-mentalism" controversy on which the results of modern linguistics bear, then, is not actually a behaviorism-mentalism controversy at all. It is rather simply one over the kind and complexity of functions required to connect environmental occurrences with behavior. It is thus a controversy *within* Stimulus-Response theory in the broad and basic sense rather than between S-R theory and some (to Chomsky inconceivable) alternative. As such it will of course require empirical research rather than merely conceptual analysis to resolve. This does not mean that the issue is unimportant for psychology and for linguistics, but it does mean that it is completely lacking in the kind of general, basic or "philosophical" importance that a genuine behaviorism-mentalism controversy would possess.

In consideration of all of these facts one can hardly conclude other than that statements to the effect that the results of modern linguistics demonstrate a "mentalism" and are inconsistent with "behaviorism" are somewhat over-simplified at best. But so is it also with "rationalism," "empiricism," "innate ideas" and "induction."

RATIONALISM AND INNATE IDEAS

The definitive issue between rationlists and empiricists over innate ideas and induction has been a matter not of acquisition or origin at all, but rather of validity. "Nothing in the mind that was not first in the senses" has actually functioned basically not as a bastard psychological hypothesis but rather as an attempt to assure empirical applicability and validation. Neither classical nor modern empiricism has held that either concepts or, *a fortiori*, judgements, laws and theories are somehow simply imposed upon us by objects in the world. Even raw sensations themselves have been universally recognized as arising from at least the interaction between objects and ourselves and as possessing characteristics and structurings dependent at least in part upon us and our characteristics and structurings. Both concepts and theories are widely regarded as being, in Einstein's splendid, if less than completely informative phrase "free creations of the human mind." The distinctive position of the empiricist consists solely in insisting that in so far as concepts and theories are to be regarded as being empirical, as being about the world, so far must they be tested for the adequacy with which they do in fact cope with the data, do in fact succeed in organizing our experience.

When Chomsky says such things as, of the child, that "His knowledge of the language, as this is determined by his internalized grammar, goes far beyond the presented primary linguistic data and is in no sense an 'inductive generalization' from these data," (1965, p. 33) he is apparently using the term 'induction' for what is ordinarily called 'complete induction' or 'induction by simple enumeration,' that is, induction in which the "sample" is the entire reference class. This is, of course, one sense of 'induction,' but a limited, derivative and trivial sense indeed. By 'induction' in general and without qualification is meant just exactly such an extension beyond the given data of an hypothesis which works for them. If it were not for this extension there would be no problem at all to the famous "problem of induction."

More significantly, however, much of what Chomsky has to say about "inductivist, empiricist theories of language" even in the normal sense of 'induction' is quite correct. These are not good, or at least not complete, theories of language acquisition. What Chomsky's idiosyncratic usage conceals is that the reason for this is not that they are bad theories of language acquisition, but rather that they are not really complete theories of language acquisition at all. Because the issue is one of validation rather than of origin, "induction" is at best a very partial explanation of the acquisition of anything. To say that something, linguistic or otherwise, has been learned by induction is to say that concepts and hypotheses have been tested by experience, but it is to say nothing whatsoever about how these concepts and hypotheses have been developed in the first place.

Interpreted literally, Chomsky is simply talking nonsense in statements such as the following:

In general, then, it seems to me correct to say that empiricist theories about language acquisition are refutable whenever they are clear, and that further empiricist speculations have been quite empty and uninformative. On the other hand, the rationalist approach exemplified by recent work in the theory of transformational grammar seems to have proved fairly productive, to be fully in accord with what is known about language, and to offer at least some hope of providing a hypothesis about the intrinsic structure of a language acquisition system that will meet the condition of adequacy-in-principle and do so in a sufficiently narrow and interesting way so that the question of feasibility can, for the first time, be seriously raised. (1965, pp. 54-55)

In the normal acceptation of the terms there is and can be no such thing as an "empiricist theory of language acquisition" unless by this one means a theory which has been or is to be tested empirically. Nor can there be a competing "rationalist" theory unless by this one means a theory deduced by pure reason from some kind of a priori principles and thus neither requiring nor permitting any empirical check. On this interpretation the type of theory Chomsky proposes would be doubly empircal and not in the slightest way rationalist. Such theories would themselves be perfectly good empirical theories, and the procedure they envisage the learning child going through, involving as it does rejection, on the basis of experience, of grammars of languages other than that he is learning, would be a perfectly good empirical procedure.

What Chomsky actually means by such statements, on the other hand, is quite well taken if somewhat less exciting than what he says. Unless we regard as an acquisition theory the methods developed by taxonomic linguistics for relatively mechanically developing grammars from given bodies of data, methods which were certainly never intended to be taken as such a theory and which function rather unhappily when thrust willy-nilly into that role, there simply are no detailed theories of language acquisition. Competing theories cannot, therefore, serve as any kind of ground for resisting the development of theories involving inherent and species-specific mechanisms nor can they serve as a ground for rejecting such theories should they be developed—providing the theories meet the empirical tests.

The only objection one could raise to this is to suggest that it is too good to be limited to linguistic behavior but could be applied to any or all of the vast range of behaviors more or less specific to the human species. There is nothing in any of this which implies, as MIT seems sometimes to infer, a sharp distinction between such other behaviors and the linguistic.

Nor does any of this pertain particularly to generative grammars. The basic point Chomsky seems to overlook in his discussion of acquisition is that since our generative grammars do not give us models or theories of performance, they do not actually give us models or theories of what is acquired. The competence metaphor is undoubtedly one of the factors causing confusion here. Chomsky's idiosyncratic use of the term 'competence' makes it harder to see that competence in the ordinary sense would be competence to do, that is, to perform. Our generative grammars characterize what is put out but not the way in which it is put out, although it is actually the latter which is actually acquired.

Thus Chomsky tells us, you will recall, in the passage quoted on p. 12 that "The problem for the linguist, as well as for the child learning the language, is to determine from the data of performance the underlying system of rules that has been mastered by the speaker-hearer and that he puts to use in actual performance." (1965, p. 4)

But once again this cannot be taken literally. The "speaker-hearer" to the products of whose performance our generative grammars would actually apply does not exist, it is to be recalled. The phrase "that he puts to use" would imply that our generative grammar does indeed provide us with a theory of production, of how, or at least partly how, speakers actually go about producing sentences. But, as we have seen and as we have seen that Chomsky has seen, this is not at all the case. The problem for the linguist, then, is not at all that of determining *the* system of rules, but rather *a* system of rules more or less adequate to the data and to such other constraints as simplicity, consistency, non-redundancy, effectiveness and so on which we may impose on them. The problem for the child is still less one of discovering *the* rules; it is rather one of learning to come up with—in whatever way he can—linguistic behavior more or less like that of the rest of us.

This identification of the learning child and the working linguist which looms so large in Chomsky's exposition, although hardly in the substantive portions of his work, is thus surely whimsical at best. Such an identification, in addition to overlooking the non-congruence I have emphasized between grammar and performance, also overlooks the very substantial differences between knowing how and knowing that, differences again exactly comparable to those between learning to walk or to catch a ball, on the one hand, and formulating theorems of mechanics on the other. Let me cite only one example of the sort of confusions to which such an identification leads. Chomsky as a particularly ingenious and imaginative linguist usually finds available to him a multiplicity of grammatical hypotheses, each of which is compatible with any given finite body of linguistic data. He therefore needs principles of selection or justification for choosing among these. He therefore assumes that the child learning the language must have similar principles of selection. But clearly (even ignoring for the moment the differences between grammar and performance and between what one might call a "physical" as opposed to an "intellectual" performance) for the child, as opposed to the linguist, anything that will do the job is actually quite adequate. The child has merely to speak and understand as best he can. He does not have to defend to his colleagues or even to himself the "principles" by which he does so.

Generative grammars, insofar as they provide better characterizations of languages than do alternative types of grammars, will certainly be relevant to theories or models of language acquisition. But they cannot themselves provide or directly contribute to such models any more than, and in fact even less than, they can provide models of performance.

EXPLANATION

These considerations lead naturally to the question of explanation in linguistics. As far as I am aware, the only ground ever explicitly offered for taking the mentalistic myth literally is that unless we do so linguistic results are not and cannot be explained. It is therefore essential for an evaluation of literal linguistic mentalism to consider this aspect at least briefly.

Chomsky has on occasion distinguished three "levels of success" for grammatical description. The first and lowest of these he has characterized as merely presenting correctly the data of performance in his sense of that term. The second and higher level is supposedly achieved when a correct account is given of linguistic intuition. The third and highest or explanatory level is reached when a basis is found for selecting a grammar that achieves the second level over alternatives which do not (1964, pp. 62-79). Now I have already noted that this way of describing the distinction between "levels" one and two is most misleading. Chomsky, in fact, himself abandons it in the later *Aspects*, there distinguishing only between descriptive and explanatory adequacy (1965, pp. 24-27). In actuality, however, the original three-fold distinction which Chomsky had in mind, while not at all what he described, is, as it emerges from his practice, an entirely reasonable one.

Consider an example Chomsky gives us from phonology. There is an English word 'pick' but there is not or at least was not until it was introduced by R. M. Hare, a word /blik/ nor is there a word /ftik/. The first level of adequacy would then be attained by an English grammar that contained a lexical rule introducing /pik/ but not /blik/ or /ftik/. The second level of adequacy would be attained by a grammar that contained in addition a general rule excluding /ftik/ but not /blik/. The third level would provide a ground for including this latter rule but excluding the factually correct "rule" that in the context #b__ik#, a liquid is necessarily /r/. What Chomsky actually has in mind, in short, is a simple list as opposed to a neat calculus as opposed in its turn to a broader theory containing this. But there is nothing mentalistic in all this: /blik/ is the *sort* of thing that does occur in English even though it itself specifically may not, and not only does /ftik/ not occur, but nothing else of that *kind* does either. It is just this sort of occurrence and non-occurrence of *kinds* in the objective data which even our third level of theory needs to attain—and not some obscure occurrence or structure in the nethermost regions of the soul.

Consider an example from syntax. Take an array of English sentences and non-sentences such as the following which illustrate similarities and differences in functioning between the word 'find' and the word 'be': ('John found the book' – 'John was a farmer'), ('the book was found by John' – *'a farmer was been by John'), and so on. One could then merely list these differences, thus attaining the first level of adequacy. Chomsky can and does, however, give five simple rules from which all the sentences and none of the non-sentences can be generated, thus attaining the second level of adequacy. These rules, moreover, can be justified or explained, thus attaining the third level of adequacy, by the entirely practicable proof that they would have to be complicated considerably before they *would* generate the non-sentences.

This latter type of explanation or justification is the kind most frequently used in actual linguistic practice. Chomsky's preferred method of explanation, that in terms of linguistic universals, is not often actually employed, if only because if there actually are any linguistic universals, we know very little of them at the present time. The essential thing to see here, however, is that neither of these kinds of explanations involves anything whatsoever that is mentalistic. The one is largely based upon formal logical characteristics, the other upon more specific regularities within broader regularities. Explanation of grammars as it occurs in actual linguistic practice, then, like grammars themselves owes nothing whatsoever to the myth of mentalism.

Still in all, one may think—and some like Katz have not only thought but said—such "explanations" in terms of mere brute regularities or formal characteristics of rules are not really explanations at all, but mere descriptions. In order really to explain grammatical results, it is essential to hypothesize that they actually duplicate, are actually isomorphic to, actual neural structures in the brains of actual speaker-hearers. Without this hypothesis there is a gap in the chain of causality and thus in our explanations. But the response to this is obvious and decisive. One does not explain by hypothesizing. If physiologists were to discover that and how neurological mechanisms produced speech acts, whatever this might mean, then they might be said, in one sense at least, to have explained these. But one certainly does not explain or justify grammatical rules simply by supposing, as I for one certainly should, that speaker-hearer performances might have some sort of physiological basis, nor yet by supposing that this basis might somehow be precisely isomorphic to the grammar explained—just or even approximately how being left quite obscure.

To say this is not to say, on the other hand, that theoretical constructs in linguistics or elsewhere are "fictions." Those who have used this term were themselves speaking metaphorically. No one has ever actually thought that the atom has *just* the status of Mr. Pickwick or Hamlet. To be a theoretical "entity" in a successful scientific theory is as different from being a character in a successful play or novel as the criteria for success are different in the two cases. Nor, since the use of such theories is itself a part of what we mean by "explanation," should we argue that such a theory cannot "really explain" unless its theoretical terms function more or less as do the names of cats or dogs.

Now of course nothing I have been saying is intended to or should suggest that one could not use a grammar as the basis for formulating psychological or perhaps even physiological hypotheses. One could also use the crossword puzzle in last Sunday's *Times* as such a basis for that matter. But it is important to realize that formulating such an hypothesis from a grammar is by no means an easy task. Grammars, even generative grammars, are not ready-made psychological, and still less, neurological hypotheses, the myth of mentalism notwithstanding. This should be quite clear to anyone who has more than glanced at the various attempts to test the "psychological reality" of various grammatical elements and the numerous and profound difficulties encountered in these attempts. The even more formidable difficulties involved in deriving from grammars anything like meaningful neurological hypotheses have not even been approached, except perhaps by those philosophers who have struggled with the mind-brain identity theory and in doing so come up with far more problems than solutions.

It is perhaps more important to realize that even if such psychological or neurological hypotheses could be formulated, they would be psychological or neurological hypotheses and not linguistic ones. Suppose we are playing the parlor game of "John is. . . ." This game consists of trying to think of and state as many characteristics of John as possible. The player whose turn it is but can't think of another characteristic of John loses. We have been at it for half an hour now and are running out of ideas. "John is six feet tall," I say. "John is eager to please," you retort. "John is . . ." I pause searching, and then it comes: "easy to please," I conclude. Suppose now, as seems quite reasonable, that what I have actually thought is just exactly what I have actually said, that in my thought "John" is the subject and "easy to please" is as fully a predicate, a characteristic of John, as is "eager to please." Is this to be considered any kind of evidence at all against Chomsky's assertion that while 'John' in 'John is eager to please' is the logical subject of 'please,' 'John' in 'John is easy to please' is the direct object?

Chomsky's statement is a grammatical one which must comprehend such factors as that 'John is easy to please' is approximately equivalent to 'It is easy to please John' while 'John is eager to please' is scarcely so to 'It is eager to please John.' But in my game I, as opposed to Chomsky in his, need not have thought of any of this; it need never have entered my mind. So too with the fact cheerfully cited by Chomsky himself that in such expressions as 'This is the cat that caught the rat that stole the cheese,' the intonation breaks are ordinarily inserted in the "wrong" places. That such expressions are not divided in speech and thought in the way Chomsky or any other reasonable grammarian would divide them cannot by any stretch of the imagination be taken as evidence against the adequacy of Chomsky's grammatical formulations. The only casualty of such facts is the myth of mentalism.

L'ENVOI

The contributions of MIT linguistics when shorn of myth can be seen to accord quite precisely with those conceptions of science formulated, discussed, understood and accepted by the vast majority of contemporary empirically minded philosophers of science. As such these contributions constitute not a challenge but a confirmation. For the psychologist and the philosopher of mind these contributions are of interest in just the way any accurate grammar is—as a type of characterization of certain types of behavior. Insofar as generative grammars are more accurate representations of these phenomena than are alternative formulations, they will presumably be that much more interesting. But here again these linguistic theories themselves do not and cannot constitute a challenge. For they are not themselves psychological theories and still less philosophies of mind. Linguistic theory, however high-powered, is still just linguistic theory, and the constructions of imagination wrought by grammarians, however necessary and natural they may appear to their discoverers, are not given realities mental or physical but constructions of the imagination still.

REFERENCES

Bloomfield, L., 1933. *Language.* New York: Holt, Rinehart, and Winston, Inc.

Chomsky, N., 1957. *Syntactic Structures.* The Hague: Mouton.

Chomsky, N., 1959. "Review of Skinner's Verbal Behavior," *Language, 35,* pp. 26-58. Reprinted in *The Structure of Language: Readings in the Philosophy of Language,* ed. J. A. Fodor and J. J. Katz. Englewood Cliffs, N.J.: Prentice-Hall, Inc., 1964.

Chomsky, N., 1964. "Current Issues in Linguistic Theory," in Katz and Fodor above. A revised and expanded version of a report presented to the session: *The Logical Basis of Linguistic Theory,* Ninth International Congress of Linguists (Cambridge, Mass.), 1962.

Chomsky, N., 1965. *Aspects of the Theory of Syntax.* Cambridge, Mass.: M.I.T. Press.

Chomsky, N., 1966. *Cartesian Linguistics.* New York: Harper and Row.

Katz, J. J., 1964. "Mentalism in Linguistics," *Language, 40.* Reprinted in *Readings in the Psychology of Language,* ed. Jakobovits and Miron. Englewood Cliffs, N.J.: Prentice-Hall, Inc., 1967.

Katz, J. J., and P. M. Postal, 1964. *An Integrated Theory of Linguistic Descriptions.* Cambridge, Mass.: M.I.T. Press.

2

Comprehension and Expression

Rulon Wells

The relation between thinking and speaking concerns both psychology from the side of thinking and linguistics from the side of speaking; it also somehow concerns philosophy, whose appearance on the scene is perhaps uninvited. Psychology and linguistics may find themselves united in the sense that both of them are sciences in contrast to philosophy which is unscientific. The position I defend here is that this is true and deeply significant, though not at all to the discredit of philosophy, and that, contrary to the prevailing assumption, a certain conception of philosophy should be held which entails, among other things, a sharp and fundamental distinction between the philosophical and the natural-scientific enterprises. When the conception of philosophy that I advocate is brought to bear on recent behavioral psychology, it yields some valuable points, some of them being conceptual clarifications and others methodological precepts. Inasmuch as, on account of the Transformational Approach, there is much current interest in the psychology of language and in the implications of linguistics for psychology, I will pay particular attention to my agreements and disagreements with this approach.

PSYCHOLOGY AND LINGUISTICS

Serious and widespread interaction between psychologists and linguists is fairly recent, a matter of the last fifteen years or so. Since the late fifties, with the energetic promulgation of transformation theory, it has come to be

NOTE: I was prevented by illness from attending the Thought and Language Symposium at the University of Arizona in February, 1968, nor did I submit this study at that time. I am grateful to the editor for asking me to include it in this volume.

widely thought that linguists have posed new challenges to psychologists, challenges which had not been posed to them before. In a sense this is true and in a sense it is false. I want to make both of these senses clear.

The encounter between linguistics and psychology is concentrated in the subfield of learning theory, and upon the approach, or school of thought, called Stimulus-Response theory. More particularly the claim has been advanced that the new linguistics *overthrows* S-R theory because it presents us with a body of knowledge—everyman's ability to speak and understand a language—which could not be learned by the methods that S-R theory provides.

The claim of novelty, I remarked, is true in a sense and false in a sense. It is true in the sense that, de facto, and speaking now of psychologists in the concrete and not of psychology in the abstract, transformational theory seems to have driven home various insights that had not been driven home before. It is false, however, to claim that the new linguistics has discovered previously unknown basic facts which have a new bearing on psychology. The central fact of transformational theory is that speech may be regarded as generated by various recursive processes. But recursive processes are not new, nor are they claimed to be; nor is it new that recursive processes are used in the daily activities of every normal human being.

What is new then is (1) the detailed application of the insight and (2) the psychological impact whereby this insight was appreciated, brought home, where it had not been appreciated before. A comparison with Darwinism may be made. Darwin's theory had novel points, but its impact was not so much because of these novelties as because of the fact that it caused people to think as they had not thought before about the relation of science and religion. Similarly, though of course not on the same scale, the transformational approach has made psychologists take notice of facts which they had not permitted themselves to take notice of before. Previously their attitude had been like the attitude of some descriptive linguists to the recursive aspects of syntax: "We're not ready to grapple with those facts yet." The facts were not denied, but attention to them was given low priority. And the psychological impact of transformational theory upon psychologists, as upon linguists, was to cause them to revise their priorities.[1]

THE TYPE OF CRITIQUE

What I have to say in the present paper about transformation theory will be largely negative criticism. The reason is that we can distinguish two ingredients in transformation theory—its facts and its interpretation of these facts. My judgment is that its facts are in large part correct and its

---

[1] Cf. my discussion of vividness, p. 53. Transformational theory has made some basic but long-known facts *vivid* to psychologists.

interpretation in large part unwarranted. To say that its interpretation is unwarranted is not to say that it is untenable. Rather it is to say that the same facts admit of other interpretations.

The present study is not a comprehensive critique even on the negative side, much less on the positive and constructive side of presenting alternative tenable interpretations. I review the old question of the relation of thought to its expression with the effect of intimating that the contrast is only an aspect of a much profounder contrast, the one mentioned near the outset: the contrast between the subject-matters of philosophy and of empirical science. As for transformational theory, the central mistake in its interpretations is that of putting forward 'creativity' as though it were a factor alongside of other factors in speech production.[2]

THOUGHT, SPEECH, AND LANGUAGE

In agreement with ordinary usage, and for the sake of style, I will speak of thought and speech, rather than of thinking and speaking, whenever there is no danger that 'thought' will be taken as 'that which is thought' rather than as 'thinking,' or that 'speech' will be taken as 'that which is spoken' rather than as 'speaking.' On the other hand, it would be too constantly misleading if I followed ordinary usage in contrasting thought with language, rather than with speech. Linguists have found it useful to distinguish speech from language, even if there is no general agreement as to how the distinction should be drawn, and I need not elaborate on the distinction here in order to make the point that in the present paper it is speech, not language, that is the focus of my attention. There is a contrast of thought with language, but it is not the same as the contrast of thought with speech.

Sir William Hamilton has said: In "the process of tunneling through a sand bank . . . it is impossible to succeed unless . . . almost every inch of our progress be secured by an arch of masonry before we attempted the excavation of another. Now language is to the mind precisely what the arch is to the tunnel . . . Though . . . every movement forward in language must be determined by an antecedent movement forward in thought, still, unless thought be accompanied at each point of its evolutions by a corresponding evolution of language, its further development is arrested."[3] This statement of the

---

[2] See particularly Chomsky's *Cartesian Linguistics,* pp. 5, 9, and 32 (but also *passim*). Chomsky is there expounding Descartes, but the whole point of the book is to show that after the chaff is winnowed out much wheat remains. Without being willing to reckon Descartes's two-substance theory as part of the wheat (though also without showing that it can be separated from those doctrines that Chomsky does regard as wheat), he declares his sympathy with a theory that *alongside* of the mechanical principle in man posits a creative principle. I don't deny that there is something distinctive in man, but I deny that it can be dealt with by empirical science in the way Chomsky seems to have in mind.

[3] Quoted by Max Müller and, in turn, by Samuel Butler. Butler's discussion is reprinted in Black, 1962, pp. 13-35; see especially p. 34.

reciprocal dependency has not been improved upon to the present day. The participants in George Revesz's symposium, published in 1954, do not seem to have been able to do better than rehearse it. (See the review by G. A. Miller and E. Lenneberg in *Am. J. Psychol.*, 1958, *68*, 696-698.)

But what about the influence of language on thought? Even though we distinguish speech from language it is appropriate to speak of the influence of language, rather than of speech, on thought. If we spoke of the influence of speech on thought, we would want to mean that particular speeches influence particular thoughts. But what speech could influence a particular thought? It could not be the speech in which that thought was expressed, for if a thought can be distinguished at all from the speech which expresses it, it must come earlier than the speech, or at least no later, so that it cannot be an effect of the speech. Nor can any preceding speech have such an effect either. Not that preceding speeches are without influence, quite the opposite, but theirs is not the kind of influence we are here interested in, for they are influential *qua* expressing thoughts of their own. What we mean is rather this: the languages that a person speaks, or knows, influence his thought in that they more or less gently, or more or less forcefully, cause him to think certain thoughts and not to think certain other thoughts.

We need a word that will apply to all kinds of human mental activity. No word of ordinary English fills this role. It has been customary with English speaking philosophers to press the verb 'think' into this service, just as (and no doubt because) Descartes similarly pressed the Latin verb *cogitare* and the French verb *penser*. Philosophers are on the whole clear that this use is distinct from such narrower uses as are illustrated in 'I don't just *think* it's good, I know it,' and 'I'll stop thinking about the problem as soon as I've solved it.'

THE EXTREME VIEW

I will begin with brief consideration of the extreme view that thought and speech are outright identical, and (in the search for plausibility) successively consider various modifications of this view. As I mentioned earlier, the popular view is that thought and speech are distinct. Speech is the expression of thought; this relation is often put metaphorically by saying that speech is the *clothing* of thought.[4] One can, and often does, think without speaking; the speech which expresses a thought follows that thought in time. This popular view has been elaborated in various philosophies, such as Cartesianism.

If one wanted to show that thought and speech were simply identical, he would need to show either (1) that replacing one of the two words 'thought',

---

[4] Many references are culled in Hirzel, 1927, pp. 1-8; in Cassirer, 1955, pp. 40 ff,; and In Ullmann, 1951, p. 94. See also Peirce, *Collected Papers* 6 section 199.

'speech' by the other never changes the sense, or never changes sense into nonsense, that it has at most a stylistic effect, or (2) that any effect on sense can be accounted for otherwise than by the *diversity* of thought and speech. It is not necessary to elaborate a proof that (1) cannot be done; as for (2), I can't conceive all conceivable theories, and so am not in a position to declare it impossible, but neither am I acquainted with nor able to conjure up any such account. The generally agreed-upon fact that both 'thought' and 'speech' have more than one sense would be a complication, for (1) requires that in that case the several senses of 'thought' can be put into one-one correlation with the equally numerous senses of 'speech', unless the identity theory were to be somehow retrenched and qualified. Another complication stems from the fact that 'speech' does not stand in the same semantical relation to 'speak' as 'thought' to 'think', for whatever one thinks is a thought, but not whatever one speaks is a speech.

It would be more plausible to claim identity between the verb 'speak' and the verb 'say', whose relations (grammatical and semantical) to one another are close to what linguists call 'noncontrastive distribution.' Replacing 'say' by 'speak' in 'He says that it is two o'clock' turns sense into nonsense, so requirement (1) is not met. Requirement (2), however, is met by the theory that though speaking is saying, obligatory rules of mere grammar require the form 'speak' in some contexts and 'say' in others. My picture here is simplified and not quite accurate, but it comes close enough to adequacy to show what might be expected of 'thought' and of 'speech', or of the verbs 'think' and 'speak', in order to infer simple identity.

If there is no near prospect of identifying thought and speech outright, serious efforts have been made to establish some looser identity, some sort of assimilation. Understanding 'think' and 'thought' in the comprehensive way mentioned above, and using 'express' and 'expression' comprehensively to apply not only to speech and gesture but to any other publicly observable and manifest doings that we would say were (1) done by a human being and (2) meaningful, we may say that attempts have been made to show that there cannot be thought without expression nor expression without thought. (Oftentimes thought as "inner" is contrasted with expression as "outer"; the clothing-metaphor mentioned earlier drew this contrast.)

TWO KINDS OF NECESSITY

Perhaps, then, thought and expression are, as Chomsky puts it (1966, p. 31), *virtually* identical. What might this mean?

Oftentimes by virtual identity we mean constant concomitance: if A does not occur without B, nor B without A, they are virtually identical. Let us look at "constant concomitance" more closely. We might say that the concomitance is perfect if A never occurs without B nor vice versa. If we mean more than to report that A never has been found without B and never will be, and vice versa, we are entitled to use the word 'can' in one of its ordinary senses and say 'A cannot occur without B, nor B without A', or 'Necessarily, B occurs with A, and A with B', or 'It is not possible for A to occur without B, or vice versa.'

But 'possibility' and 'necessity' have more than one meaning. Some philosophers have distinguished two main kinds: a priori, and empirical (or factual). I defend this distinction and argue that much confusion has resulted from failure to draw it. There is a certain relation between this distinction and that between philosophy and empirical science. It is not one of simple correlation; philosophy is not simply the study of a priori truth, nor is empirical science simply the study of factual truth. Empirical science, as I conceive it, *uses* a priori truths but does not *study* them. Philosophy, for its part, doesn't study all a priori truths—by that criterion it would include logic and mathematics—and moreover there is a part of philosophy, so-called phenomenology, which is not clearly a priori in a narrow sense but isn't clearly mere matter of fact either. Since the delimitation of philosophy is not the central concern of this study, it must suffice here to assume that whatever else philosophy may deal with, it does deal with (a) the distinction between a priori and factual truth, (b) the criteria of apriority, and (c) phenomenology.

'Possible' and 'Necessary' have various senses; it is sufficient here to distinguish between an a priori and a factual sense of each. In other words, when we say that something is possible, we may mean that it is possible a priori ("logical possibility" is a variety of this), or that it is possible in point of fact, or that it is possible in some other sense. (For example, one such sense is based on knowledge: we call that 'possible' which we do not know to be false.) The former possibility includes the latter, that is, whatever is factually possible is possible a priori, but not vice versa.

There is a variety of factual possibility that deserves to be singled out for special mention because it is involved with human beings and with freedom. It has no fixed standard name; the term 'feasibility' comes as close as any. When we say that A, a normal mature human being, can do B, it is ordinarily not mere logical possibility that we have in mind, but what I am calling 'feasibility.' Actually, 'feasible' in its ordinary use isn't quite right, because it suggests that the thing can be done without effort, even without inconvenience. My alternative to adopting this ordinary word would be to coin a phrase or a neologism. All voluntary actions are feasible in my semi-technical sense, but so also are certain involuntary ones. It is feasible for me to digest meat, but not cellulose or glass.

The distinction of two kinds of necessity may now be applied to our central topic, the relation between thought and its expression. To say they are 'virtually identical' may be taken in two ways: either as asserting that they are concomitant by a priori necessity or by mere factual necessity.

Russell, the earlier Wittgenstein, the logical positivists, and C. I. Lewis explored the conception of private language—a language that would not, or perhaps even could not possibly, be used to communicate, and whose sole use was to express. The later Wittgenstein launched an attack on this conception, with such effect that it is now widely considered to be obsolete. I don't need to take a stand on this matter; it is enough to point out that those who defended the conception were not asserting its factual, but only its a priori possibility. (Even its a priori possibility has been attacked, but some of the criticisms of the conception were only apropos if factual possibility were claimed for it.)

A SHIFT OF STATUS

It often happens in science that a proposition is at first advanced as a factual truth, and then, in the course of defense against attack, is reconstrued in such a way as to function as an a priori necessity. This happened, in the discussion of thought and expression, in the work of Professor Max Müller.[5] I will describe Müller's move.

In the 1880's Francis Galton gave experimental evidence against the widely held view that all thinking takes place in images. In reply to Galton's alleged instances of imageless thinking, Muller contended that if there was thinking without images there must have been some other signs present that did essentially the same work as images, since there *could not* be thinking without signs. He, however, was prepared to admit that these signs might escape our introspective notice, and thus his contention lacked observational support. A latter-day defender might say that Müller's thought-signs had the status of constructs in his theoretical framework. I would make two comments. First, it remains to be shown that, as constructs, they serve any useful purpose; second, the prevailing contemporary view of constructs does not undertake to distinguish a priori from factual ingredients as I do. On my view, it is quite possible that some propositions about constructs should be regarded as a priori propositions, and Müller's proposition that all thought is in signs appears to me to deserve that status.

On the view that I am advocating, it is neither a promotion nor a demotion if a proposition changes from factual to a priori status. But one ought to be clear about the distinction, and if the status changes one ought to acknowledge this. A fuller discussion of this matter would explain the sense in which it is "the same proposition" before and after status-change, and the sense in which it is no longer the same. A controversialist like Müller is

---

[5] See the exchange between Galton and Müller reprinted in an appendix to Müller, 1888. (This book is distinct, by the way, from Müller's *The Science of Thought*, also published in 1888.) The exchange is discussed in Hadamard, 1945, because it involves Galton's recognition of the unconscious.

subject to the criticism that he heeds the first sense and ignores the second, so that he doesn't make what he is doing completely clear. (In Müller's case, what he was doing was throwing out a smokescreen.)

Sometimes (if not always), when people maintain a priori propositions, their philosophical motives for doing so can be usefully stated. Why, then, should one wish to stipulate, or have it be true a priori, that all thought is in signs, or—whether this is a mere paraphrase or a distinct doctrine—insist that thought is always accompanied by expression? I am aware of four lines of argument.

THE ARGUMENT FROM GENERALIZATION

Often our thinking is manifestly accompanied by overt and audible speech; often, too, we speak very softly, or deliberately move our lips as if really speaking, while at the same time refraining from phonating. Sometimes, too, we talk to ourselves without being aware of it; that is, we think we are silently thinking, when in fact we are thinking noisily. And often enough we do think, and are conscious that we are thinking, without giving the least audible or other sign to anyone else—no gesturing or posturing or twitching of the body, not anything even that we ourselves, functioning by feedback as monitors of ourselves, could detect in the way of anything physical or sensible. This is the "discourse of the soul with itself." [6]

But the opposite experience is equally familiar. We intend to say one thing but, when it comes right down to it, blurt out another; and sometimes afterwards admit that we actually said what we meant. Then there are times when we "speak without thinking"—not that we don't think at all, but only that we don't think of the social consequences, the emotive meaning of our speech and so forth. And there is the experience, generalized as an aphorism by Joubert:[7] "We only know just what we meant to say after we have said it."

In short, it appears *prima facie* that when we are thinking we sometimes speak and sometimes don't. Now scientists are taught to seek universal propositions,[8] and it has occurred to people that if we shift our concepts around somewhat—alter our "segmentation of reality," in Whorf's phrase, we might be able to turn our particular proposition ('particular' in the sense of formal logic: 'Some S's are P's') into a universal one ('All S's are P's'). Let us formulate the project: what terminological or semantical changes would we

---

[6] Plato, *Theaetetus*, 189e, 206d, 208c; *Sophist*, 263e-264a; *Philebus*, 38e.

[7] James, *Principles of Psychology*, 1.280.

[8] On the misguided search for universality, I may cite two papers of mine in which I have argued that two very great thinkers—Gottlob Frege and Charles Peirce—pursued this will-o'-the-wisp: Wells, 1963, *passim*, and 1964, p. 315.

have to make in order that the universal proposition 'All thought is accompanied by expression' would become true? An informed investigator would immediately pose the counter-question, "Which of the two kinds of truth is intended here?" Different changes will be required to insure a priori truth than would be needed to insure factual truth. This clear distinction, however, is not commonly made.

Max Müller quickly retreated to the a priori kind of truth-claim. Since World War I the concept of subvocal speech has often been used in support of a *factual* claim. This concept modified the familiar concept of speech. According to the familiar concept, it is true universally and a priori that speech can be heard. The modified concept discards this truth, dividing speech into that which can be heard and that which cannot. But what I have called the modifed concept comes in several varieties.

According to one variety, speech need not be audible, but it must be detectable by direct observation. Speech is movement of the speech organs; these organs may not move enough to produce something audible, but they must move enough so that some observation or other (aided, if need be, by instruments) can observe the movement. One of the neater observations along this line was the observation with deaf mutes whose speech organs were their fingers, that their fingers twitched when they were having dreams.[9]

According to another variety, which builds on the physiological distinction between peripheral and central processes, the essence of speech is some central process which is ordinarily but not invariably accompanied by peripheral processes. This variety will still be maintaining a factual truth, provided that suitable central processes can be observed in any subject who we would say was thinking. It also has the advantage that the universal proposition 'all thought is accompanied by expression' can be maintained in the utter absence of observable movements of the speech-organs. It has the disadvantage, or in any case the consequence, that the meaning of 'expression' has had to be changed. To begin with, it was, to use Tolman's contrast between molecular and molar, a kind of molarity. With the giving up of audibility, molarity was jeopardized; with the giving up of peripherality, it was completely abandoned. In its new way of being construed, the proposition is simply an assertion of mind-body correlation; it does not differ from Huxley's "epiphenomenalist" thesis. Huxley proposed the term 'psychosis' for a state, or a process, of consciousness, and 'neurosis' for a state, or a process, of "the physical basis of consciousness."[10] Epiphenom-

---

[9] Experiment by L. W. Max (1935). See Dunkel, 1948, p. 44; Osgood, 1953, pp. 650-1; and Henle, 1958, p. 263.

[10] Huxley, *Method and Results,* 240; *Darwiniana* 158; cf. James, *Principles of Psychology* 1.129, 186.

enalism teaches, in James' words, "No psychosis without neurosis." (Most people today are only familiar with these two terms in the very different senses that they came to have in Freud.) I may add here Huxley's own famous statement,[11] "I believe that we shall, sooner or later, arrive at a mechanical equivalent of consciousness." The concept I am now discussing— the concept that thought is in fact always accompanied by a "central process"—differs from Huxley only in a somewhat different and somewhat more precise account of the "physical" or "mechanical" basis.

There is also, of course, at least as an a priori possibility (whether or not it has actual advocates) the claim that the accompaniment of thought by some physical process—molar or molecular, peripheral or central—is an a priori necessity. Those who have declared thought to be "nothing but" this or that physical process may be interpreted in this way. In some cases it is difficult or impossible to tell whether an a priori or a factual claim is being made. I find myself unable to decide which status should be assigned to Osgood's mediating processes.

So much for the first line of thought: we shift our concepts in order to make it true, whether a priori or factually, that all thinking is accompanied by expression. To make it true a priori involves a shift that reduces to epiphenomenalism, to make it true factually involves a shift away from molar behavior. To say that the a priori view reduces to epiphenomenalism is not (for me) pejorative; I myself hold the epiphenomenalist view. But I have the impression that such people as Müller thought they were holding more than that.

THE PRAGMATISTIC ARGUMENT

I am not proposing anything so rigid as to take this line of thought as characteristic of all and only pragmatists, but it is in the spirit of pragmatists' emphasis upon action.

On this conception, all thinking is response, is a *doing* of some kind. In order to make this at all plausible, it is necessary to consider non-action to be a kind of action. The beginnings of this may be found in Aristotle ("The privation of form is form, in a way"), but its full flower belongs to the nineteenth century, with its quasi-mathematical concept of generalization (cf. fn. 8). Not all non-action is considered action, but when a person might have acted (in the ordinary, positive sense) and didn't, then in that special case we say that his doing nothing amounted to doing something. (And if it was a sin, it was a sin of omission rather than of commission.) And if a distinction is introduced between actual thinking and a disposition to think, this will be

---

[11] Huxley, *Method and Results,* p. 191.

matched by a corresponding distinction between a disposition to respond and an actual response.

Although before pragmatism it was customary to contrast thinking and doing, words and deeds, still the thesis that thinking is doing only sounds novel unless some more definite meaning is specified for 'doing.' Pragmatism ran into trouble in its attempts to specify a duly definite meaning. It kept sounding energetic, like Teddy Roosevelt; as Peirce wrote in 1902 of James's version, "the doctrine appears to assume that the end of man is action—a stoical axiom which, to the present writer at the age of sixty, does not recommend itself so forcibly as it did at thirty" (Peirce, 5, p. 2, section 3). Peirce's own attempts, and Dewey's, fared no better; the basic problem was the same: to equally avoid the Scylla of untenable stringency and the Charybdis of relapse into the uncontroversial.

If thinking is construed as response, then since responses are (in principle) public, thinking is public too, not inherently private. In the eyes of pragmatists this was a desirable consequence. But the task remained, and remains, of specifying a satisfactory sense of 'doing.' Dewey welcomed behaviorism when it came along, partly, no doubt, because it seemed to offer a prospect of doing this. When Hobbes had said that words are the counters of wise men and the money of fools, this was only a metaphor, even though he elaborated the metaphor by characterizing thinking as reckoning (calculation). The task of pragmatism was to take this sort of talk as more than a metaphor yet not in a way that was plainly false.

THE IDEALISTIC ARGUMENT

Besides his pragmatistic view of thinking, Peirce put forward an idealistic theory. This theory (more prominent in his early than in his later writings) argues as follows: An unknowable (an "incognizable") is nonsense. The doctrine of an unknowable thing-in-itself, a thing other than appearances, must be given up. But all knowledge is interpretation, i.e. all knowledge treats its object as a sign of another object. This must be true, then, even of our knowledge of our own thought; our own thought, being knowable, must consist of signs. This doctrine of course involves Peirce's pragmatic conception that all reality consists in future consequences. It also involves a certain kind of infinite regress. (A regress which, according to Peirce, is not vicious because it is like the infinite regress of Achilles pursuing the tortoise: every object of an interpretation is itself an interpretation of a previous object. This follows from a principle which Peirce accepts from Berkeley: "Only an idea can be like an idea." Peirce's idealistic argument is stated especially in *Collected Papers* 5 sections 213-263; on the regress see 250 and 263.)

THE EMPIRICIST COMPARISON

A fourth line of argument differs almost diametrically from Peirce's. In Locke, in Berkeley, and in Swift (*Gulliver* III.5), with a revival in Alexander Bryan Johnson and in Russell, we find the doctrine that it is difficult but possible to dispense with language. Language makes a veil or curtain which we can raise to contemplate things bare. It is not their proposal that we dispense with language, as Swift mischievously suggests. Rather, judiciously exercising our power to dispense with it, we do so just often enough to keep language in its place, and prevent it from becoming our master when it should be our servant. This empiricist view, ambiguously, is either an argument *for* or an argument *against* the dependence of thought upon speech, depending entirely on whether the bare contemplation is treated as coordinate with thought or subordinate to it. If coordinate, then the differential mark of thought is its use of speech or other expression; if subordinate, then it is only the non-contemplative species of thought which requires expressions.

A PRIORI ARGUMENTS, CONCLUDED

Here, then, are four lines of thought that have motivated some philosophers to maintain a priori that all thought involves expression or signs. Before leaving this group of arguments I should point out an asymmetry in the mutual involvement of thought and expression. Opinions differ as to whether thought involves expression by a priori necessity, by factual necessity, or not by either one but only as a frequent and probable consequent. With the reverse relation it is quite different. Expression involves thought by its very concept, which is the simplest kind of a priori necessity: expression is a relative term, an expression is the expression *of* something, and if it doesn't express anything then it is at most a pseudo-expression.

DEPENDENCE: FACTUAL AND METHODOLOGICAL

Most writers who maintain the dependence of thought upon expression do not distinguish between a priori and factual independence. Factual dependence may be maintained as really true or as a methodological position. One treats thought as methodologically dependent upon expression if, when he is supposed to be discussing thought, he always brings in a discussion of expression. If, methodologically, he treats the dependence as a priori and as total, he will, when he is supposed to be discussing thought, simply discuss expression. A dependence that is less than total, whether it is a priori or factual, will bring both thought and expression into the discussion. A person might maintain dependence as a methodological position even though not accepting it as true. For instance, he might regard dependence in the way that Kant regards "regulative principles," as a guide to inquiry. He might regard dependence as false, or he might be uncommitted as to its truth or falsity, and yet nevertheless, for methodological reasons, proceed as if it were true.

In particular, an empirical scientist might accept dependence methodologically. If he did this *simply as a scientist*, this would mean that, on his view, empirical science could not treat thought except as dependent upon expression. This would, for such a person, leave open the question whether thought really is dependent. That question could not be closed except with the help of the premiss "There is nothing of which empirical science cannot treat." Similarly (although this topic falls outside the scope of the present study) someone might maintain—many people actually do—that the empirical scientist, as a scientist, must methodologically assume that every thought has a physical cause, whether or not it has one in reality.

THE INFLUENCE OF LANGUAGE UPON THOUGHT

For two centuries arguments have been marshaled for an influence of language (not speech) upon thought. Basically they all undertake to show, as a first step, that in point of fact people who speak differently think differently. (If this proposition were given a priori status, for instance, by taking difference in speech as an infallible sign of difference in thought, then the discussion of it would not belong here.) In the actual discussions by Whorf and others, one is at pains to select examples where the languages, and allegedly the modes of thought, are quite markedly different from one another. How a person speaks, that is, the set of habits or rules to which his speeches conform, is called his language. The alleged empirical fact is that differences in mode of thought are correlated with differences in language, so that there is either chance coincidence or causal connection. Supposing the former to have been ruled out as improbable, we may proceed to infer that it is the language which is the cause and the mode of thought which is the effect, for the opposite relation—that it was an individual's mode of thought that determined which language he learned—is generally regarded as empirically refuted. (But a third possibility should not be overlooked, namely that some third factor is the cause both of what language one learns and of how one thinks. I refer readers to an earlier study of mine [Wells, 1962] for discussion of this.)

Differences between one language and another come to the attention of the translator, for translation is, precisely, the matching-up of a speech in one language with a speech in another language which expresses the same thought. It seems to be widely agreed that in general there is one respect in which translation is possible and another in which it is not. Granting that different languages adopt or embody different conceptual frameworks, we see it is obvious that translation from one framework to another must change something, and thus lose something, to wit, the original framework. What is not obvious, but is generally agreed to be somehow true is that there is something that is not lost in the translation; something that is preserved. Using the convenient polar terms 'matter' and 'manner' (or the even more convenient, but badly ambiguous terms 'content' and 'form'), we may say that translation preserves content or matter and loses form or manner. The claim that translation is impossible is tantamount to the claim that matter cannot be separated from manner.

The claim that translation is impossible is one end of a spectrum, the other being that perfect translation is always possible. Neither extreme is plausible, but positions near the extremes have enough plausibility to have been maintained from time to time; for instance, near one extreme the claim that in general, though not with every pair of speeches from every pair of languages, there is an appreciable loss in translation and near the other extreme the claim that in general only inessential features are lost in translation.

Let us consider the second extreme position, in order to bring out a new point about dependence. Suppose that perfect translation is always possible; that a thought expressible in one language is expressible in any language. Take any speech, S_L, in language L, and take any language M other than L. Then there is in M a speech, S_M, which is the perfect translation of S_L. This is, of course, only an assumption, and a false one. What I want to point out is that even if it were true, it would not follow that thought is independent of language and of speech.

What is needed here is a distinction between distributive and collective dependence. We learn in elementary logic about the fallacy of composition, illustrated by the following reasoning: a person can live without meat, and he can live without vegetables; therefore, he can live without meat and without vegetables. Now we commit the same fallacy if we reason thus: Let L_1, $L_2, \ldots$ be all the languages. Then thought is independent of L_1 (because it can be expressed without the use of L_1), and it is independent of L_2, and so on; therefore, it is independent of all languages. But if thought is independent of all languages, we are entitled to employ the general term 'language' and say that thought is independent of language. It is easy to avoid the fallacy, if we are on our guard against it. We have only to note that our argument proved thought to be distributively independent of language, but did not prove it to be collectively independent.

ADEQUACY OF EXPRESSION

We have spent most of our time so far considering arguments that thought depends on speech, and on language, whether totally or partially. But our ordinary ways of talking about thought and speech recognize a fact of everyone's experience which emphasizes the independence of thought from speech or other expression. I mean all those locutions in which we recognize that our expression may be an *inadequate* expression of our thought.

As soon as we speak of inadequate expression—which is tantamount to dividing expression into the adequate and inadequate—we change the meaning of 'expression.' Before, when we were considering whether every thought requires expression, it went without saying that adequate expression was meant; in other words, to speak of adequate expression was redundant. The shift is like that involved when we ask if a poem is good poetry. In one sense of the word 'poetry,' 'good poetry' is redundant; what is not good poetry is not bad poetry but pseudo-poetry. But just as two senses of 'poetry' are current, two senses of 'expression' are current. It is the broader sense that is now engaging our attention.

Whenever we have partial dependence we have partial independence; these will stand in a Gestalt-relationship such that, when by an act of will (in particular, of attention) we make one our focus, the other will recede into background-status. Previously dependence has been our focus; now it is independence's turn. And it is when we are focusing on independence that the broader sense of 'expression' and the possibility of inadequate expression become germane.

We are certain that expression can be inadequate, whatever account we may finally have to give of adequacy. Our certainty has a twofold basis: feelings, primarily about ourselves, and judgments, primarily about others. This same twofold basis can be arrived at from another direction. 'Adequacy' is a relative term; something is adequate or not for a use (or a purpose). Now what are the purposes of speech? One common answer cites two: expression and communication. But it sounds foolish if we question whether a given expression is adequate for the purposes of expression; it sounds trivially redundant. To say that the purpose of an expression is expression seems vapid. But it isn't really so; two different senses of 'express' are involved.

When we express our thought, we do so by producing a physical object—an ephemeral one, if we speak with the voice, or a longer-lasting one, if we write. This physical object is the expression. It may avoid some confusion if I refer to the distinction between token and type. On the view that I am adopting, expressions in the primary sense are tokens; when we have assigned tokens to types, a type may be said to be an expression (in a secondary sense) of the same thing as all its tokens are.

When we speak of expression as a use of language, what we have in mind is *self*-expression. We express ourselves in various ways; one of these ways—only one—is to produce token-expressions. Let us call expressions that are either tokens or types T-expressions; then we may say that producing a T-expression is one of the means of self-expression. Throughout, when we have contrasted thought and its expression, we have meant thought and its T-expression. And the problem now facing us is twofold: When is a T-expression inadequate for self-expression? When is it inadequate for communication?

It may be that the two basic purposes of language are fundamentally connected in some way—perhaps by the desire for self-expression always being ultimately a desire for communication. But we must beware of the genetic fallacy. Oftentimes when people say 'ultimately' they mean 'originally'. What we must beware of is thinking that our original purposes must still, however cryptically, be our present ones. In this study I shall treat self-expression and communication as purposes that are not only distinct but also independent a priori and factually.

COMMUNICATIVE ADEQUACY

In discussing adequacy, I will so far as feasible discuss adequacy of self expression and adequacy of communication separately.

"Tristram Shandy, as we know, took two years writing the history of the first two days of his life, and lamented that, at this rate, material would accumulate faster than he could deal with it, so that he could never come to an end. Now I maintain that, if he had lived forever, and not wearied of his task, then, even if his life had continued as eventfully as it began, no part of his biography would have remained unwritten." (Russell 1918, p. 90; 1938, p. 358) This is the Tristram Shandy paradox.

We are presented here in exaggerated form with one of the most commonplace facts: the fact that things happen faster than we can describe them. Let me for the moment make these two assumptions: (1) that perceptual experiences shall be counted as thoughts, and (2) that the communicatively adequate expression of an experience in language L (say English) consists of a minute description of it. Under such assumptions we would have daily experience of the communicative inadequacy of speech, for it is not physically possible to produce the T-expression that minutely describes an experience as fast as one has the experience.

Our practical solution is to renounce Tristram Shandy's ambition, and to describe on a smaller scale. Whether deliberately or otherwise, we *select* experiences for description. And thus, in effect, we acknowledge the distributive-collective contrast once again: we acknowledge that even if *any* experience can be described, not *every* experience can be described. (The like is not true of "central processes"; if we count these as T-expressions, the condition which gives rise to the Tristram Shandy situation—the discrepancy between experience-duration and expression-duration—is not fulfilled.)

A quite different limitation on communicative adequacy is this. We cannot judge communicative adequacy except on a premise stating what communication is supposed to do. But there is no general agreement on this point, no generally accepted account. The older account—that communication is supposed to cause the hearer to think the same thought that the speaker had when he spoke—is seen to be naively inadequate; for one reason, it doesn't do justice to emotive meaning. But nothing to take the place of this account has come into general acceptance.

A still older view—what I have called the surrogate conception (Wells, 1954)—is still less acceptable in the last analysis, though it has a good deal of merit as a first approximation. What I now wish to point out is that the failure of the surrogate conception determines a sense in which, in general, T-expression is communicatively inadequate. That sense is simply this: words don't fully take the place of things. The fact that they do in some respects take the place of things is the fact that encouraged the surrogate theory in the first place. In some respects speech not merely takes the place of but is actually superior to direct experience, much as in some respects coins are superior to cattle and paper money to coins. The mistake lies in trying to generalize this fact and to make it out that the very essence of signs, or T-expressions, is to take the place of something.

If not always, it is certainly sometimes true that we want to communicate how we feel, or how things seem to us. And sometimes we use as a criterion of success that if we succeed in communicating our feeling or experience to our hearer, he will then have the same feeling; he will come to share that feeling with us. By this criterion everyone sometimes fails in communication, not from ineptitude but because there is no way of doing better. In the light of this fact (it is a fact, not an a priori necessity, because it concerns cause and effect), we may modestly revise our ambitions and give up the expectation that our expressions will always, if properly carried out, have the same effect as the direct experiences which they describe.

However, there are cases in which it merely seems that there has been a failure in surrogation; cases in which our description was incomplete or inaccurate. Tristram Shandys all of us, our description of our experience is surely not as detailed as the experience. How can we rule out the possibility that it was because of what we left out (or because of what we inaccurately put in) that our description didn't have the same effect upon our hearer as the direct experience would have had? We may reply that a description should have the same effect on a hearer as the direct experience, provided that the description leaves out nothing essential. This, however, is an empty reply, for the mark of the inessential is that leaving it out does not alter the effect. The question of what is essential and what is inessential in description (relative to a particular hearer) turns out to be an empirical question, which for the science of empirical psychology has some fragmentary findings but no very striking general theory.

If we are to conclude, then, that there are cases of genuine failure of a surrogate, it will have to be by indirect argument. For instance, we may with the help of some theory *indirectly infer* that the reason why an incomplete description didn't have the same effect as a direct experience was not that it was incomplete.

We get some clue about the obstacles to communication if we consider our attempts to communicate with ourselves. What we want to examine more closely is cases where the attempt fails. For example, at a time when I am much engrossed in some inquiry, I make notes on my thoughts. My thoughts seem to me to culminate in some insight, which I formulate to my satisfaction and write down among my notes. Forced by external circumstances to abandon the topic, I return to it months later and find that my notes "leave me cold." They do not, in other words, have the effect of putting me back in the state of mind in which I was when I wrote them. Is this because they are incomplete, because they are only notes? No. The reason why I select this particular case for discussion is that, at the time I was engrossed, I had the feeling that my thinking had culminated in an insight, the expression of which should be enough. And there before me is my expression of this insight, which at the time seemed to me perfectly adequate, and now, as I say, leaves me cold. It is not that I don't understand the insight which I expressed, but that it doesn't seem to me like an insight at all; I don't puzzle over its meaning and don't question its truth, but it doesn't seem to me as important, as it did when I had it and wrote it down.

Then, as I ponder over these old notes, thoughts flash across my mind; my notes remind me of things, association sets to work, I re-engross myself in the topic, and after a while I say to myself, "Oh! Now I see what I had in mind!" And then I am in the state of mind that I would describe as "being warmed up again."

As I said, this kind of experience, the experience of re-engrossment, is particularly valuable for throwing light on surrogation, because it presents us with a perplexing borderline case. Shall we say that my notes, the expression of my former thoughts, did finally function as a successful surrogate, since in the end I warmed up and returned to my former state of mind? The question is not whether I returned to my former state but whether reading my notes was the cause of it. I should think one would say that my own active efforts were a considerable part of the cause and that reading the notes was more an incentive, an impetus, than a main cause. The criterion seems to be this: if reading the notes is a main cause, then its effect will occur right away and without effort. This settles the treatment of the case in question, which then ceases to be on the borderline. (Such a criterion, however, with its vague terms 'right away' and 'without effort' inevitably will give rise to other borderline cases.)

But the case at hand does not cease to be of interest by being removed from the borderline. It still forces us to attend to the question of what we shall say about vividness. There is a dimension of experience partaking both of the cognitive and of the affective dimensions, or at least resembling them both, which we may call vividness. It is this dimension which is the special province of literature, and which gives rise to the troublesome impression that literature purports to be true (and so to be operating in the cognitive dimension) and yet does not capture any very profound or startling truths. The answer is that what literature does with truth is to make it vivid; it doesn't exhibit truth, it brings truth home to us. That was what my notes failed to do: to bring home to me the truth that they recorded for me, to make me *appreciate* their message. Thus, for communicative adequacy, we demand not only truth but also vividness.

SELF-EXPRESSIVE ADEQUACY

A person may have the feeling that he has said just what he wanted to say or, at the other extreme, that he has failed utterly. This "feeling" might be a judgment that he had communicated what he wanted to communicate; and so far as the judgment concerned communication, regardless of whether the judgment was true or false, it would concern communicative adequacy and so would not fall under the scope of the present section. But, I believe that sometimes, in fact often, the feeling of success or failure does not exclusively concern communication; insofar as it does not, I would ascribe it to the other main purpose of expression, namely self-expression.

As regards communication, it is clear that the judgment of the speaker is not decisive. He may exaggerate or underestimate his success; he may even be under a delusion. It is not so clear that feelings and judgments about self-expression are subject to the same possibilities. The question here is simply one aspect of the general question of self-knowledge, which in turn involves the question as to whether there is any private knowledge (inherently private, that is, private in principle; there is no question that in fact much knowledge is private). The question of private language, mentioned earlier, is another aspect of the same larger question. My purpose in the present paper is not to offer any answer to the question, even my own, but rather to allocate questions according to whether empirical science may hope to answer them or may not.

My underlying contention is that there are concepts, and therefore questions, that fall outside the province of empirical science but within the province of philosophy. I take it as one of the criteria of empirical science that it deals with the public (in which can be included the private-as-reported, but not the private-as-decisive), and that in conformity with this criterion it might very well refuse to recognize as decisive a person's feelings as to whether he had succeeded in expressing himself. (Though on the other hand it would hardly dismiss these feelings altogether as irrelevant to the question.)

If this is so, then any viewpoint from which a person's feeling that he had expressed himself well or ill is decisive must be a viewpoint which, falling outside of empirical science, falls by default within philosophy.

It is sometimes said that symbols are arbitrary; that "a word has sense if I give it a sense." By considering self-expressive adequacy, we can see a sense in which this dictum is false—or at least misleading by suggesting something false. The dictum suggests that giving a sense, or more generally, giving a use to an object (so as to make it a T-expression), is an easy matter; we have merely to say (or even to think) "Let it be so," and it is so. No. Within limits and for certain abstract kinds of meaning it is so, but not for the kind of meaning which is constituted by the feeling that one has expressed oneself satisfactorily or unsatisfactorily. If the power of arbitrarily instituting symbols by an act of volition extended to this kind of meaning, then one could by an act of volition satisfy one's desire. It is true that, if I desire an ice cream cone, then I can by an act of volition satisfy my desire, but the phrase 'by an act of volition' must be rightly understood. I don't simply will "Let my desire be satisfied"; I will "Let me get an ice cream cone." Not just any volition, but a suitable volition, and one whose suitability is determined by external standards, is required to satisfy my desire. But according to the theory that T-expressions are arbitrarily instituted, I don't find something that conforms to a standard, or even make something that conforms to a standard, but rather I make a standard. And for the self-expressive kind of meaning this is simply not so.

SOME OTHER KINDS OF ADEQUACY

It is often said, vaguely, that there is more than tongue can tell, that if one were to trace out all the consequences of a statement they would be infinite, and so forth. In these remarks there is the germ of an important truth.

If a person knows a truth, P (knows that P is true), does he know all its logical consequences? If he understands P (whether P is true or false), does he understand all its consequences; does he know (realize) that they *are* its consequences? One customary answer is that he understands and knows these things implicitly. What does 'implicitly' mean? As clear an answer as we are going to get is that X implicitly knows that P, if and only if he would explicitly know P if he thought about the matter long enough. In other words, the notion of implicitness makes use of the notion of counterfactual conditionals.

The use of counterfactuals is tricky; it is easy to pass beyond the bounds of the physically possible into the realm of fantasy. (Russell did this in supposing "if he had lived forever.")   In the case of understanding consequences implicitly it is certain that the bounds of physical possibility will be exceeded by the demands of this account. Take a universal a priori truth of the simplest sort such as that every integer has a successor. This truth has infinitely many logical consequences: One has a successor, two has a successor, etc. Our account (not *my* account, please notice) says that each of these would be arrived at by one who thought long enough (in other words, by one who was given a sufficiently long period of time for thinking). But no matter what units of time we use there is an integer such that to think out the consequence for that integer would take a period of time so long that it would make no physical sense to speak of a human being or other physical organism continuously living for that period of time. At some point, even if at no unique and definite point, the bounds of the physically and factually possible will have been exceeded. And there are infinitely many integers, indeed 'almost all integers,' in the technical mathematical sense, such that to think out the consequence for them of 'Every integer has a successor' is infeasible and beyond the range of physical possibility.

Either, then, the proposed account of implicit knowledge won't do, or else no one knows that every integer has a successor. If we didn't try to treat implicit knowledge as what *could* become explicit knowledge, we wouldn't get into the difficulty, but we wouldn't have given any account of implicit knowledge, either.

The important conclusion to be drawn is this: We must avoid an account of implicit knowledge in terms of 'would' or 'could' or 'can'; all these terms are ambiguous as between an a priori and a factual sense. Taken in their a priori senses, they simply don't give an 'account' of the required sort, whereas if taken in their factual senses, although the account they give is of the required sort, it is false. That is, it doesn't account for implicit knowledge of the infinite. In particular, our knowledge or understanding of languages cannot receive such an account, for (as Chomsky has so well emphasized) such knowledge will include knowledge of sets of rules whose generative output is infinite. And thus we cannot, to account for this knowledge, appeal as Chomsky has done to some infinite capacity of speakers and hearers.

THE ARGUMENT SO FAR, SUMMARIZED

The seventeen sections of this paper so far have argued for the following points:

1. Sections 1 ("Psychology and Linguistics") through 6 ("A Shift of Status") conclude that thought can be neither identified with nor reduced to speech, *unless* the identification or reduction is converted into a stipulative a priori truth. In particular, no plausible sense can be given to the proposition that thinking is a *disposition* to speech.

2. Sections 7 ("The Argument from Generalization") through 11 ("A Priori Arguments, Concluded") consider identification and reduction as

stipulative truths. Four ways of making them true by stipulation are considered; all are found possible, none is found plausible.

3. The upshot of the first two theses, restated in still broader terms, is that thought can be neither identified with nor reduced to speech in any a priori way except the trivial way of stipulative or built-in apriority. Other sorts of dependence than identification and reduction remain as possibilities. Below I will speak about statistical correlation.

Perhaps the main interest of the first two theses is the discussion of the shift by which verbally the same proposition is shifted from factual to stipulative, a priori true status.

4. Sections 12 ("Dependence: Factual and Methodological") through 17 ("Some Other Kinds of Adequacy") bring in a new line of thought. When we introduce the concept of adequacy, we think of various reasons for saying that this or that expression is inadequate as an expression; from which the conclusion is that there are thoughts that we can think but cannot adequately express.

Now it is time to put these theses to use.

IMPORT FOR BEHAVIORAL PSYCHOLOGY

My remarks are addressed primarily to behavioral psychologists. They are intended as part of a critique, from a certain philosophical standpoint, of recent behavioral psychology. I articulate my critique partly by direct comment and partly by a critique of Noam Chomsky's critique.

Very broadly stated, my contention about behavioral psychology is this. We can distinguish between behavioral (and behavioristic) psychology in general and the particular versions of it that have been cultivated so far. Much of what has been cultivated so far should be discarded. The discardable part consists, in turn, partly of hypotheses that were at one time worth testing, but which the now available evidence shows to be probably false, and partly of pseudo-hypotheses about fact and of pseudo-maxims of method which correct philosophical reflection would have shown to be absurd (nonsensical, meaningless) all along.

Included in the part to be discarded is a simplistic view about conceptual analysis and about structure. A sensitive conceptual analysis, such as I have tried to sketch of thought and of speech, is disregarded by science at the expense of accuracy and without adequate compensating gain in manageability.

Also discardable: the belief that a framework without innate dispositions is possible; the belief that it is possible to hold that all knowledge can be assimilated to inductive knowledge; the belief that all inductive knowledge can be reduced, or otherwise assimilated, to the results of learning by association.

CHOMSKY'S CRITIQUE OF BEHAVIORAL PHSYCHOLOGY

The fundamental point that I wish to defend concerning Noam Chomsky's criticisms of behavioral psychology is that in the main they are logically independent of his technical contributions to linguistics. This point is obviously consequential, for it undermines any argument *from* these outstanding contributions *to* the conclusion that they have shown in a way that could not have been shown before that the stimulus-response approach to human psychology is inadequate at its very foundations.

The fact is that I agree to a fair extent with Chomsky's criticisms, but disagree with his reasons.

To begin with, the issue of empiricism versus innatism has been badly put. A fuller discussion of this issue (going beyond what was said in "Innate Knowledge") is reserved for another occasion, but I may briefly say that it is a fundamental mistake to treat thoroughgoing empiricism as false in fact rather than, which is how it should be treated, as impossible a priori.

To distinguish the meaningful from the meaningless, and, within the meaningful, the a priori possible from the a priori impossible, is the task of a priori inquiry, and (in part) of philosophy. Within the a priori possible to distinguish the factually true from the factually false, so far as this can be done by intersubjective means, is the task of science. (Throughout, I use 'science,' for convenience, as short for 'natural science' or its synonym 'empirical science.') From the point of view of one who accepts those distinctions, just as it was a mistake of the a priori sort for the psychologist to take inductive knowledge as the model of all knowledge, so it is a mistake of the same sort for the linguist to treat truths that are known a priori as 'language universals.' But the transformationalists (so far) have made this mistake, and it deeply infects Chomsky's account of language learning.

But another mistake has gone along with this one. In pressing his innatist version of language-learning, Chomsky has given the impression that it is such rules as the Principle of Cyclic Application that show empiricist versions to be untenable. Whether this impression is intended or not, examples of this sort will be misleading until they are matched by others as different from them as possible but which still make the same point. The insight which it would be important to communicate is that principles used in the phrase structure component of a grammar serve as well, if not as dramatically, to make the points of criticism that Chomsky wants to make.

Chomsky urges that the theories of Skinner, Osgood, etc., are almost without empirical content. I fully accept the implication (which fits well with my discussion above of the status-shift from empirically true to true a priori) that we should be as clear as we can about the empirical content of the various propositions we are discussing, but am bound to urge that Chomsky's own crucial concepts of 'creativity' and 'appropriateness' will turn out to yield propositions that are no better off in this regard. Relatedly, "the assumption that linguistic and mental processes are virtually identical" (1966, p. 31, cited above) is pointlessly strong; the linguist can make exactly the same contribution under the assumption that linguistic processes are also mental processes, while remaining uncommitted (because it is irrelevant to him) as to whether (all) mental processes are also linguistic processes.

The last point in my critique of Chomsky is that his critique has thrown out the baby with the bath water. Not all of behavioral theory need be discarded, and he has slighted the part that may be kept. A clear example is afforded by his recent suggestion (1968, pp. 78-9; 1969a, pp. 64, 159) that Peirce's theory of abduction has a valuable contribution to make. I agree with this (see Wells, 1967, pp. 108-12), but would add that behavioral psychologists had a similar theory (the doctrine of a hierarchy of responses), even if they didn't apply it as extensively as they might have to the treatment of language-learning. It is perverse to characterize this theory (1965, p. 47; 1969a, p. 90) as an empiricism different in kind from the 'rationalism' of Peirce and Chomsky, when there is a viewpoint from which the difference is one of degree, or, even slighter, a difference as to what particular responses are hypothesized to be hierarchically ordered.

In denying an inner connection between Chomsky's critique of behavioral psychology and his transformational linguistics, I have no thought of denying the originality of his critique. I do mean to say that a person subscribing, let us say, to the linguistic doctrines called "Descriptive Linguistics" could without inconsistency have made such a critique (from which it follows as a corollary that if, in point of fact, descriptive linguists instead of critiquing behavioral psychology went along with it, this too was a fact without an inner logical necessity), but I do not mean to claim that any such person did so. We are indebted to Chomsky for the vigor, the persistence, and the impact of his critique.

I will now pass to a more detailed discussion of some of these theses.

PHILOSOPHY AND SCIENCE, RESUMED

In Section 1, near the end, I implied that philosophy deals with thought and science with expression. In Section 5 ("Two Kinds of Necessity"), the relation between the contrast of philosophy with science and the contrast of a priori with a posteriori truth was discussed. In the present section I will sketch certain conceptions about philosophy, not undertaking to argue for these conceptions, but only to show how they bear on the topics of (a) thought, (b) speech, (c) psychology, and (d) linguistics. The air of dogmatism with which these are laid down is the result of limitations of space and pressures of time.

Philosophy does not have exclusive prerogative to thought; psychology and linguistics can study thought too. But they, as sciences, have inherent limitations, stemming from the scientific demand for verifiability of a certain sort. These same limitations affect too their treatment of speech.

For example — perhaps the most important example — freedom is beyond the reach of science. Science may try to deal with, or handle, freedom, and can do so up to a certain point, but that there is such a limiting point is shown by the fact that under scientific treatment, freedom is indistinguishable from chance (random behavior). In other words, science can, to an extent, deal with freedom, but not to an extent that would enable it to distinguish freedom from chance.

The same is true of 'creativity' (Chomsky, 1964, p. 918, and see footnote 2 above) and 'appropriateness' (Chomsky, 1969b, p. 523, Column B near the bottom). It is misleading to introduce these, as Chomsky does, into a critique of psychology in such a way as to suggest that a psychology that does not deal with these is neglecting its paramount task. Clearer analytic thinking would show that science in general, and psychology in particular, *could* not deal with these in a distinctive way, i.e., in a way that would treat them differently from the way in which they treat chance.

Owing to the difference between philosophy and science, the following two propositions are compatible:

(1)Thinking is peculiar to man and is not reducible to speaking. There are features of thought that are reflected in speaking and that make speaking too, so far as it reflects these features, not amenable to scientific treatment any more than thought is.

(2)Psychology should treat thinking and speaking as responses similar in fundamental kind to other human responses, and to all the responses of other organisms.

From these two propositions we can respectively deduce two others, which are likewise compatible: Man, (3) though different in kind from brute animals, (2) should be treated by science as the same in kind.

INNATENESS AND ACQUISITION

Science in general, and psychology in particular, will need to admit beings with various innate dispositions. (See Walls, 1969, for detail, including pp. 107-8, the important difference between a disposition and a capacity or power.) There will be a general problem of distinguishing innate from acquired dispositions, and since from the methodological viewpoint 'acquired' is the positive property and 'innate' the negative one (for that is innate which has not *in any way* been acquired), there will be a derived maxim of method, to try treating each disposition as acquired and only when such attempts fail to begin treating it as innate. The question of when it is time to declare that attempts to prove that something has been acquired are a failure is a practical question. As a corollary, there will be a maxim to treat beings (even structurally, organically different beings such as man and ape) as the same in their innate dispositions unless there is reason — sufficient reason for the time being — to think this unworkable. The organic differences are not by themselves to count as sufficient reason to think this.

It is not possible for a science to avoid a conceptual framework which treats some dispositions as innate, and the reason is this. Every explanation of such and such a disposition as acquired will demonstrate that it is acquired from some other disposition, assumed by the explanation, under such and such conditions. A disposition which is treated by a certain theory as acquired is a disposition which that theory explains as derived from some other disposition by stating that owing to that other disposition of the acquiring organism, the acquirer acquires it under such and such conditions. And so, for every theory, and for every disposition which that theory treats as acquired, there will be some other disposition which that theory does not treat as acquired. Finally, if a theory treats of a disposition at all and does not treat it as acquired, we will say that it treats it as innate.

Although every theory treats some disposition as innate, it does not follow that some disposition is treated by every theory as innate. For one theory may differ from another as to which dispositions it treats as innate.

Since (as noted) innateness is a negative property, it will be a maxim of method that, for each disposition that one wants to provide for in a psychological system, psychology should first try hypotheses which treat that disposition as acquired, and if such attempts fail, only then to fall back on treating it as innate. (It is because innateness is conceived negatively, and not, or not only, as Chomsky seems to think, because the hypothesis that something is innate is thought to be less simple than hypotheses that it is acquired, that an innateness-hypothesis is a last resort.) There is no definite objective answer to the question when a set of attempts shall be declared to have failed; but I agree with Chomsky that S-R psychology in general should have given that answer long ago, as regards attempts to show that all of man's intellectual dispositions except conditioned or associative learning can be treated as acquired dispositions; I disagree as to the reasons. He says (if I may offer a very rough paraphrase) that it was gratuitous; I say that it was absurd. There is a difference. From the epistemological standpoint, conditioned learning corresponds to inductive knowledge; and the attempt to treat all cognitive dispositions, other than the disposition to induce, as dispositions learned (acquired) with the help of the disposition to induce, is absurd — is nonsense — because the attempt to treat all knowledge (of the knowing-that variety) as inductive knowledge is nonsense. Now with the testing of nonsense there is no question as to how long is long enough; a nonsensical pseudo-hypothesis should never be tested at all.

There was a time when hypothetical entities[12] were to be eliminated in favor of logical constructions. Except for saying that the abandonment of this aim is to be regarded as justified empirically by its failure, rather than (as Chomsky seems to hold) as dictated *ab initio* by good sense, I will steer clear of the debate about the ideals of description and explanation, and the admissibility of hypothetical entities, and will assume the point that hypothetical entities will be admitted. There is still a question of method to be settled. This question is whether accuracy or simplicity is to be given prior claim as a goal.

ACCURACY VERSUS SIMPLICITY

It would be widely agreed that accuracy is an important goal and that simplicity is also, but there is disagreement as to which to prefer in a case where the two prove incompatible. My own hierarchy of goals is that accuracy takes precedence over simplicity; several of my criticisms of psychologists and of linguists presuppose this hierarchy, and correspondingly the views criticized presuppose the opposite hierarchy in which simplicity is rated above accuracy. If the disagreement about the hierarchy cannot be settled, then the merits of the criticizing and the criticized positions cannot be settled either, and the point of presenting the criticism would then be not to settle the issue but to clarify it. Let it be borne in mind that it is comparative accuracy and comparative simplicity that are in question: the question I am raising is whether to prefer theory A or theory B where A is the more accurate theory and B is the simpler one.

Roughly speaking, and within some limit, the more distinctions a scientific theory makes, the more accurate it can be. We know that there must be a limit to this because if, for example, a scientific theory tries to distinguish

---

[12]Also called inferred entities, theoretical entities, and constructs. Clark Hull's 'intervening variables' are a variety. The term 'construct' has historical priority over Russell's term 'logical construction'; we find it proposed in 1891 by Conway Lloyd Morgan, in *Animal Life and Intelligence*. Karl Pearson, who adopts the term (*The Grammar of Science*, second edition, 1900, p. 41), is in turn quoted by Henry Margenau, *The Nature of Physical Reality*, 1950, p. 71. Margenau carefully explains the difference between his sense and that of Morgan and Pearson. Russell, 1914, p. iv, credits to Whitehead "the whole conception of the world of physics as a *construction* rather than an *inference*"; however Whitehead himself subsequently employed the phrase 'extensive abstraction.' Russell's term 'logical construction' is defined as meticulously as is the term of Morgan, Pearson, and Margenau, and is closer to the connotation of the verb 'to construct' in its ordinary use which implies that what is constructed is constructed out of given materials. Constructs whether in Morgan's and Pearson's sense or in Margenau's would be more aptly called 'invention.' I suspect that some of those who have used the term 'construct' have — unwarrantedly — ascribed to constructs the logical properties of Russell's logical constructions.

freedom from chance, it will find that it has made a distinction without a difference, that is, without a *scientific* difference; the situation will be similar, perhaps, if a scientific theory tries to deal with the concept of adequate expression. It may be that science can no more adequately deal with adequacy than it can with freedom, creativity, and appropriateness. In that case, scientific theories could not be reproached for not tackling the notion of adequacy; and it would further follow (in view of the meaning of 'insofar as') that insofar as it is the possibility of inadequacy that precludes a reduction of thought to speech, science is at liberty to attempt the reduction. For where it fails, insofar as possible inadequacy is the reason for the failure, it will not be because it was a *poor* scientific theory, but just because it was a *scientific* theory.

It is impossible to deal in a brief compass with a doctrine so subtle, on the one hand, and so out of favor, on the other, as a sharp and *prinzipiell* distinction between philosophy and science. But I could not forbear from trying, with the hope that in the future I can converge upon this point from different approaches as upon a hub by traveling along different spokes.

REFERENCES

Black, M. (ed.), 1962. *The Importance of Language.* Englewood Cliffs, New Jersey: Prentice-Hall.

Cassirer, E., 1955. *The Philosophy of Symbolic Forms.* Volume 2, *Mythical Thought.* New Haven: Yale University Press.

Chomsky, N., 1964. "The Logical Basis of Linguistic Theory." In Horace G. Lunt (ed.), *Proceedings of the Ninth International Congress of Linguists, Cambridge, Mass., August 27-31, 1962.* The Hague: Mouton.

Chomsky, N., 1965. *Aspects of the Theory of Syntax.* Cambridge (Mass.): M.I.T. Press.

Chomsky, N., 1966. *Cartesian Linguistics.* New York: Harper and Row.

Chomsky, N., 1968: *Language and Mind.* New York: Harcourt, Brace & World.

Chomsky, N., 1969a. "Linguistics and Philosophy." In Hook, 1969, pp. 51-94.

Chomsky, N., 1969b. "Knowledge of Language," *Times Literary Supplement* No. 3,507,523-25 (London, May 15, 1969).

Dunkel, H. B., 1948. *Second Language Learning.* Boston: Ginn and Company.

Hadamard, J., 1945. *An Essay on the Psychology of Invention in the Mathematical Field.* Princeton, New Jersey: Princeton University Press.

Henle, P., et al., 1958. *Language, Thought, and Culture.* Ann Arbor: University of Michigan Press.

Hirzel, R., 1947. *Der Name* (zweite Auflage). Leipzig, Germany: Sächsische Akademie der Wissenschaften, Philologisch-historische Klasse, Abhandlungen Bd. 36 Nr. 2.

Hook, Sidney (ed.), 1969. *Language and Philosophy: A symposium.* New York: New York University Press.

Müller, F. N., 1888. *Three Introductory Lectures on the Science of Thought.* Chicago: The Open Court Publishing Company.

Osgood, C. E., 1953. *Method and Theory in Experimental Psychology.* New York: Oxford University Press.

Peirce, C. *Collected Papers.* Cambridge (Mass.): Harvard University Press, 1931-58. 8 Vols.

Russell, B., 1918. *Mysticism and Logic.* London: Longmans, Green.

Russell, B., 1938. *The Principles of Mathematics.* 2nd ed. London: Allen & Unwin.

Saporta, S. (ed.), 1961. *Psycholinguistics: A Book of Readings.* New York: Holt, Rinehart, and Winston.

Ullmann, S., 1951. *The Principles of Semantics.* Glasgow: Jackson, Son and Company.

Wells, R., 1954. "Meaning and Use." *Word, 10,* 235-250. Reprinted in Saporta, 1961, pp. 269-283.

Wells, R., 1962. "What Has Linguistics Done for Philosophy?" *Jour. of Philos., 59,* 697-708.

Wells, R., 1963. "Is Frege's Concept of Function Valid?" *Jour. of Philos., 60,* 719-730.

Wells, R., 1964. "The True Nature of Peirce's Evolutionism." In *Studies in the Philosophy of Charles Sanders Peirce* ed. Edward C. Moore and Richard S. Robin. (second series). Amherst: The University of Massachusetts Press.

Wells, R., 1967. "Distinctively Human Semiotic." *Social Science Information (Information sur les Sciences Sociales), 6,* 103-124 (Paris, France).

Wells, R., 1969. "Innate Knowledge." In Hook, 1969, pp. 99-119.

3

Understanding

Paul Ziff

On occasion some of us are concerned to understand what is said. What is it that we are then concerned to do? To understand, of course, but what is that?

This question, so cast, can invite the blankest of stares, but it can be construed: let something be said to two persons such that, though each heard it, one did but the other did not understand what was said. Then presumably there was some difference then and there between these two that obtained simply in virtue of the fact that one did and the other did not understand what was said. What was that difference?

1. The difference between one who understood and one who did not need not have been a difference in actual overt behavior, verbal or nonverbal.

If each heard what was said then even if neither gave any indication, neither responded in any way, possibly one did and the other did not understand. If this were so then perhaps we would not know that one did and one did not understand. But that possibility would remain: such is our common conception of understanding.

2. Perhaps the difference is that though neither did anything in any way noticeable or overt or evident, one could have done something of that sort that the other could not, thus a difference in potential overt behavior. For suppose what had been said was "Open the safe: the combination is left 23, 4, 21." Then perhaps the one who understood could have opened the safe and perhaps the other could not.

But as against this it is conceivable that, with respect to such overt behavior as opening a safe, the one who did not understand what was said could nonetheless have done what the other could have done, and it is conceivable that the one who did understand could not have done anything that the other could not have done. For first, the one who did not understand might already have known the combination to the safe and so could have opened the safe even though he had not understood what was said; secondly, each could have been encased in concrete with only ears protruding and these rendered immobile and so since neither could have done anything noticeable or overt or evident, the one who understood could not have done anything of that sort that the other could not.

3. To claim that the difference between one who understood what was said and one who did not was not a difference in overt behavior, either actual or potential, verbal or nonverbal, is not to deny that there was, in the case in question, something which the one who did not understand could not possibly have done which possibly the one who did understand could have done. For only the one who understood could possibly have obeyed the given order.

If the one who understood the order to open the safe were then to have opened the safe, in so doing he would have been obeying the order. Whereas if the one who had not understood what was said had nonetheless then opened the safe, in so doing he would not have been obeying the order even though it could certainly have seemed as though he were.

But such a difference makes no difference here. The difference between obeying an order to open a safe and merely behaving in such a way that constitutes compliance with an order to open a safe is not an overt behavioral difference.

4. Understanding what is said is, in the respects noted, somewhat on a par with having a pain. For just so there is no piece of overt behavior, either actual or potential, that necessarily serves to differentiate between a man who is in pain and one who is not. There is nothing that a man who is in pain does or can or could do that is noticeable or overt or evident that a man who is not in pain could not do equally well.

Understanding what is said is also like having a pain in that just as some minor pains, say a slight pain in one's head, can hardly be specifically manifested in overt behavior, just so one who understands what is said when what is said is something like "The Löwenheim-Skolem theorems have remarkable implications," can hardly specifically manifest his understanding in overt behavior. Just as there is no specific overt behavior that is indicative of a slight pain in one's head, so there is no specific overt behavior that is indicative of an understanding of any of innumerable statements.

But understanding is in a way worse than pain. For though neither understanding nor pain need be evidenced nor can be unmistakably evidenced by overt behavior, at least a person in pain can hardly have much doubt whether he is in pain: he has the pain, he experiences pain. But one who understands what is said need not experience anything at all and on occasion he may be in considerable doubt whether he understands what is said.

5. Since evidently there need not have been either an actual or potential overt behavioral difference between one who understood what was said and one who did not, if there was any difference between two such persons we must look elsewhere to find it. Is it that the one who understood what was said, say S, made an inference from S, whereas the one who did not understand did not?

How are we here to construe making an inference from S? If someone says "It is raining" and I then say "Then we shall have to call off the game," my so saying could be held to exemplify the making of an inference. But my actually saying that is in itself merely another piece of overt behavior, verbal rather than nonverbal, but still not to the present point. Suppose, however, on hearing what is said I then think, it then in consequence occurs to me, that then we shall have to call off the game. This could be held to constitute the making of an inference. Let us say that to make an inference from S, where S is something that is actually said, is to infer P from S, where P is something expressible in words and having some of the properties of its verbal expression; in particular, it too may be understood just as its verbal expression may be understood, and if its verbal expression can be associated with a truth value, so it too can be. (In traditional terms I suppose P would thus correspond more or less to an "entertained proposition" at the moment of festivity.)

Is it that one who understood S must have made an inference from S? There is, I think, no reason to think it. Let S be a query about the time; if I understand S I may simply glance at a watch and then say what time it is by way of reply. On introspection one is not apt to find any indication that any inference was made. (Possibly here some could be inclined to speak of an "unconscious inference" but little is likely to be gained by doing so.)

6. Is it that the one who understood S was able to make an inference from S whereas the one who did not was not? This can hardly be correct but, as will be seen, the question is somewhat complex.

To begin with, one can have good reason to believe that S is a statement having a truth value even if one does not understand S. Thus one may have good reason to believe that a person who said "Differential puffing is an expression of differential *in situ* transcription" in so saying made a statement having a truth value even if one does not understand the statement one believes to have been made.

The question whether one is able to make inferences from a statement if and only if one understands it is complicated by the fact that understanding admits of degrees. One may fully understand or one may only partially understand, or understand roughly, or only more or less. To hope to have some understanding of a statement is not to be overambitious.

A man who has no conception of what differential puffing is may hear and not understand the statement in question. But to claim that he does not understand that statement is not to deny that even so he may have some understanding of what was said. He may have some understanding of it but not enough to warrant the unqualified claim that he does understand it, and his understanding of it may be sufficiently insufficient to warrant the unqualified claim that he does not understand it.

7. That one may be able to make an inference from what is said even if one does not understand it may be argued in three different ways on the basis of three different kinds of example. Let what is said be 'Differential puffing is an expression of differential *in situ* transcription' and let this be S.

First, one who does not understand S may nonetheless be able to infer P from S, where P is expressible as 'Something is an expression of something.' For though his understanding of S is sufficiently insufficient to warrant the unqualified claim that he does not understand S, he may know that if S is true then P must be true.

But in reply it may be said that the case supports rather than confounds the claim that one is able to make an inference from S only if one understands S. For though it is true that the man in question can rightly be said not to understand S, he nonetheless has some understanding of S and it is that aspect of S that he does understand that accounts for the inference he is able to make. Thus the inference he is able to make is as it were in some sense proportional to his understanding of S.

8. Secondly, one who does not understand S may know that S is a statement having a truth value and so he may be able to infer P from S, where P is expressible as 'Some statement, that could be made by uttering the words "Differential puffing is an expression of differential *in situ* transcription" in some appropriate way and under appropriate conditions, would be true.'

But in reply it may be said that the inference to P is not an inference from S but rather an inference from the fact that a certain speech act was performed by uttering certain words. It is not what was said that warrants the inference to P but simply the fact that something was stated by using certain words.

9. Thirdly and more importantly, one who does not understand S may know that S is a statement having a truth value and so he may be able to infer

P, where P is expressible as 'Either differential puffing is an expression of differential *in situ* transcription or snow is white,' and this on the grounds that from any S having a truth value one may infer the disjunction S *or* Q.

As against this it may be argued that one has not made a genuine inference from S if, as we are supposing, one does not understand S; for if one does not understand S then one does not understand the disjunction S *or* Q either: if one is genuinely to infer P then that which is inferred must itself be understood.

10. If the replies just indicated were correct, it would follow, I think, that one is not able to make an inference from a statement that one does not understand. And this is to say that being able to make an inference from S would be a sufficient condition for understanding S. But if this were so then the reply just given to the third argument must be inadequate to the point at issue.

One who knows some elementary logic and knows merely that S is a statement having a truth value is able to infer P from S, where P is expressible as a statement of the form: S or Q_1 or Q_2 ... or Q_n, where the Q's are such statements as 'Snow is white,' 'The sky is blue,' and so forth. (Although one may plausibly argue that one does not understand the disjunction S *or* Q if one does not understand one of the disjuncts, one cannot plausibly argue that one does not understand the disjunction S or Q_1 or Q_2 ... or Q_n simply in virtue of the fact that one does not understand one disjunct. If one understands all but a single sentence of a lengthy novel, should one say that one did not understand the novel?) That the one who infers P from S understands P is then indicated by the fact that he is able to make inferences from P. And since he is able to infer P from S, he must understand S, contrary to our original hypothesis. This would mean that knowing some elementary logic and knowing merely that S is a statement having a truth value is sufficient for understanding S. Since this is clearly absurd, it is equally clear that being able to make an inference from S is not a sufficient condition for understanding S.

11. Is being able to make an inference from S a necessary condition for understanding S? That is, if one understands S does it follow that one is able to make an inference from S?

Let it be clear what the letter 'S' is here supposed to designate. The letter 'S' is here being used for the moment in connection with the present example to designate a statement that we are supposing to be made at a certain time and place. Thus 'S' here refers to a supposed temporal event, the performance of a particular declarative speech act. Suppose another statement is made at a different time or place such that this statement is sufficiently similar in the relevant respects, whatever they may be, to warrant classing this statement as a statement of the same type as the first. Let 'S_i' designate the statement then made. Then in so far as we are here concerned with questions of understanding, we cannot here identify S_i with S. The reason for this is simply that even though one might understand S, it does not follow that one understands S_i: it is fortunately the case that even if one does not understand a statement at one time, one may manage to understand its equivalent at a later time. To take account of such a possibility, we are here using the letter 'S' to designate a statement at a particular time and place such that no recurrence of S itself is possible. Thus we are concerned with what may be called "statement-tokens" rather than "statement-types."

On the hypothesis in question, if a man understands S then he is able to infer P_i from S, where P_i is expressible by some statement-token or other, possibly one of the same type as S. For this to be a genuine inference, however, he would have to understand P_i. To understand P_i on the hypothesis (and on our assumptions about making an inference (see section 5), he would also have to be able to infer P_j from P_i. And so of course he would have to be able to infer P_k from P_j, and so on *ad infinitum*. This means that to understand S, he would have to be able to make not just one but all of an infinite series of inferences.

It is essential to realize that what is required here is not simply that the man be able to make any inference of the infinite series but that he be able to make all of the inferences, for if he cannot make all, he cannot make any. For suppose a man is able to make any but not all of the inferences of the series from S to P_1 to P_2 to .... Since he is not able to make all of the inferences, there must be an inference, I_i, that he is not able to make. This means that there must be a P_i in the series such that he is not able to make the inference from it. (It won't do to argue here that since by hypothesis he is able to make any inference of the series, he must be able to make them all, and this on the grounds that since he can make any inference, P_i cannot be P_1 since he is able to infer P_2 from P_1, and P_i cannot be P_{n+1} since he can infer P_{n+1} from P_n. If an usher has only 10 seats available and 11 people to be seated, though he is able to seat any one of the group, he is not able to seat them all. If he is not able to seat them all then there is at least one member of the group that he is not able to seat. Hence being able to seat any one of a group is not incompatible with not being able to seat some one of the group.) Given that the man in question is not able to make the inference from P_i, this means that on the hypothesis in question he does not understand P_i and hence the inference to P_i was not itself a genuine inference. From which it follows that he was not able to make inference I_{i-1} either. From which it follows that he was not able to make the inference from P_{i-1}, and thus not able to make the inference from P_{i-n}, and so not able to make any inference from S. Thus if he cannot make all of the inferences of the series, he cannot make any. (The analogous difficulty could be created for an usher who has only 10 seats but 11 people to be seated if he were instructed that he is not to seat a person unless he is also able to seat an unseated friend of the person. Suppose all 11 people waiting to be seated are friends, and suppose 10 of them are then hastily seated by the usher. There was, as there was bound to be, one person, p_i, who was not seated. But if so, p_i's friend p_{i-1} was seated in violation of the rule that he was not to be seated unless his unseated friend were also seated; on realizing this a conscientious usher would have to unseat p_{i-1}; but then of course he would have to unseat p_{i-2}; and so on. The consequence would be that the usher would not be able to seat anyone.)

Although it may seem strange to say so, it takes time actually to make an inference. It does not take much time. But given the speed of conductivity in the brain, it would appear that 20 inferences per second would be the upper limit that a human being is capable of. And given a life expectancy of 65 years this means that the upper limit for the number of inferences an average human being is able to make is in the neighborhood of 41 billion (enough, no doubt, to pass the time).

Given that there is a finite upper limit to the number of inferences a human being is able to make, and given that the condition in question would require one to be able to make an infinite number of inferences, that condition must be rejected. And this is to say that if being able to make an inference from a statement to a statement one understands were a necessary condition for understanding any statement, no one would understand any statement.

One could of course avoid this conclusion by not requiring that one understand that which is inferred and thus no further inference need be possible from that which is inferred. So construed, the condition that one be able to make such an inference from S if one understands S could perhaps more plausibly be supposed to be necessary, but it would be quite unilluminating since with a minimal understanding of logic one could always, for any statement whatever, infer the denial of its denial, and so forth.

12. The difference we are looking for is not to be found in the ability to make inferences; possibly it is to be found in the possibility of providing paraphrases. Is it that one who understands what is said could paraphrase what is said but one who does not could not?

That the ability to provide a paraphrase cannot suffice here as a sufficient condition for understanding what is said can be seen in a glance. If one has a thorough grasp of the syntax of a language then even if one has virtually no knowledge of its semantics one can nonetheless readily provide paraphrases. Thus without understanding S one can, on the basis of syntactic considerations alone, paraphrase it as 'Differential *in situ* transcription is something that differential puffing is an expression of' or as 'Differential *in situ* transcription and differential puffing stand in a relation such that the latter is an expression of the former.'

13. The view that being able to provide a paraphrase is a necessary condition for understanding what is said is at best a mare's nest.

Assuming that it is not altogether unclear what is to count as a paraphrase, to provide a paraphrase of a statement, *S*, requires one to say (or to write) something, *P*, such that *P* is a paraphrase of *S*. If the condition in question were a necessary condition for understanding what is said it would follow that no nonhuman animal we know of ever understands anything that is said. (Don't horses and dogs, on occasion, understand and obey oral commands? That either makes inferences is doubtful; that neither could provide paraphrases is certain.) Furthermore, it would follow that such creatures as infants and unlettered mutes cannot understand anything that is said.

To suppose that being able to provide a paraphrase is a necessary condition for understanding what is said is to suppose that one cannot understand a use of words unless one is oneself able to use words. But there is no reason to think that and good reason not to.

14. The marshalling of evidence in support of the counter claim that one can understand a use of words even if one cannot oneself use words here admits of an avid eclecticism. Information theory, psychology, common sense all lend credence to the view.

The familiar phenomenon of being able to understand a foreign language but not to speak it, of being able to read it but not to write it, is not something phenomenal. (An inability to speak in Italian need not be confused with an incapacity to speak. Leopardi *sensa lingua* would not be *sensa linguaggio*. But an unschooled tongueless Texan lacks both the capacity to speak and the ability to speak in Italian.)

Studies of aphasics indicate that two relatively distinct types can be discerned and that instances of each are in fact to be encountered: expressive aphasics and receptive aphasics. Expressive aphasics can understand a use of words but cannot themselves use words. Receptive aphasics cannot understand a use of words directed by others to them but can themselves use words.

15. The robot-minded among us are wont to construe using words and understanding a use of words in terms of encoding and decoding processes. It is not an impossible point of view.

If, in Martian manner, we think of the process of using words as some sort of encoding process in which something, *a*, is encoded as something, *b*, it is then not implausible to think of understanding a use of words as something connected with the completion of a decoding process. If so, the separation of the hearer from the speaker can seem immediate and complete. That one can decode *b* as *a* in no way necessitates one's having the ability to encode *a* as *b*. From an engineering standpoint, decoding and encoding are far from symmetrical processes: think of the differences between a television receiving station and a television broadcasting station. Receivers are not generally transmitters.

More precisely, think of a general all-purpose computer capable of computing the values of some function *E* (for encoding) and capable of computing the values of some function *D* (for decoding). Despite its capacity to compute both *E* and *D*, the machine may be programmed to compute *D* and yet not programmed to compute *E*. If the machine is programmed to compute *D* but not *E*, it is the analogue of a person who can understand but cannot speak a foreign tongue because of the lack not of a tongue but of the requisite knowledge, or better, "know how." The analogue of the tongueless hearer can be supplied either by a suitably programmed but partially damaged all-purpose computer or by, what comes to much the same, a special-purpose computer having a relatively rigid structure rendering it incapable of computing the requisite function.

16. Our question is this: if two persons each heard and made out what was said but one did and the other did not understand it, what was the difference then and there between the two that obtained simply in virtue of the fact that one did and the other did not understand what was said? So far we have concluded that that difference was not a difference in overt behavior, actual or potential, neither was it a difference in an ability to make inferences, neither was it a difference in an ability to provide paraphrases. That it is not any of these things was, I think, rather plain to begin with even though I have been at some pains to make it so. This travail could have been considerably curtailed had we come by another way, had we reflected on a simple ambiguity of the phrase 'to understand what is said.'

The ambiguity of the phrase arises from and is owing to the ambiguity of the subphrase 'what is said': for, among other things, 'what is said' may refer either to the utterance uttered or to the statement made. If while pointing to me a person says "That person is in pain" then what he has said, in the sense of the utterance uttered is 'That person is in pain'; but what he has said, in the sense of the statement made, is that I am in pain.

We are here concerned with understanding what is said in the sense of understanding the statement made. We are not primarily concerned with understanding what is said in the sense of understanding the utterance uttered. But the difference between understanding the statement made and understanding the utterance uttered is not a difference with respect to understanding. The ambiguity of the phrase 'to understand what is said' does not arise from and is not owing to any ambiguity of the word 'understand.' The sense of that word here appears to be univocal. But if so, understanding what is said in either sense of the phrase can hardly sensibly be supposed to be a matter of behavior or of making inferences or providing paraphrases.

17. To understand what is said, in the sense of understanding the utterance uttered is (not so simply) to hear and make out the utterance. Thus if from the lecture platform one asks students at the rear of the room "Can you understand what is said?", the answer is yes if they can hear and make out the words: thus even Heidigger can hope to be understood. It is necessary merely not to mumble overmuch.

Understanding the utterance uttered would then appear to be a matter of data processing of some sort. A hearer is supplied with auditory data which are to be processed in such a way that, on completion of the processing, the hearer will have made a correct phonemic morophologico-syntactic identification and classification of the constituents of the utterance.

If a hearer does understand the utterance uttered then in the ordinary run of things one would expect him to be able somehow to utilize this knowledge. And in the ordinary run of things hearers on occasion do utilize such knowledge in supplying verbatim reports. But an exercise of the ability to supply a verbatim report depends on factors over and above a knowledge of what was said. And on occasion, as in the case of aphasics, or of mutes, and so forth, hearers may lack the requisite abilities even though they have the requisite knowledge. That the means of expression are not available to a hearer cannot ever suffice to establish that he lacks the requisite knowledge to be expressed.

18. Understanding what is said, in the sense of understanding the statement made, also appears to be essentially a matter of data processing of some sort. Again a hearer is supplied with auditory data which are to be processed in such a way that, on completion of the processing, the hearer will have made a correct semantic identification and classification of the constituents of the statement made.

If the hearer does understand the statement made then in the ordinary run of things one would expect him to be able somehow to utilize this knowledge, either in the modulation of overt behavior, or in making inferences, or in providing paraphrases. And in the ordinary run of things hearers on occasion do so perform. But again an exercise of the abilities requisite for so performing depends on factors over and above a knowledge of the statement made. And again on occasion a hearer may lack either the opportunity or the requisite capacities or abilities even though he has the requisite knowledge.

19. That understanding what is said is essentially a matter of data processing of some sort is not a claim about the use of words. What is at issue here is our conception of understanding, not our use of the word 'understand.' But support for the view being urged can be gained by considering why we use that word as we do.

Suppose there is at hand a concrete slab with an inscription carved on it. The inscription reads: "Take two paces forward, three to the left, four more forward, six to the right, and then salaam!" A man who had paused to look at the slab then did precisely that, swiftly and surely. How are we to account for the fact that he behaved in precisely that peculiar fashion? To suppose he just happened to behave so would be to suppose a minor miracle had taken place.

Since his peculiar behavior occurred immediately subsequent to his having attended to the inscription, and assuming that no equally attractive alternative explanation is available, to explain what would otherwise appear to be a miraculous coincidence between the immediate significance of the inscription and the evident modulation of his behavior, we must suppose that the visual data he was supplied with were somehow rendered efficacious by means of some internal processing. We baptize such successful processing 'understanding' and we attribute to him an understanding of what was inscribed.

To realize that understanding what is said is essentially a matter of data processing of some sort is not, unfortunately, enough to achieve a clear conception of what understanding is. For one wants to know precisely what the character and form of that processing is.

20. Unhappily the character and form of the data processing that can culminate in understanding is today much of a mystery. But one important feature of our present conception of understanding can readily be discerned.

To understand what is said, in the sense of understanding the utterance uttered, is to hear and make out the words. Thus in effect one performs a morphological analysis of the utterance; the utterance is segmented, decomposed into its morphological constituents. This indicates that the data processing that can culminate in understanding has a specific character: it is an analytic process. Understanding, not surprisingly, is akin to figuring out, deciphering, decoding, and the like.

21. Further support for the view that the process in question is essentially analytic in character can be uncovered in connection with the following sort of question. Suppose we have before us the concrete slab on which there is a

carved inscription. Then although we can perhaps set ourselves the task of attempting to understand the carved inscription, we cannot set ourselves the task of attempting to understand the slab: a concrete slab cannot be understood and not of course because it is inscrutable. But what is the difference between the slab and the carved inscription in virtue of which only the latter can be understood?

I have claimed that understanding is essentially a matter of analytical data processing of some sort. This in turn may suggest that the reason why the inscription can but the slab cannot be understood is that the inscription can but the slab cannot be processed in the appropriate way, whatever that way may prove to be. But that won't do at all.

First, it is not the carved inscription but the visual data supplied by the inscription that can be processed. Secondly, a slab certainly can supply visual data that can be processed in an appropriate way, whatever that way may be; for one may attempt to understand and one may succeed in understanding the structure of the slab on the basis of a visual inspection.

22. A concrete slab may have a complex structure: it may be reinforced, pretensed, and so forth. And this structure can perhaps be understood. And yet the reason that one cannot, without linguistic deviation, speak of 'understanding a slab' is that only that which is composite, complex, and thus capable of analysis, is capable of being understood. Even though a slab may in fact be something composite, complex, to speak of it as 'a slab' is to speak of it as something uncomplex, unitary. Suppose on encountering a concrete slab lying in a field, one were told to count it. Assume that one was not then in the process of counting concrete slabs lying about. Possibly one might respond to the order by saying "One!" but even that seems somewhat absurd. And yet a slab is a collection of molecules and one might madly enough be enjoined to count the molecules of the collection.

If one is to speak sensibly of 'understanding' something then that which is to be understood must be characterized in such a way as to indicate that it is capable of the requisite sort of analytical data processing. So one speaks of understanding a statement, an utterance, a person's behavior, the structure of a slab, and so forth. (We do speak of 'understanding a person' but this is a matter of understanding his behavior, personality structure, and so forth; the expression is an evident trope on a par with 'believing a person' which is a matter of believing what he says.)

23. To understand that understanding is the resultant of some sort of analytical data processing is to have some understanding of understanding. But not much and not enough to warrant an unqualified claim to understand understanding.

More could be conjectured here, albeit some what airily. Unquestionably the process in question involves synthesis as well as analysis: the utterance that is understood is analyzed into words but synthesized into a sentence. But to understand the nature of this synthesis we shall have to have a much clearer conception than we have at present of the constitution and character of the set of elements to be synthesized. In the case of understanding what is said, in the sense of understanding the statement made, this means that we shall have to have a clearer conception of the elements of the analysis, thus of the set of factors that serve to determine the immediate significance of the utterance uttered. Furthermore, it should be altogether obvious that if we are to understand the processes involved in understanding what is said, we shall have to disentangle them from the little-known and ill-understood processes involved in perception. There too, one supposes, the data are subject to some sort of systematic synthesis. Consideration of perceptual processes is of course inescapable in so far as understanding what is said requires one to hear (or at least to witness something in connection with) what is said.

When one broaches such topics as these, one can no longer avoid the dismal conclusion that to understand understanding is a task to be attempted and not to be achieved today, or even tomorrow.

4

Say What You Think

Zeno Vendler

The real man, to Descartes, is the soul, and the essence of the soul is thinking; man, and only man in this world, is a thinking thing. For man, and man only, is capable of speech, which is "the sole sign and the only certain mark of the presence of thought hidden and wrapped up in the body."[1] This relation of thought and language is not merely psychological. If it were only that, if it registered a mere empirical truth, it would be of no interest to Descartes. The connection he points out is on the conceptual level, it is a metaphysical relation. Thought, in the strict sense of the word, is inconceivable without the idea of language, and the use of language, in the full sense of the word, is essentially the expression of thought. This is so because the object of thought and the object of speech belong to the same category: what we think and what we say are things of the same kind. In the following pages I intend to specify, in some detail, what these things are; to use philosophical jargon, I shall give an outline of the ontology of propositions.

To my mind, the most promising study yet made of what it is to say something is Austin's investigation of illocutionary acts (Austin, 1962). Unfortunately, not even Austin has paid enough attention to the Aristotelian principle that the nature of an act is specified by the nature of its object. The varieties of saying things have to be understood in terms of the variety of

---

[1] Letter to Henry More, February 5, 1949 (translations from R. M. Eaton, *Descartes Selections*, New York: Scribner, 1927). In the full original context:
"... nunquam tamen hactenus fuerit observatum, ullum brutum animal eo perfectionis devenisse, ut vera loquela uteretur, hoc est, ut aliquid vel voce vel nutibus indicaret, quod ad solam cogitationem, non autem ad impetum naturalem, posset referri. Haec enim loquela unicum est cogitationis in corpore latentis signum certum, atque ipsa utuntur omnes homines. . ." *(Correspondance*, ed. C. Adam & G. Milhaud, Vol. VIII; Paris: Presses Universitaires, 1963).

what is said. In linguistic terms, my complaint is that he failed to consider, in sufficient detail, the various kinds of verb-objects illocutionary verbs take. Had he done so, the remarkably perceptive classification of illocutionary acts with which he concludes his work would be still more accurate, and what is more, would be supported by argument rather than mere intuition, albeit a penetrating one. There is another, and for the present study crucial, shortcoming in Austin's work. The grammatical tools at his disposal did not permit him to draw a sharp enough criterion of illocutionary verbs, such that it would clearly exclude some other verbs which obviously belong to the domain of thinking rather than saying. He repeatedly wonders about *doubt, know* and *believe* and verbs such as *value, understand, envisage, favor, resent, overlook, intend* and *regard* turn up unquestioned in the final list. Nothing could illustrate the close affinity between the acts of thinking and saying better than this propensity of thinking words to sneak into the domain of saying words, eluding the vigilance of such a valiant guard.

By this time, just a dozen of years later, we have the equipment to underpin Austin's doctrine of how and what one can say, and to extend the inquiry to the various forms and objects of thinking without any fear of confusing the two domains. Accordingly, as a first step I shall define the class of illocutionary verbs, and give an outline of their classification. This will be followed by a corresponding treatment of the verbs of thought, which group, as the reader probably guesses, will roughly correspond to the class known to philosophers as verbs of propositional attitudes. Finally, a glance at the common object of both speech and thinking—the proposition—will provide the metaphysical frosting on the multilayered cake.

PROPOSITIONAL VERBS

Falling through Austin's prism, the concept of saying something spreads out in a spectrum of illocutionary acts.[2] Such an act consists in the production of an utterance with a certain illocutionary force. Language has many devices to specify this force (intonation-patterns, certain transforms such as question, imperative, and so forth), but by far the most versatile and indeed the most universal means of indicating the force is the employment of an illocutionary verb. To Austin, therefore, the normal form of saying something is the issuing of an utterance prefixed by the first person singular present indicative active occurrence of an illocutionary verb.[3] This verb functions as a bracket, or container, in which the content of the utterance is

---

[2] Here I exclude the sense of saying in which one can say words or sentences. Later on I shall be more specific on this point.

[3] In much the same way, Kant claims that "the proposition 'I think' . . . contains the form of each and every judgment of understanding." *Critique of Pure Reason* (ed. N. Kemp Smith, London; Macmillan, 1963), B. 406.

offered with one force or another. The content is, of course, nothing but the verb object of the illocutionary verb in question. It appears, then, that the class of these verbs, which I shall henceforth call 'performatives,' belong to the broader class of prenominal container verbs, verbs, that is, the objects of which are nominalized sentences.

In order to illustrate this point before continuing our theoretical investigations, I shall give a list of utterances, the production of which, provided it is "happy" in Austin's sense, amounts to the performance of an illocutionary act. After each utterance I shall add the sentence from which the particular verb-object has been derived by the nominalising transformation. In this list I purposely include examples from the whole range of illocutionary acts.

    (1)   I suggest that Joe committed the crime.
   (1a) Joe committed the crime.
    (2)   I deny having seen the victim.
   (2a) I have seen the victim.
    (3)   I call it murder.
   (3a) It is murder.
    (4)   I urge you to proceed.
   (4a) You should proceed.
    (5)   I appoint you to the presidency.
   (5a) You will become the president.
    (6)   I promise to pay on time.
   (6a) I shall pay on time.
    (7)   I praise you for having helped the lady.
   (7a) You have helped the lady.

This list is instructive for many reasons. First of all, it displays the wide variety of forms in which nominalizations of the relevant kind may appear. Since it is impossible for me, within limits of this study, to discuss morphological details, all I can do is hope that the reader will catch on to the idea on the basis of these and the yet forthcoming examples.[4] Later on, I shall have to spell out some details anyway.

As I mentioned above, the use of a performative is the most prominent, yet by no means the only way of indicating illocutionary force. I leave it to the imagination of the reader to envision situations, transforms and intonation patterns in which, or with which, the (a)-forms in my list could be produced without the performative, yet with the same force.

Austin has noticed in the course of his quest for a grammatical criterion that the primary occurrence of a performative is the first person singular of

---

[4] Detailed discussion of this topic is to be found in Vendler, 1967 and 1968.

the simple non-continuous present, which is not the case with most other verbs. *I am smoking* is the usual form of reporting my concurrent smoking; *I smoke* is used to admit a disreputable habit. *I promise to pay on time,* on the other hand, exemplifies the normal form of promising, and does not say anything about my habit of promising. The continuous present, moreover, is quite alien to performatives, except for a few colloquial emphatic uses such as *I am warning you.* Unfortunately for Austin, but fortunately for us, this preference for the simple present is by no means a prerogative of these verbs. The whole host of propositional attitude verbs, such as *believe, know, understand, doubt, remember* and *expect* share this feature together with some other verbs of attitude like *love, hate, prefer* and *detest.* It turns out, then, that the preference for the simple present marks a much wider class and that all "propositional" container verbs, be they performatives or propositional attitude verbs, belong to this class.

This aspect is of great value because it helps us to distinguish container verbs of this kind from another kind, the object of which is also a sentence nominalization, but one of a different sort. The following short list should suffice to illustrate this latter species:

> I am watching the sunset.
> I am listening to his singing.
> I am observing the passage of Venus.
> He is imitating the walk of a bear.

Elsewhere (Vendler, 1967, c.5) I have described in great detail the differences between these two kinds of nominalization. By way of a rough summary, one can say that the product of the former kind, which I have called 'imperfect' nominal, expresses a proposition, whereas the product of the other kind, called 'perfect' nominal, denotes an event, process or action. Since these things, unlike propositions, are temporal entities which take place somewhere in the world, it is not surprising to find "perceptual" container verbs in the list just given, and these occurring in the continuous tense, indicating temporal progress. The simple present, on the other hand, neatly corresponds to the atemporal nature of propositions.

Nevertheless it is exactly a temporal aspect that will split the class of propositional verbs into performatives and verbs of propositional attitudes, a feature which has escaped Austin's grammar. It is quite clear that whereas the simple present tense, in the case of a performative, singles out the moment at which the illocutionary act occurs, in the case of a propositional attitude verb, the same tense does not indicate a unique moment, but an indefinite time span which includes the moment of the utterance. To use the terminology I introduced in an earlier study, performatives are achievement verbs, but propositional attitude verbs are state verbs according to their time schema (Vendler, 1967, c.4). *When (at what moment) did you promise such and such?* and *For how long did you believe such and such?* are the proper questions, and *At 5 p.m.* and *For a year or so* are the appropriate answers respectively, and not the other way around. Again, compare *I still believe* with *I still promise*. The first phrase needs no explanation; the second does. It might mean that I have not withdrawn my promise, or that I am still willing to promise, but certainly not that my promising has not yet come to an end.

This difference in their time schema would be sufficient to distinguish thinking words from saying words were it not for the fact that there are some propositional verbs with the achievement schema which, nevertheless, are obviously words of thought and not of saying. *Decide, resolve, realize, identify, recognize* and the like are achievement verbs, yet, typically, not performatives. Their behavior with respect to the present tense, however, is very different from that of the performatives. With a performative, the first person singular present form is the most characteristic, and indeed, the primary occurrence. Members of the *decide* group, on the contrary, do not occur in this form except when accompanied by grammatical adjuncts indicating general scope. There is nothing missing in such a sentence as *I promise to pay on time* or *I warn you that the bull is going to charge*. On the other hand, the sentences **I decide to go home* and **I resolve to quit smoking*, are distinctly deviant. *I decide* and *I resolve* are only acceptable in such contexts as *I always decide on the spur of the moment* or *I never resolve a problem without first sleeping on it*. This feature is not so obvious with the other three verbs just listed. Looking closer we realize, however, that in case they are acceptable in the simple present without a modifier indicating general scope, they occur as a performative or as a propositional attitude verb, for example, *I realize that such and such is the case* permits *still: I still realize . . . . Realize,* therefore, doubles as an attitude verb. *I identify* and *I recognize,* on the other hand, may function as performatives as in: *I hereby identify the accused as the man who . . .* or *I hereby recognize the deputy as the representative of . . . .*

We can safely conclude, then, that the class of propositional verbs falls into three groups: (a) performatives, with achievement time schema and unmodified first person singular present occurrence; (b) the *decide*-group, with the same time schema but no unmodified first person singular present; and (c) propositional attitude verbs with state time schema. For the sake of simplicity I shall refer to the last two classes as verbs of propositional achievement and verbs of propositional state. As we see, the correction of Austin's criterion for performatives has led us to the recognition of the two main groups of thinking verbs. Furthermore, we are going to see that the classification of performatives, begun by Austin, can be parallelled by a similar classification of thinking verbs.

PERFORMATIVES

Within these limits I can only summarize the subdivision of performatives. It turns out that the intuitive classification given by Austin can be recast, with only few and unimportant deviations, in terms of the syntactic structures that the appropriate verb-objects display.

To begin with, the simplest, and indeed paradigm, form of propositional object is the *that*-clause. The class of performatives that normally take such an object corresponds to Austin's "expositives": *state, assert, suggest, concede, admit, deny, argue, report, testify, confess, predict, warn* and many others. Of course, there are optional structures available such as the ones appearing in, say,

> I confess having seen her.
> I concede his superiority.

but the *that*-form is always easily available.

Austin's "verdictives" are similar to this class, except for the fact that the sentence that gets nominalized contains the copula rather than some other verb. This leads to another structure, which, in this case, obligatorily replaces the *that*-clause: the subject of the nominalized sentence becomes the direct object of the performative, and the copula is omitted or replaced by *as*. Some examples:

> I *call* it murder.
> I *rank* him second.
> We *find* him guilty.
> I *classify* the piece (as) a novel.

Other members of this class will be *place, rate, grade, diagnose, describe, define* and so forth.

In the class of "commissives" two new elements enter the picture: a noun-sharing between the subject of the performative and the subject of the nominalized sentence, and an auxiliary (*shall* or *will*) in the same sentence. *Promise* belongs to this class:

> I promise (you) to pay on time.

which codes the full form:

> *I* promise (you) that *I shall* pay on time.

Some other commissives: *undertake, covenant, vow, pledge* and *guarantee*.

There are two structures corresponding to Austin's "exercitives." The first one, for which I shall retain the name, is shown in sentences such as

> I *order* you to proceed.
> I *advise* you to remain silent.

The infinitive construction in the nominal once more conceals an auxiliary (in this case *should*), and the subject of the nominalized sentence again appears as the direct object of the performative. This is almost always *you*. Spelled out in full:

> I order *you* that *you should* proceed.
> I advise *you* that *you (should)* remain silent.

This is a large class comprising many other specimens, e.g.: *urge, command, request, beg, dare* and *challenge.*

The other structure is similar to this, with the difference that the nominalized sentence contains a copulative verb, in this case (most likely) *become*. This feature permits the following kind of contraction:

> I nominate *you* that *you should become* the president.
> I nominate you to become the president.
> I nominate you for the presidency.

The same pattern is followed by *appoint, promote, degrade, dedicate, recommend* and a few others. I shall call these 'operatives.'

The "behabitives," too, conform to a typical pattern. Consider:

> I *thank* you for having helped me.
> I *praise* you for what you did.

Also note:

> I *apologize* for having hurt you.

Obviously, there is a noun-sharing here between the subject of the contained sentence and either the direct object (as with *thank*) or the subject (as with *apologize*) of the container. The contained sentence, however, does not have a modal verb, but a verb usually in the past tense. The verb phrase of this sentence is brought in by means of a preposition (*for, upon, against*). Other behabitives: *commend, congratulate, censure, pardon* and (with a slightly different structure) *protest.*

A small but important class of performatives has to be added to this list. The verbs *ask, question, inquire* are followed by what the grammarians call 'indirect question.' This is nothing but a nominal formed out of a sentence by either prefixing *whether* or by replacing a noun or adverbial phrase by the appropriate *wh*-word: *who, what, when, where, why, how, etc.* Examples:

> I *question* whether he has succeeded.
> I *ask* (you) how he did it.

These, naturally, can be called 'interrogatives.'

These are, then, the main species of saying something. If our hypothesis about the identity of what we say and what we think is correct, then a parallel classification will be forthcoming in the domain of thinking words.

VERBS OF THOUGHT

The time schema of the performatives is uniform. The very nature of their employment implies that they are all achievement verbs: the issuing of an utterance with a certain force, the illocutionary act, occurs at a given moment and, ideally, does not last through a period of time.[5] We recall, however, that thinking verbs can be either achievement verbs or state verbs. To anticipate a little, a proposition can be obtained at a given moment or held for a period of time. This distinction stipulates that with respect to each object-structure, we will have to collect two separate groups of verbs: first the verbs denoting propositional achievements, then the ones denoting propositional states. The boundary-line separating them will not be very sharp; there will be clear cases on either side, but many verbs will straddle the line.

What, then, are the propositional achievement verbs corresponding to the *that*-clause? The following short list will do as a sample: *notice, learn, find out, realize, discover, understand, guess, conclude,* and *establish.* Some of these, notably *realize* and *understand*, double as state verbs: think of *I realize that* .... Others are pure: the sentences **I still find out that* ... and **I discover that* ... are deviant. I shall call this class 'apprehensives.'

The corresponding state verbs also come in great variety: *think, believe, suspect, assume, surmise, imagine, see, remember, recall, expect, agree,* and many others. The verb *know* is so important and complex that it will merit a special discussion later on. These verbs I call 'putatives.'

Turning to the mental verbs corresponding to the verdictives, we find two typical achievements: *recognize* and *identify*. The structural similarity is obvious. Note the verdictives in:

> I classify the book as a novel.
> I diagnose the ailment to be pneumonia.

Compare them with *recognize* and *identify* in:

> I recognized the lady as the one who ...
> I identified the bird to be a sparrow.

The fact that, say, *recognize* also occurs in the first person unmodified present does not change the picture. *I recognize him* ... is an ellipsis for *I can recognize him* .... To be able to recognize is, of course, a state. The point is, however, that the *can*-version is out of place with respect to a real state verb, e.g., *regard*. *I regard him as a coward* is not an ellipsis for *I can regard him as a coward*. It is not easy to find a name for this small class of propositional achievements; I suggest the trivial 'recognitives.'

---

[5] Owing to the "leakage" between the verbs of thinking and the verbs of saying, some performatives, notably expositives, may take on the state time schema, e.g.: *Descartes claims that there are innate ideas, Locke denies that there are such ideas.* Notice the present tense here; the timeless nature of the proposition conveys "immortality" to the thinker.

There is a much greater variety in the state-equivalents of verdictives. In addition to *regard*, the verbs *take, consider, value, interpret, deem, esteem view, look upon, see (as)* will belong to this class. For a name I suggest 'assessives.'

Commissives, too, have their cognate families. On the achievement side, we find *decide* and *resolve*. As you promise or vow to do something, you decide and resolve to do something. To name them I resort once more to the trivial and suggest 'resolutives.'

There is no difficulty in naming the next class, the state equivalents of commissives. The rich and important class of 'conative' verbs emerges: *want, wish, desire, intend, plan, aspire, contemplate, mean, prefer,* and so forth. The structural similarity between these and the commissives and resolutives is too obvious to waste words on it.

To our initial dismay, we find the classes corresponding to the exercitives and operatives almost empty. This stands to reason, however. Exercitives are words of command, while operatives are tied to institutional or ritual contact between persons; think of the obligatory *you* in the performative use: *I order you . . .* or *I promote you. . . .* Now there are no unexpressed commands or imperceptible contacts between people. If we still want to describe some exercitive thinking, we borrow a conative verb: *I want him to go, I prefer him to do the job* or we use a more complex (but very expressive) phrase: *I have him in mind to do the job* (or *for the presidency*). On the achievement side we have a couple of originals: *choose* and *select*; e.g. *I selected him to. . . . Consign* and *relegate* may also belong here.

Are there mental achievements fitting into the syntactical slot inhabited by behabitives? I can think of one: *forgive. Blame, approve, condone, sympathize, resent* and *regret*, on the other hand, are some of the state verbs that belong there. This latter class deserves a name; so I suggest 'emotives.'

Finally, the interrogatives will have the lone 'inquisitive,' *wonder,* for a counterpart. This, of course, is a state verb. (See table.)

I have neither space nor inclination to go into minute details concerning the many imperfections that can be found in the given schema. Admittedly, there are many verbs that can function now as performatives, then as propositional state or achievement verbs. Think of *identify, agree* or *approve*. Others, again, like *see*, go beyond the limits of propositional verbs altogether: think of seeing cats.

What is crucial is the possibility of matching the division of performatives (imperfect as it is) with the division of propositional state and achievement verbs (imperfect as it is). It is important that the same things that can be asserted, suggested or denied in words, can be realized and understood, believed, suspected or doubted in thought; that things regarded, considered, looked upon and recognized to be such and such in thought, can be judged

TABLE

Structure	Performatives	Propositional Achievements	Propositional Status
	Expositives	Apprehensives	Putatives
NV that S	state assert suggest concede admit deny argue report testify confess predict warn	notice learn find out realise discover understand guess conclude establish	think believe suspect assume surmise imagine see know remember recall expect agree
	Verdictives	Recognitives	Assessives
NVN as N/A	call rank find classify place rate grade diagnose describe define	recognize identify	regard take consider value interpret deem esteem view look upon see (as)
	Commissives	Resolutives	Conatives
NV to V+	promise undertake covenant vow pledge guarantee	decide resolve	want wish desire intend plan aspire contemplate mean prefer
	Exercitives		
NVN to V+	order advise urge command request beg dare challenge	(choose) (select)	(want) (prefer)

TABLE (Cont'd)

Structure	Performatives	Propositional Achievements	Propositional Status
	Operatives		
NVNP nom (become N)	nominate appoint promote degrade dedicate recommend	(choose) (select) (consign) (relegate)	(want) (prefer)
	Behabitives		Emotives
NVNP nom (have V^{en+})	thank praise commend congratulate censure pardon (protest) (apologise)	forgive	blame approve condone sympathise resent (regret)
	Interrogatives		Inquisitives
NV wh. . .	ask question inquire		wonder

and rated, described and defined in similar ways in words; that what one may decide to do, want, wish or intend to do in thought, one also can promise, vow or pledge to do in words; that the things that are worthy of blame, approval, resentment or forgiveness in thought, can be censured, praised, objected to, and pardoned in words; that, finally, what you wonder about in thought, you can ask about in speech.

To put it more briefly: you can say whatever you can think and you can think *almost* whatever you can say. This last qualification is necessary in view of the fact that the vocabulary of performatives is much richer, in types and in items, than the vocabulary of thought. The problem is not: can we express in words whatever we can think? It is rather: can we think everything that we can say? I hazard a guess: speech is the primary phenomenon, thought is the derivative one. It is true that speech is the expression of thought, but it is also true, and I would like to say, more true, that thought is the suppression of speech. It is like typing or just touching the keys without pressing them.

It will be objected that I misrepresent here the concept of thinking, that thinking, primarily, is thinking about . . . , not thinking that . . . . And these two are quite different things: thinking about is an activity, thinking that is a state. Indeed, *What are you thinking about?* is in the continuous tense. I reply that this is like saying that talking, really, is talking about. . . and not saying that. . . . The question, *What are you talking about?* asks about an activity too. Talking about something involves a process of talking: producing a patterned sequence of noises. A parrot or a machine can do this, yet they cannot talk about anything. To talk about anything one has to say something, that is, perform some illocutionary acts. And this parrots cannot do.

Thinking about something also involves a process of "thinking": hearing sound-patterns or visualising shapes "in one's head." But this, by itself does not constitute thinking about something, unless these "images" carry mental acts. Animals, probably, can "think" in the sense of having internal experiences of a similar kind; what they cannot do is think about something. In talking about something a person performs a series of illocutionary acts: he may assert, suggest or argue that something is the case; describe and rate a person or a thing; recommend, urge or advise a certain course of action; and so on. In thinking about something one goes through a series of mental acts, i.e., one reaches some propositional achievements and initiates (or "tries out") some propositional states: one may guess or assume, realize or conclude that something is the case; regard, consider or view a certain thing in many ways; contemplate, plan and decide to do one thing or another; wonder about the consequences; and so forth. The idea that one might be thinking about something without performing any of these or similar acts is as incomprehensible as the idea of talking about something without saying anything at all.

"What is a thing which thinks?" asks Descartes. And he answers: "It is a thing which doubts, understands, [conceives], affirms, denies, wills, refuses, which also imagines and feels."[6] It is interesting to note that the performatives *affirm* and *deny* slip into this list, much the same way as some thinking words turn up in Austin's list of performatives. The two kinds are related; they have the same object. Remember Descartes' *Cogito* argument as it appears in the *Meditations*: "this proposition: I am, I exist, is necessarily true each time that I pronounce it, or that I mentally conceive it."[7]

What one can say and what one can think may be the same thing. Yet, obviously, thinking and saying are not the same thing. What is the difference? Is it merely that speech is a noisy form of thinking, and thinking is a silent way of talking to oneself? That the difference is much less trivial can be gathered from the fact that most thinking verbs are state verbs, whereas the

---

[6] René Descartes, *Meditation II.*
[7] *Ibid.*

performatives are one and all achievement verbs. But there is another much more illuminating way of approaching the problem. There is a common device of reverbalizing a nominalized verb by using an ad hoc auxiliary. Instead of saying *I kicked*, I can say *I gave a kick*; instead of *I looked, I took a look,* and so on. The same move is possible in regard to most propositional verbs. One speaks of giving a promise, holding a belief or arriving at a decision. The auxiliaries involved are more or less metaphorical, but this is not a reason for disdaining their aid. For, as we are going to see, the consideration of these auxiliaries casts an extraordinary light on the relation between a person and a proposition, which relation is either that of saying or thinking.

To begin with the performatives, the most common auxiliaries are *make, give* and particularly *issue*. One makes a statement, gives a promise and issues a denial. There are a number of offbeat forms: one offers a proposal, hurls a challenge, pronounces a verdict, hands down a decision and sounds a warning. The verb *issue* is the most typical in that it goes with almost all the performatives. This is no surprise: after all, these verbs, as Austin has noted, are verbs of issuance; the proposition in question is issued, pronounced (*pro-nuntio*), given out.

The verbs of thinking call for a totally different set of auxiliaries. With respect to the state verbs, *have* is the most common: one has beliefs, opinions, suspicions, desires, regrets and what not. The off-beat auxiliaries add color to the picture. Take *belief*. It is like a child: it is conceived, adopted, or embraced; it is nurtured, held, cherished and entertained; finally, if it appears misbegotten, it is abandoned or given up. The same is true, with lesser variety, of thoughts, suspicions, intentions and the like. This image is *toto coelo* different from the one evoked by the set corresponding to the performatives; no issuance here, these states are "in" or "with" the person, they are "held" in one way or another, they can be hidden, concealed, or, on the other hand, shown, manifested or given voice. What we hold (for a time) in a propositional state, we can issue (at a time) in an illocutionary act.

Propositional achievements share *make* with some performatives: we make decisions, identifications, realizations and so on, as much as we make statements, proposals, declarations and the like. *Make* seems to mark achievements in this domain. Yet the difference remains between the two kinds. Statements, proposals, declarations can also be issued, which is not true of identifications, resolutions or realizations. True, one can issue a decision. But obviously *decide* in that case will function as a performative. The less standard auxiliaries, such as *reach* (a decision) and *arrive at* (a realization) illustrate the achievement aspect of these verbs. Whereas a propositional state is like possessing something, a propositional achievement is like finding or getting hold of something.

Man lives in two environments, in two worlds: as a "body" he is among objects and events in the physical, spatio-temporal universe; as a "mind" he lives and communes with objects of a different kind: he perceives and acquires these, holds them and offers them in various ways to other citizens of this world, to other minds. The body and the mind are related as the utterance of a string of phonemes in a given situation is related to the act of saying something, or as the buzzing-blooming confusion of one's stream of consciousness together with one's overt behavior is related to the act or the state of thinking something. In anticipation of what is to follow, one can say that man's world, *qua* man's, is not the world of things, but the world of facts and possibilities.

PROPOSITIONS

One can say words and sentences but, as I mentioned above, this is not saying something in the full sense. To point out, as Austin has done, that saying something incorporates an illocutionary force, is certainly true, but even this is not enough. For after all, this force merely specifies the *modus quo*, the way in which the object is produced, but not the *id quod*, the thing itself, which is produced. We have seen that the same thing which can be issued in various ways in an illocutionary act, can also be acquired and held as an object of thought. It is time to inquire into the nature of this thing.

Philosophers traditionally have felt the need to distinguish the carrier of saying something, the sentence, from the thing that is said, which they called the proposition. Moreover, as the name "propositional attitude" eloquently shows, they have also realized the similarity, if not the identity, of the objects of speech and thought. Unfortunately, however, I cannot think of any account that would render the notion of a proposition really understandable. Recently a great deal of effort has been expended by partisans of the so-called nominalistic tradition, to reduce the notion of a proposition, with respect to speech and thinking, to the notion of an utterance or an inscription, or a set of isomorphic utterances or inscriptions, in a historical context. These attempts are doomed to fail. The object of speech and thought, the proposition, is not a thing, or a set of things, in the physical world; it is an abstract entity.

First I intend to show that what one says, in the relevant sense of the word, cannot be a sentence, and still less a set of individual marks encoding a sentence. If this can be demonstrated, then, by virtue of what we have found thus far, the same thing will *a fortiori* hold of what one thinks.

As I implied at several points in this essay, the phrase *the thing one says* is ambiguous. It may mean the word, the phrase or the sentence one utters, or the product of the illocutionary act one performs. This duplicity is reflected in the two ways of reproducing what one said, which are commonly known as direct and indirect quotation; e.g.: *He said, "Abracadabra"* versus *He said that I should not take the job.*[8] *Say*, in the first sentence is replaceable by verbs such as *shout, whisper, mumble* and the like. In the second case it is a blanket for, and replaceable by, a variety of appropriate performatives. There is something unnatural in sentences that attempt to cross the line: *He shouted that I should not take the job* or *He advised, "You should not take the job."* Again, one cannot say anything (in the illocutionary sense) in an unknown language. A child, uninstructed in Latin, can say "Omnia sunt vanitas," but in uttering this he would not say that everything is vanity. Finally, parrots and talking dolls can say things in the first sense, but not in the second. The knowledge of a language is a *conditio sine qua non* of saying something in the full sense.

It appears, then, that the natural way of reporting what one said in an illocutionary act is the indirect quotation. Now in most cases we enjoy a considerable structural or even lexical freedom within this form. If Joe said (in the appropriate context), "I stole the watch," how am I to report what he admitted? He admitted *that he stole the watch, that it was stolen by him,* he admitted *having stolen the watch, the theft of the watch,* and so on. Is any one of these ways wrong? Obviously not, since Joe himself might have cast the same admission in several forms: *I admit that I stole it . . . having stolen it . . . the theft of the watch,* and so forth. The structural variations exhibited in these examples form a paraphrastic set, and any one of them can be taken as a representative of the entire set.

This freedom of choice extends to the lexical domain as well, to words or phrases, that is, which are synonymous, at least in the given context (think of *theft* replacing *stealing* above). What is the reason for this freedom? We have just mentioned that the mastery of the language is a logically necessary condition of the ability to say something. The speaker who says something does so as a speaker of the language, who therefore has to be credited with the knowledge of what words and phrases mean, and consequently, with the ability to recognize synonyms and paraphrases. Joe, for example, cannot challenge the variants of reproducing his admission without, *ipso facto*, challenging his own right to say something or, for that matter, his very ability to issue a challenge . . . .

What is said, the proposition, is not a sentence or an utterance, nor a set of sentences or utterances, nor any of these things as produced in a given historical context; it is the abstract unity of a paraphrastic set of imperfect nominals, which may be represented by any member of this set. The

---

[8] A further ambiguity of the phrase *what one said* is indicated by the unexpected consistency of the sentence *I know what he said, but I do not believe it.* Obviously what one knows in this case must be different from what one refuses to believe. I have attempted to solve this puzzle in Vendler, 1969 (in press).

abstraction involved here is the same as the one developed in the Middle Ages to account for the unity of a universal, *abstractio totius a parte*: "If there were a single corporeal statue representing many men, it is clear that the image or species of the statue would have an existence singular and proper according as it existed in this matter, but it would have a ratio of community according as it were a common thing representing many."[9]

As to the object of thought, there is not even a temptation to view it as a physical object or event, or as a class of physical objects or events. If Joe thinks that he and Jane are going to get married, then there is no sense in asking whether this is exactly what he thinks, or, rather, that he will marry Jane, or that Jane will be married by him, and so forth. Thoughts, unlike, say, promises, need not be formulated at all. The expression of thought, of course, is usually done in words, but, as we have seen, it is not the words themselves that are the expression of thought; they are mere carriers of what is said, of the thought now given voice.

It has been pointed out, particularly by Quine, that the freedom of selecting equivalent linguistic forms in expressing what one said or what one thinks does not extend to equivalent referential devices (Quine, 1953, c. 8). To use Quine's example, the man who claims that Tegucigalpa is the capital of Nicaragua cannot be accused of the idiocy of thinking that the capital of Honduras is the capital of Nicaragua. The reason for this restriction is easy to see in the light of the principles just outlined. It is the knowledge of the language, and not of geography, that is prerequisite to the ability to say something. What one says, or what one thinks, the proposition, is "transparent" with respect to synonyms and paraphrases, but "opaque" in regard to equivalent media of reference. There is, of course, a "penumbra" even around the core of the idea of knowing a language. Sodium chloride is a synonym for kitchen salt. Yet if the maid orders kitchen salt from the store, I have no right to report that she just ordered some sodium chloride. The maid is not supposed to know scientific terms, yet her knowledge of English is not impaired by this deficiency. This situation has a counterpart: if the speaker can obviously be credited with the knowledge of a referential equivalence, I do have the right to treat what he said and what he thinks as transparent in this particular respect. If Joe says "Jane is a good cook" I can correctly report what he did by saying that he boasted that his wife (who happens to be Jane) is a good cook. In cases of egocentric particulars such a freedom is indeed indispensable.

In footnote 6, I alluded to what Descartes said. That *is* what he said, although he did not say it in English, but in French or Latin. I can make this

---

[9] Thomas Aquinas, *Concerning Being and Essence* (ed. G. G. Leckie). New York: Appleton-Century-Crofts, 1937), Chapter III.

claim, because he knew these languages and because sentences formed in them are translatable into English. In general, there are two necessary conditions that must be fulfilled whenever X claims in a language L_1 that Y said or thought such and such: (1) Y must have the mastery of a language L_2 and (2) L_2 must be identical with L_1 or inter-translatable with L_1. The domain of speech and thought—the realm of the mind—is confined within the limits of linguistic inter-translatability. Animals cannot think, concludes Descartes. "Can only those hope who can talk?" wonders Wittgenstein (1953, p.174).

OBJECTIVITY

Earlier I spoke of man as living in two worlds, the world of the body and the world of the mind. As a body, man enters various relationships with parts of the material world: through active and passive physical contact, and through perception, he affects, or is affected by, this environment. These relationships, of course, do not abrogate, but presuppose, the objective existence of the physical world. The situation is similar in the world of the mind. Thus far, we have considered the furnishings of the mental environment only as propositions, that is, as terms of the active relations of saying and thinking. Accordingly, as we just described it in detail, in this perspective they appeared afflicted by the imperfections of the human agent, showing the traces of human ignorance. Yet here too there is a need for the objectively given.

One important aspect of certain illocutionary acts and of some mental states and achievements is the dimension of truth. Statements, verdicts and the like, though not orders and promises; beliefs and opinions, but not wishes or regrets, are true or false. Now truth and falsity do not depend upon the maker of the statement or the holder of the belief. What is stated, what is believed, is true if it agrees with what is the case, if it fits the facts. Facts, as I have shown elsewhere, are "made of the same stuff" as propositions (1967, c.5). Yet it is not enough to say that a fact is a true proposition; a true proposition is not a fact, it merely fits or corresponds to the facts.

There is another reason, too, for attributing objective existence to facts and, for that matter, to possibilities. We are often affected by entities of this kind. The fact that my friend is ill may shock or surprise me, and the possibility of his loss may upset or worry me, whereas the same fact and the same possibility may please or delight his enemy. There are not only "propositional actions," such as thinking or saying, but "propositional passions" such as surprise or delight. Of course, in all these cases one might also say that it is the thought of my friend's illness, or the idea of his possible demise, that really shocks or upsets me. This, however, by no means proves that the fact or possibility in question is a merely subjective, thought-dependent entity. These things are apprehended in the form of a proposition, but this is merely the subjective appearance of an objective reality. Suppose I do not know that my friend is your cousin. Is it true, then, that the illness of your cousin worries me? Yes and no. Yes, if one focuses one's attention on the fact, the objective element, but no if the subjective appearance, the proposition, is considered. Think of the analogy of sense perception. Often a particular appearance of a harmless object, a tree or a rock, may frighten even the bravest soul. Is it then true that he was frightened by a tree? Yes and no.

How can one form the concept of a fact or possibility, of an "objective" proposition, of a "belief," as it were, without the restrictions of a believer?

Think of an omniscient being, demon or god. Since he knows everything, he knows all languages, so that there is no difficulty in attributing thoughts to him in a straightforward sense. Moreover, for the same reason, he would be able to see all things from all possible points of view (including temporal relativity), that is, according to all possible ways of referring to them. Consequently there would be no "opaqueness," no subjectivity in his beliefs at all (seeing the world *sub specie aeternitatis*). All his beliefs, finally, would be correct. He would know everything that is the case, all the facts, and more: he would know what is not the case, though it could be the case; he would know all possibilities. The world of facts is a subset of the sum total of all possibilities. Clearly, we have just reconstructed Kant's "transcendental ideal." [10]

Then forget the demon and retain the facts and possibilities. This ideal represents the "objective" element, with respect to which statements, beliefs, verdicts and opinions are assessed in the dimension of truth and possibility. Since the ideal is postulated as something objectively given, the referential (and, for that matter, intensional) opaqueness marking propositions gives place to the perfect transparency we attribute to the world of facts. As the proposition is the result of an abstraction from the variety of synonymous linguistic media, so facts (and possibilities) are the result of a further abstraction, this time from equivalent referring media. A proposition is the subjective appearance of an objective possibility, and, if true, of a fact. That Joe is married to Jane is a different propostion from his being married to my sister, but, if Jane is my sister, they will express the same fact, and are true or false together.

Once language is given, and the world is given, all the facts are given. Statements are made, orders are issued, opinions are formed, and beliefs are held by people; facts are not. They are to be found, learned or discovered. One's statement may fit the facts, but is not a fact. What one states, however, in one sense, may be a fact. After all, people often state facts. This

---

[10] Kant, B. 599ff.

corresponds to the ambiguity in *what the painter paints*. In painting a picture of a rose he is painting a rose. So, in a sense, what he is painting is a rose, yet his painting is not a rose. "We make to ourselves pictures of facts." (Wittgenstein, 1922, 2.1)

Finally, about knowledge. It differs from belief not only in the necessity of truth and evidence. The state of knowing something is quite different from believing firmly what is true on good evidence. This difference is like the one between imagining an object vividly and accurately and seeing it, or like the one between desiring something and possessing it (etymology is suggestive here: *believe* is related to *love* and *know* to *can*). One has reasons for believing (assuming or suspecting) but not for knowing something; one can refuse to believe, but not to know. "You ought to believe ..." is a recommendation, "You ought to know ..." is a reminder. The attitude of "I don't want to believe ..." is like a struggle against a compulsive image; the attitude of "I don't want to know ..." is akin to closing one's eyes. Compare what cannot be believed with what cannot be known. The unbelievable strikes you as unlikely, outrageous or impossible; the unknowable does not strike you at all: you have no access to it. Once more, it is like imagining and seeing. The unimaginable defies the power of the imagination; the invisible may be quite simple, but hidden. Knowledge is the mind's vision of facts, but, as with seeing objects, they appear in a perspective, through the opaque medium of a proposition.

REFERENCES

Austin, J. L., 1962. *How to Do Things with Words.* Oxford: Clarendon.

Quine, W. V., 1953. *From a Logical Point of View.* Cambridge, (Mass.): Harvard University Press.

Vendler, Z., 1967. *Linguistics in Philosophy.* Ithica, N.Y.: Cornell University Press.

Vendler, Z., 1968. *Adjectives and Nominalizations.* The Hague — Paris: Mouton.

Vendler, Z., to appear. On What One Said. In *Proceedings of the XIVth International Congress of Philosophy, Vienna.* Herder, Wein (Vienna): Universität Wien.

Wittgenstein, 1922. *Tractatus Logico-Philosophicus.* London: Rutledge & Kegan Paul.

Wittgenstein, 1953. *Philosophical Investigations.* Oxford: Blackwell.

5

Words, Lists, and Categories:

An Experimental View of Organized Memory

George Mandler

The aim of this study is to present some theoretical notions and experimental results about memory and specifically about the storage of the vocabulary of our language. We shall address ourselves to several questions: How is access achieved to words in the vocabulary? How are lists of words learned and recalled? In general, how does human memory deal with language in its essentially nonsyntactic state, that is, with one of the elements of our language—words?

When we are required to deal with words—unconnected words out of their usual syntactic context—we are usually faced with single words or with lists or groups of words. Instead of moving directly into the psychological laboratory, let me present an analogous situation—the shopping list problem— the memory task set for the husband sent to the store to do some last minute shopping for the weekend. We assume that the wife in question is the forgetful type, that there are no less than about a dozen items that must be bought, that she can't find pencil and paper, and that our experimental spouse has to remember all the items without any aid from accompanying children, written lists, or repeated phone calls from the supermarket. Let us also assume that he had better not forget anything—he is highly motivated— the payoff is high.

The list he is given consists of the following items:

coffee	butter	pickles	milk
cookies	bacon	pork chops	mustard
crackers	beer	peanut butter	mushrooms
cat food	baloney	pastry	melon
	iceberg lettuce		

[1] The preparation of this paper and the research reported here were supported by Grants GB 5282 and 7807 from the National Science Foundation. I am indebted to several coworkers and students, particularly to Zena Pearlstone for assistance in all stages of our research, and to Peter J. Dean, Terry Jackson, and Barbara Cragin.

I have used one principle of mental organization here, namely alphabetical organization. This is one system the husband might use to remember the four items within each initial letter category. However, a list is generally not given in alphabetical order, nor is it subsequently arranged in this manner. A more likely arrangement would be the following:

Meat: catfood, bacon, pork chops, baloney
Dairyfoods: milk, butter
Fruits and Vegetables: mushrooms, melon, lettuce

But what are we to do with the rest of the items under this kind of arrangement? No single category appears to accommodate them, and our poor husband is much afraid that he will forget some of them. He then hits upon the idea of imagining the shelves in the kitchen cupboard, placing the required items on well-known places on the shelves. And here we add:

Shelf One: coffee, peanut butter
Shelf Two: cookies, crackers
Shelf Three: pickles, mustard

This leaves beer, but he easily remembers this item by saying to himself, "Remember what I will need if I ever get back from this expedition." He then recounts the list to his wife, remembering three categories of food and the items in those and three shelves in order and the items on them and, lo and behold, he has misremembered because it was to be iceberg lettuce, not just lettuce. So he reminds himself that a lot of all this stuff will go into the refrigerator—icebox to him—and that will help him remember *ice*berg.

He goes to the store, and not only has he successfully remembered the list, just as he had recited it, but he has also demonstrated three major principles of long-term storage: categorization, seriation, and relational imagery. He has remembered some of the items by remembering the categories which contain them; he has remembered others by using an ordered serial system—the shelves; and he has remembered two—beer and iceberg lettuce—by special mnemonic devices, which we shall provisionally call relational imagery.

Before going into a more detailed discussion of these three processes and the nature of organized memory, we should briefly delineate some general characteristics of the human memory system.

THE MEMORY SYSTEM

Before dealing specifically with long-term or organized memory, it will be useful to review some of the prior stages of information processing. How does verbal, semantic information get into organized memory?

A generally satisfactory picture has been developed by a number of different investigators. Without being theoretically determinate, the following outline suggests that experimental and theoretical work in different laboratories is looking at phenomena that fit into the same general location in a flow chart of the system.

In another presentation (Mandler, 1967a), I suggested that three successive systems filter information flow from input to output—the sensory buffer, followed by buffer storage (or short-term memory), and finally, long-term storage. "Long-term storage" and "short-term storage" have become fairly common terms in psychological parlance, but I would prefer to abandon them at this point, for it is not necessarily useful to conceive of the two systems they describe in terms of temporal flow, rather than function. Preferable descriptions might be "primary storage"[2] and "organized storage" (or "primary memory" and "organized memory.") A potent reason to substitute such non-temporal designations is the possibility that the function of buffer storage is *not*, as has been generally suggested, time dependent, but, in fact, item dependent. It has been suggested (Norman, 1968, for example) that in the absence of displacing, interfering input, the capacity of the primary system is fixed at about five to seven items, and that the apparent time-dependent limitation of the system is occasioned by the flow of information into the system, which displaces items out of primary storage at a generally constant rate. Whatever the mechanism, material in primary storage apparently is available for about 10 to 20 seconds following presentation. If it is not transferred to secondary, long-term or—to use our preferred term—organized storage, it is lost.

The system that precedes the primary storage (or memory) system is one with clear time limitations in the order of 200 milliseconds. We have previously referred to it as the sensory buffer. The sensory storage has been primarily investigated in the visual mode by Sperling (1967) and by others. Sperling suggests a visual information storage which precedes the equivalent of primary memory. In any case, visual material is available for about 200 milliseconds before a limited aspect of this information is recoded and transformed into primary storage.

Our concern here is with the characteristics of the final storage system—the organized storage. We need only remember that the previous filters or buffers permit a limited amount of coded material to enter this storage over relatively short periods of time. Our concerns are with the storage of large amounts of material over long periods of time.

Finally, nothing need be assumed about the identifiability of two distinct, primary, and organized storage systems. For purposes of exposition, such a distinction is useful, but what follows can easily be accommodated to a single dual-process system, where primary and organized storage are "different

---

[2] "Primary," William James' term for the short-term system, has been introduced into the modern literature by Waugh and Norman (1965).

properties of the same physical device," as Norman (1968) has suggested, and as Melton (1963) has argued in a different context.

ORGANIZED MEMORY

Organized storage is the repository of all material, verbal and otherwise, that the organism can retrieve given the proper conditions and cues for retrieval. Quite clearly it contains a vast number of mechanisms and materials that we will not even touch on in this discussion. For example, the machinery for sentence production must be a part of this system, as are visual recognition systems, motor skills, and so forth.

When an item—a word—enters this system for permanent storage, it is stored in an organized fashion. By organized we refer to the structure of the storage, not to the items themselves. Obviously, the items are stored, that is, their address is uniquely located, but the relations among these addresses are what concerns us in trying to provide an adequate description of the system. An item or a set of items is said to be organized when (1) a set of objects or events displays a consistent specifiable and stable relation among the members of the set, and (2) the functional characteristics of the members of the set depend upon the characterization of the set and the relations among its members. This definition recalls Wertheimer (1921) and can be found in more recent expositions such as Garner's (1962).

In the present context we shall talk about the organization of words in lists of various sorts. These items are said to be organized when the functional aspects of a word, specifically its meaning, depend at least in part upon the set of words of which it is a member, and the relation of the members of the set to each other.

At the present time, there are three types of organization that are adequate to deal with most aspects of word and list memory. These are the three demonstrated by our hypothetical husband: *seriation, categorization,* and *relational imagery*. It must be added immediately that various kinds of organization can be found that do not seem to fall immediately into one of these three types, but upon analysis these seem to reduce to one of them or, frequently, to some combination of two or three of these mechanisms.

We shall discuss briefly each of these three major mechanisms with special reference to experimental evidence concerning their mode of operation. However, it should be noted that we are not talking solely, or even primarily, about the organization of words that are given to an experimental subject in a laboratory (or in a kitchen), but rather claim that these experiments and characteristics apply to the storage of words in general, and that the storage of the dictionary of previously learned words can be characterized by the kind of organization discussed here.

It follows from this that we will only be talking about words learned sometime previous to our investigation. "Learning" is not what concerns us here. The husband on his shopping tour has learned the words 'milk' and 'meat'; he has adequately handled the problem of connotation and reference, but he is faced with the problem of recalling them at the supermarket. Similarly, all our experiments deal with English words, typically nouns, that the subject has previously learned. They are all words that occur with a high frequency in normal spoken and written English, and problems of response learning (Mandler, 1954) do not arise.

Finally, we assume that for formal presentation both seriation and categorization can be represented in tree structures. For example, one of the most powerful serial organizers, English syntax, can generate a tree structure from its formal description. We shall have occasion to refer to the tree structure as a model for some of these organizations.

SERIATION

The attempt to impose constant serial orders or generally ordered sequences on behavior is one of the most pervasive processing strategies imposed by the human mind. More pervasive and impressive, though, is the persistence of the associationistic-behavioristic establishment in ignoring this phenomenon as a distinct and basic law of human learning. For some 80 years, the vast majority of research in the area of serial learning and sequential behavior had been devoted either to an exploration of the atomistic chaining hypothesis and its consequences or to an attempt to show how the chaining hypothesis can explain data inconsistent with it. The chaining hypothesis is an attractive, if simple-minded, way of looking at serial verbal behavior and reducing it to pairwise associations. It says—in varying degrees of confusion and complexity—that in the learning of a serial list successive members of the list act as stimuli and responses, and that each member has a double function of acting as a response to its previous members and as a stimulus to its succeeding member of the list. Despite the fact that the most impressive serial achievement of human behavior—the production of language—is quite clearly not amenable to such an explanation, the general acceptance of the chaining hypothesis has been maintained.

During the past ten years increasing evidence has been adduced to show that the chaining hypothesis is not only not the basis on which one might explain sequential behavior, but is in fact wrong. This had been rarely considered a possibility before the mid-1950s. One of the most imaginative researchers in the area, R. K. Young, who has provided impressive evidence against a chaining interpretation, cannot quite believe what he found and ends up denying that serial behavior may be of fundamental interest because it fails to conform to the associative interpretations. He says ". . . serial learning emerges as a relatively poor method to use for the analysis of the processes which are assumed to underlie verbal behavior." (R. K. Young, 1968, p. 145) The processes that are *assumed* to underlie verbal behavior are, of course, associative S-R processes. In contrast to this declaration of faith, Young, in the same article, also concludes that the well-known serial position effect, the general advantage in serial learning of early and late items ". . . is produced if the subject responds to the ordinal character of a set of items which are perceived as varying along a continuum such as time, position, color, line, length, etc." (Young, 1968, p. 144)

The notion of the underlying process of seriation, or of a syntax of action, should not be surprising to the contemporary psychologist, since Lashley in a programmatic article in 1951 proposed just such an alternative to the chaining hypothesis. In the same volume in which Young throws in the towel as far as the importance of serial learning goes, N. F. Johnson also reviews sequential verbal behavior. He recapitulates Lashley's program for "a mechanism which both elicits and orders the elements prior to emission" (Johnson, 1968, p. 446) and concludes that the evidence supports the argument that "some arousal and ordering of response elements must occur before the [subject] attempts to generate a response sequence." (Johnson, 1968, p. 446)

The power of sequential programs is not new to experimental psychology. The history of mnemonic systems shows that the importance of sequential governing programs was at least known to the early Greeks. Yates (1966) has provided us with a most illuminating history of the applied art of memory and shows that ancient and modern mnemonic systems rely equally on prior sequential programs. The modern "one is a bun, two is a shoe, three is a tree . . ." finds its early ancestor in images for ordering public speeches and has been maintained throughout the history of memory feats. Yates also describes at length the "memory theatres" of the Elizabethan age where the sequentially ordered image of a theater served as the basic vehicle for memorizing both simple and complex lists of items.

Our own hypothetical subject—remembering the ordering of the shelves in the cupboard—can and does search this particular set for items that are assigned to the pre-ordered system. And as he goes from the top to the bottom shelf he can pick off coffee, cookies, and pickles. Any way-station in the serial ordering serves as a cue for the items assigned to it—but the original order is prior and determines the syntax of the search.

We are some 70 years late in mounting a sustained attack on this particular problem, and relatively little is known about the serial structuring that the mind imposes on sets of items. However, it is reasonable to initiate such an attack with the use of a basic tree structure with the apex representing the initiating program for the development of the full tree and with items at the base ordered conceptually from "left" to "right." It is also possible that this seriation of lists is conceptually not far removed from the learning of much shorter sequences, such as phonemic sequences in words. Such a process of response integration (Mandler, 1954, 1962) has been extended by Jensen (1962) to serial learning.

I shall conclude this section by presenting some recent research from our laboratory which demonstrates the preference of human subjects for serially ordered structures when such ordering is presented under conditions of minimal memory load and maximal opportunity to conform to the serial ordering of input.

The Free Recall of Word Series

In the typical free recall situation, the subject is presented with a list of n words, where n is larger than the immediate memory span of about seven words, and these n words are presented for m trials, and each trial represents a new random order of these n words. Following the presentation of a list, the subject is asked to recall as many of the words as he can, usually in a limited period of time. In serial learning, one variation of procedure uses the same method as free recall, but the n items are presented in the same serial order from trial to trial. It has generally been expected that serial learning would be superior to free recall when those conditions are comparable, but a study by Waugh (1961) found no such difference. However, since Waugh's report, several studies suggest that for limited list lengths under traditional free recall conditions, free recall is, in fact, inferior to serial learning. It has been assumed that one of the reasons why serial learning is superior is that subjects use serial organization as an important cue during recall and that serial learning, or seriation, is a preferred mode of organization in the natural setting. Recent research on free recall has shown that subjects impose their own organization on their output protocols, and this has been extensively discussed in various publications by Tulving (1962, 1964) under the heading of "subjective organization." There is in free recall a tendency for subjects to cluster (organize) items, regardless of the way in which the input conditions randomize them from trial to trial.

In the experiments presented here two problems were examined: One concerns the hypothesis that any *list* of several words presents an interference situation to the subject. Clearly, he cannot learn all the items in the list; he has to learn some items. Which items does he select? Having selected an item, can he maintain memory for that item over the next trial and so on? Second, given a situation in which a subject is asked for free recall, but presented material in such a way that he can organize the material serially without interference from input trials, will such serial organization be preferred by the subject? And if it does occur, what quality of performance will it produce? The specific problems are best illustrated by the following discussion of our experiments.

EXPERIMENT. The words used were all high frequency nouns, with different lists varied across subjects, and with the restriction that each word in the list would begin with a different letter of the alphabet. Words were presented at the rate of one word per second in all five different conditions. For all conditions, the subjects were given up to one minute for recall immediately following the presentation of a trial, and, generally they took much less time than that. It should be noted that recall was free in all conditions in the sense that subjects could write down the words in any order they wished.

In all conditions all subjects were informed exactly of the conditions under which words would be presented and that they would be required to recall them.

While most of the analyses will deal with 16 trials in each condition, in all conditions we added a 17th trial which simply repeated exactly the condition of the 16th trial. However, in describing the conditions we will talk about 16 trials for ease of presentation. After subjects had learned a particular list in a particular condition, they were given a brief rest and then learned a second list. The second list was a new list but the *condition* was exactly the same as that given for the first list. In other words, the second list presented data on practiced subjects in that condition. The five groups or conditions were:

1. *Group 16 x 16R.* This was the traditional free recall group in which 16 words were presented in different random orders for 16 trials, with a recall trial following each presentation of all 16 words.

2. *Group 16 x 16S.* This was serial presentation with free recall. Sixteen words were presented in the same serial order for 16 trials with a recall trial following each presentation trial.

3. *Group 16 + 1R.* In this condition, a new word was added on each trial, such that on Trial 1 the subject was given one word followed by a recall trial. On Trial 2, he was given two words in a random order followed by a recall trial. On Trial n, he was given n words in a random order followed by a recall trial, such that on Trial 16 the subject saw 16 words in a random order and was asked for recall.

4. *Group 16 + 1S.* This group was similar to Group 3, except that the new word was added at the end of the list and the same serial order was maintained on each trial. A subject saw one word on Trial 1, two words on Trial 2 with the second word presented following the first, and on Trial n he saw n words with the nth word again in last position. Thus, the serial order of the words was constant from trial to trial, and on Trial 16, the subject saw all 16 words in the list.

5. *Group 1 + 16S.* This group was the same as Group 4, with the only change being that the words were added at the top rather than at the bottom of the list. On the nth trial the nth word was added in Position 1. Thus, in

Groups 4 and 5, we have serial presentations with a new word being added on each trial, but in Group 4 the words are added at the bottom of the list, and in Group 5 at the top of the list.

6. *Group 1 + 1.* In this group, each trial consisted of the presentation of a single word. A different new word was presented on each trial up to Trial 16. The subject was instructed on any trial to recall all of the words he had seen on that and on all previous trials. For example, on Trial 5 the subject was presented with a new word, and only that word, but he was requested to recall all the words, that is, all five words he had seen until that time. He was, of course, given no feedback. In this particular condition, since presentation is very fast, we were able to run four different lists for each subject rather than two.

In this short survey of our findings,[3] I shall report on three specific measures of performance:

1. *Trial 17 Recall.* The classical performance measure, specifically the number of words correctly recalled on the 17th trial.

2. *SO.* Subjective organization—a measure developed by Tulving (1962) which shows the degree to which subjects maintain the same pairwise grouping of items in their output from trial to trial. When SO = 1.00 on Trial N, then all pairs of words that were recalled together on that trial were also recalled contiguously on Trial N - 1. It is an index of the degree to which the subject organizes or clusters the material, independent of the input conditions intervening between the two trials.

3. *IO.* Input-Output concordance—a measure that indexes the degree to which subjects order their output on Trial N in the same way that the input was ordered on that trial. When IO = 1.00, then the ordering of words in the subject's output was identical with the input order on that trial. When IO = .50, then there was an essentially zero correlation between input and output.

Trial by trial acquisition curves showed that the groups in which one word is added at a time produce essentially similar acquisition curves. Performance was always perfect for the first six to eight words, which were within the immediate memory span, and then diverged slightly from perfect performance.

Table 1 shows SO and IO averages over all 17 trials, and also shows these measures separately for List 1 and List 2, that is, for practiced and unpracticed subjects. The performance measure in Table 1 shows that all the groups in which a word is added on each trial remember about 14 out of 16 words on Trial 17. The best of these groups is the 16 + 1S group with 15.7 words on List 2 (and 15.1 on List 1), and they are indistinguishable from the traditional 16 x 16S and R groups with 16.0 and 15.9 on List 2 (and 15.7 and 15.2 on List 1).

[3]An extensive report of these experiments, including more adequate measures of organization, can be found in Mandler and Dean (1969).

TABLE 1

Summary Performance and Organization Measures

LIST 1

Condition	Mean SO	Rank	Mean IO	Rank	Trial 17 Recall	Rank
16 x 16 S	.33	5	.71	4	15.7	1
16 + 1 S	.67	2	.93	1	15.1	3
1 + 16 S	.55	3	.88	3	14.7	4
1 + 1 S	.69	1	.90	2	13.3	6
16 x 16 R	.14	6	.55	6	15.2	2
16 + 1 R	.35	4	.64	5	13.8	5

LIST 2

Condition	Mean SO	Rank	Mean IO	Rank	Trail 17 Recall	Rank
16 x 16 S	.51	4	.79	4	16.0	1
16 + 1 S	.70	2	.95	1	15.7	3
1 + 16 S	.61	3	.90	3	14.9	4
1 + 1 S	.74	1	.94	2	14.0	5
16 x 16 R	.20	6	.54	6	15.9	2
16 + 1 R	.50	5	.64	5	13.7	6

This general finding, and especially the performance of Group 1 + 1, suggests that the major variation in list learning is related to retrieval rather than storage of material. The subjects in Group 1 + 1, for example, were given 1/16 of the presentation and 1/2 of the output time of the traditional groups, which suggests that input and output time per se are not the important determiners of performance.

For the two organizational measures, SO shows very high levels of subjective organization when the trial-to-trial load on the subject is kept to one word. SO was originally developed for the traditional 16 x 16R group by Tulving and in this condition where the changing input from trial to trial and the presence of 16 words on each trial must be particularly confusing to the subject, that is, when they load his processing system unduly, the SO measure averages .20. In our word-at-a-time groups, SO, the tendency to cluster identically from trial to trial, goes as high as .74. In particular, under conditions 16 + 1S and 1 + 1, when subjects are adding a word to the bottom of the list, they can maintain serial organization and therefore a high level of subjective organization.

The IO measure bears out this conclusion. The tendency for subjects in the serial groups to mimic the input order is very high, that is, subjects adopt the seriation procedure made possible by the experimental procedure and when IO is high, so is SO. Seriation will be adopted by subjects whenever the experimental situation permits it.

Finally, we might note that an analysis of the trial-by-trial fate of the new words indicates unequivocally that new words are added at the place where they appear in the input. If a new word appears at the beginning, it is produced at the beginning; if at the end of an input list, it is produced at the end. The 1 + 1 subjects behave as if the new word were added at the end. This is counter to the expectation that new words should be produced early during output since they cannot usually be held in primary storage long enough for adequate retrieval. A tendency to put new words toward the beginning only occurs in Group 16 + 1R condition where the output of new words occurs earlier than would be predicted from their input position. But in that condition the input does not permit seriation, of course.

It should be recalled that the subjects in these studies were permitted to recall the material in any order they wished. Thus the tendency for subjects to pick up serial orders even when they are not required to do so, to follow serial orders even if it means delaying the output of material that has just been presented, and to attempt to follow serial orders even in a random input (as we observed in the early stages of 16 + 1R) suggests that serial organization is an extremely potent method of handling information. Even in the traditional random free recall experiment (16 x 16R), the phenomenon of subjective organization suggests that subjects try to maintain serial orders in the face of confusing and interfering random inputs. The clustering found in the output protocols may reflect minimal serial ordering.

Up to now we have been talking about ad hoc seriation, the order imposed on a list that has no a priori order. There are, of course, powerful lists that have such a priori orders—either because they have been previously learned, or because they can be generated. The most powerful prelearned serial list we have is probably the alphabet, and it can easily and frequently be used as a serial device. We can frequently recall lists better when given or using the alphabet as a cue (cf. Earhard, 1967), and our first ordering of the shopping list used just such a system. A generated ordering system that is frequently used is the series of integers, which combines both learned and generative aspects. Many studies of serial learning show the use of simple numerical ordering as a mnemonic device.

CATEGORIZATION

Under this heading we shall review some evidence that, in the absence of serial order, one of the major variables that determines amount of recall is the categorical organization of the list to be recalled. Specifically, we have been studying in the laboratory the proposition that such organization is, in fact, the single most important determinant of recall, rather than time available, frequency of exposure, or other similar classical variables. Starting with the work of the Gestalt school and, in particular, of Katona in 1940, and more recently prodded by G. A. Miller's work (1956) on the limitation of the human memory span and the effect of grouping or chunking in overcoming this limitation, we have shown that memory for lists of categorized words where subjects impose their own categorization on the material is determined by the number of categories into which the material is organized. On the average, subjects recall a constant number of words, approximately five, from each such category.

Organization and Memory

Our current work in this area develops theoretical and empirical directions described in a paper titled "Organization and Memory" (O & M) (Mandler, 1967b). The basic experimental situation was originally used by Mandler and Pearlstone (1966) and involves free conceptualization followed by recall:

EXPERIMENT. The subject is presented with a set of cards (in all our current experiments, 100), each of which has printed on it a high frequency English word. He is then asked to sort these words into from two to seven categories according to any schema, rule, or concept he wishes. He is only instructed not to use any organization based on the initial letter of the words or other formal characteristics, such as length of words. The subject is given repeated trials with random arrangements of the same set of words with instructions to continue until he is able to produce an identical (or 95% identical) sorting of the set on two successive trials. Thus the subject imposes his own categorization schema on the set of words and demonstrates stability of the schema. Following the achievement of criterion, the subject is asked to write down all the words from the set that he can recall. The relationship of interest is between the number of categories (NC) used in the final stable categorizations and the number of words recalled (R). This procedure was followed in a number of different studies in O & M which varied list length, number of possible categories subjects were permitted or directed to use, and vocabularies.

The important finding in all these studies was a stable relationship between number of categories (NC) used by the subject and the number of words he could recall (R). The median correlation between NC and R in these studies was .70. The functional relationship between NC and R was adequately expressed by the line of best fit which had a median slope of 3.9, and a median intercept of 10.6. Thus, subjects add, on the average, about four words to recall per additional category used during sorting.

Two possible major artifacts in this finding were investigated in O & M. The first concerns a possible hidden relationship between number of trials (or amount of time) used during sorting and subsequent recall. Briefly, the possibility exists that number of trials is correlated with the number of categories used, so that fewer trials are needed to sort the material into two categories and more trials to sort it into seven categories. If this were the case, then the NC-R relationship would simply hide an underlying trial—or time—effect on recall. In fact, number of trials on the categorization task prior to recall was unrelated to number of words recalled; the median correlation for trials and recall was .16. When number of trials was held constant, the partial correlation between NC and R was .73. In a specific experimental approach to the problem, total time and trials were held constant for all subjects, using a technique derived from Seibel (1964). Subjects were given a constant number of trials and categorized the materials on study sheets. Even when time and trials were held experimentally constant in such a manner, the correlation between NC and R was still obtained.

The second possible artifact refers to subject's self-selection such that some individual difference variable affects the choice of low numbers of categories during categorization and also affects low recall subsequent to categorization. For example, intelligence may have such a hidden effect. In order to check on this problem, subjects were given specific instructions about the number of categories they were to use. In this manner, no self-selection took place, and the results showed that the NC-R relationship still held even when subjects were instructed on the number of categories (from two to seven) they were to use.

Other major findings in O & M were:

a) The slope relating NC and R and the intercept of that function were negatively correlated, suggesting that the more a particular organization contributed to recall, that is, the steeper the slope, the less was the amount of material recalled on some other organizational basis, that is, the lower was the intercept for a zero category value.

b) When categories with large numbers of items were used by subjects, their recall protocols indicated that these categories were subdivided into subcategories.

c) It was shown that instructions to organize the material and instructions to recall it had equivalent effects on recall, and that the combination of the two kinds of instructions produced no additional advantage in recall. This was taken to show that instructions to recall are automatically interpreted by subjects as organizing instructions in this type of task.

In O & M it was suggested that memory for lists of words involves subjective organization in a hierarchical system. We assume that the organization of lists involves the division of the items into categories of size 5 ± 2 and with hierarchies of subordinate and superordinate categories. The restrictions on the number of categories that can be recalled are similar to those which exist on the number of items that can be recalled within categories (cf. Cohen, 1963). The recall process involves the recall of 5 ± 2 categories and of 5 ± 2 items per category, corrected by the number of items that are recalled on some orthogonal organizational basis, as indicated by the intercept of the function.

Further Studies of Organization and Memory

Subsequently we extended the major phenomena reported in O & M and addressed ourselves to the following questions:

1. To what extent does recall continue to depend on the structure of the organized material after intervals ranging up to several weeks?
2. Does the categorical structure determine recognition just as it does recall?
3. How specific is the semantic storage of categorized materials?

With particular reference to the problem of recognition, it is possible, and it seemed to us likely, that recognition might not be dependent on the categorical structure of the lists. For example, each stored item could be given a list tag, and during the recognition task subjects might compare items on the recognition lists with stored items and check for the presence of tags. Such tags or other forms of storage could have various characteristics related to decay or limited short-term capacity (cf. Waugh & Norman, 1965), but would not be affected by the number of categories into which the list had been sorted. On the other hand, a relation between recognition and categorization would suggest that during recognition subjects categorize items and then check the relevant category. Two outcomes are possible: If subjects use few categories, these categories will be so all-embracing that allocation will be difficult and recognition will be impaired because the wrong category of storage will be searched. This interpretation would predict a positive relation between number of categories and recognition, that is, increasingly precise recognition with increasing number of categories. On the other hand, large numbers of categories may be, in fact, confusing when uncertain items are being examined and may result in an increasing probability of misplacement with increasing number of categories, thus resulting in a negative relation between number of categories and recognition. Finally, a recognition experiment can provide clues to the structure of the storage mechanism if the recognition lists contain filler items that are similar to, or even synonymous with, the original words used. The following three experiments will illustrate the problem.[4]

EXPERIMENT RR. In this study, 40 subjects sorted 100 words as described above. Immediately after they had achieved stable categorization, half the subjects were given a recall test followed by a recognition task, while the other half were given a recognition task first and the recall test second. The recognition task consisted of random presentation of the 100 words used during sorting, randomly mixed with 100 filler words that were taken from

---

[4]These experiments have been reported in detail, together with further extension, in Mandler, Pearlstone and Koopmans (1969).

the same pool of words. Half the subjects used one set of the 100 words which then served as filler words for the other half of the subjects, and vice versa. For each word presented during the recognition (Rg) task, the subject was to indicate whether the word did appear in the set of 100 words he had just sorted or indicate that it had not. Subjects made only yes/no judgments in this experiment.

Following the recognition and recall tasks, the subjects were dismissed, but were recalled two weeks later for the second session. None of the subjects knew he was to reappear for the second session prior to this time. In the second session, subjects were given the recall task of writing down as many of the 100 words as they could remember, then the same recognition task as in Session 1, and finally another recall task. Session 3 occurred after two more weeks had intervened, four weeks after the original sorting and recall and recognition session. Subjects were again required to go through a recall-recognition-recall sequence.

I shall only summarize the recall data here since they essentially replicate previous findings. Recall declines over two and four weeks but increases with an intervening presentation of a recognition list. In fact, after four weeks of this treatment, recall *following* recognition was at the same level it was immediately following categorization.

Figure 1 shows the recognition data. The probability of correct recognition, that is, saying yes to an old item—P(yes/old)—is very high, in fact, practically perfect at about .95 immediately following sorting in Session 1. The false alarm rate—P(yes/new)—is about six per cent.

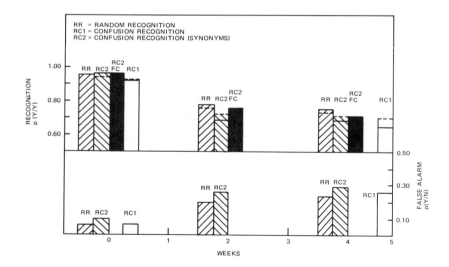

FIGURE 1

One possible mechanism in the recognition task is that subjects recognize items they can recall, but behave essentially randomly towards items they cannot recall. To determine the validity of this, a new recognition measure was developed in which all items that subjects recalled immediately preceding the recognition task were removed from the recognition performance and a new probability estimate was computed on the remaining items. These figures indicate there is little, if any, loss, and that nonrecalled items are recognized at nearly as high a level as the original set of items.

The recognition measure drops to about 75% after two weeks and stays essentially stable for Session 3 after four weeks. False alarms increase to the 25% level, and the complementarity of correct recognition and false alarms supports Parks' (1966) model. Even after two and four weeks, the removal of recall items drops recognition only slightly, again suggesting essentially long maintenance of recognition of nonrecalled items.

The data support our previous findings of a slope of about five for the NC-R relationship. The intercept of the NC-R function increases following the recognition task. This gives further support to our notion that the intercept measures the effect of organizations of the material not presented in the original categorization. Presumably, during recognition, subjects pick up and organize items that were not previously organized.

The NC-R relationship is close to .70, and statistical analysis shows no mediating effect of either trials or total time. The relationship between number of categories and recognition (NC and Rg) on Session 1 is low and positive (r approximates .35). The removal of recalled items from the recognition scores seems to have little effect on this relationship. In short, these data suggest a weak but positive relationship between recognition and categorization and support one of the notions advanced above, namely, that lists categorized with a few number of categories produce lower levels of recognition. It was suggested that this may be due to lack of category discriminability.

With these results at hand, it was decided to investigate two further aspects simultaneously. First, the question whether filler items that produced greater confusability would significantly affect recognition, and second, whether a period of time longer than two or four weeks would affect any of the relationships found for the shorter periods in Experiment RR.

EXPERIMENT RC1. In this experiment, 20 subjects were given the same categorization and recall task as in the previous experiment. The changes were as follows:

First, for the recognition task, we selected fillers such that for each word used during categorization, a high frequency English word was chosen, the meaning of which was close to, or possibly synonymous with, the meaning of the word used during sorting. Thus, the filler items should produce a greater confusability. Secondly, the second session, again consisting of recall, recognition and recall tasks, was given five weeks following the first session, again with subjects not knowing they would be recalled. Finally, all subjects were given a recall task prior and subsequent to recognition in Session 1.

Figure 1 shows very similar effects after five weeks as we found after two weeks for Experiment RR, above. Recall increased after recognition, but the drop in recall after five weeks was no different from the drop in recall after two weeks for Experiment RR. The same is true of recognition, with recognition in Session 2 being somewhat lower, but not significantly so, at .66, and false alarms at .26. Again, the removal of recalled items from the recognition measure does not seriously impair discriminability. The NC-Rg relationship is maintained, with correlation between number of categories and recognition going to .40 for all measures.

It was decided that Experiment RC1 had adequately demonstrated the stability of recall over a five-week period and a lack of decay beyond that shown after two weeks, but that it probably was inconclusive in regard to the confusable filler items. The next experiment, therefore, addressed itself directly to the problem of semantic confusion.

EXPERIMENT RC2. This experiment generally replicated Experiment RR, with two major exceptions:

A new list of words was drawn up by selecting 100 high frequency synonym pairs. Subjects were given 100 words constituting one-half of each pair during the sorting task; the other half of the pair was used for the filler items. Thus subjects saw 100 unrelated words during the categorization task, but during the recognition task, the filler items were 100 synonyms for the words they had sorted. A sample of the synonym pairs used is given below:

ache	pain	glow	shine	physician	doctor
baby	infant	illness	sickness	odor	smell
damp	moist	little	small	tale	story

One other change in procedure was that half the subjects were given a forced choice recognition task: instead of being given a random arrangement of 200 words, they were given 100 synonym pairs and asked to indicate which member of the pair was contained in the original sorting list. Figure 1 shows recognition performance for both the regular and the forced choice condition.

The general function of recall is the same. Again, after two intervening recognition tasks, recall performance after four weeks reaches the level of original recall. In Session 1, recognition under either method is as high as it was in Experiment RR with random fillers. False alarms are somewhat higher at .09. However, there was no sharp drop in the recognition performance with synonym distractor items after two weeks. There is a drop to about .70 yes/no recognition, with forced-choice recognition at about .75, and no further apparent drop after four weeks.

Figure 1 summarizes the recognition data for the three experiments. We have given, separately, data for the forced choice and the yes/no recognition groups in Experiment RC2, and the dotted lines show the forced choice equivalent for the other groups, using Green and Swets' (1966, p. 72) suggested transformation.

The graph clearly indicates the absence of very large effects among the three experiments, with the semantic relationship between words and their fillers as the major independent variable. There is an increase in false alarms in the RC2 group, but it is much below what we had theoretically and intuitively expected to be the results of semantic confusability.

Individual Changes in Memory as a Function of Categorization

One other study has been completed that relates to the category recall relationship. We presented data in O & M showing that self-selection could not be a factor in explaining the NC-R relationship. However, an additional point that needed to be explored was whether a change in the number of categories using the *same* subjects would show the change in recall that the theory demands. The following experiment was undertaken to investigate this question.[5]

EXPERIMENT. Forty-eight subjects were run in an experiment that involved four groups of twelve subjects each. In each group, all subjects were given two sorting and recall tasks. In the first task, they were asked to sort 100 high frequency words into three or seven categories and then asked to recall the words as in our regular procedure. Following a five-minute interval, they sorted a different set of 100 words into three or seven categories and recalled. The four groups were defined thusly:

	Task 1	Task 2
Group 1	7 categories	7 categories
Group 2	7 categories	3 categories
Group 3	3 categories	7 categories
Group 4	3 categories	3 categories

---

[5] I want to thank Mr. Terry Jackson for collecting the data for this experiment.

We expected that subjects who were required to sort into seven categories would recall more words than those who were told to sort into three categories, that subjects going from three to seven would increase their recall, that subjects going from seven to three would decrease, and that the other two groups would show little or no change. Such results would demonstrate that subjects' recall could be manipulated independently of individual differences and made dependent on organizational variables.

No detailed analysis of the data will be given here, except to note that all the major predictions were confirmed. Mean recall for seven-category subjects in Task 1 was 52; for three-category subjects it was 38, with an increase of approximately 3.5 words per category. The mean number of words recalled for seven-category subjects on Task 2 was 46; for three-category subjects on Task 2 it was 28, with an increase of 4.5 words per category. Both of these differences are statistically significant. As far as the groups are concerned, both Group 1 (7 - 7) and Group 4 (3 - 3) showed a mean decrease of five words from Task 1 to Task 2, while Group 2 (7 - 3) showed a decrease of 29 words. The only group that showed an increase in number of words recalled was Group 3 (3 - 7), with a mean increase of seven words from Task 1 to Task 2.

In short, the number of categories determines recall over and above individual differences or "memory ability." Furthermore, repeated tests show some apparent interference with recall on Task 2.

Other Evidence for the Hierarchical Model

In order for a model of hierarchical categorical organization to have any claim to attention, we must find some generality beyond the instances adduced so far. I shall appeal to two of several possibilities. The first is essentially anecdotal in character and refers to the nature of "associations" under different kinds of instructions. For example, if it is under a definitional set, the search appears to move typically to superordinate items in the hierarchical organization shown in Figure 2. The associations to *dog* or *cat* under such instructions are *animal* or *living thing*. Under instructions to give examples, the search is downward in the hierarchy, that is, *terriers* and *beagles* or *siamese* and *alley*. Under instructions to give similar items, the search produces items horizontally organized, such as *cow* and *horse*. Thus, instructional programming will produce very definite search patterns within such a hierarchical system.

I would like to discuss more extensively some experiments on word emissions from our laboratories. Does the free emission of words reveal the kind of structure proposed here?

In O & M and in subsequent publications (Mandler, 1968), we have used experiments on categorization and memory as initial clues to the general storage of words in long-term memory in terms of the schema shown in Figure 2. The suggestion was made that storage is hierarchical with five words per category, five categories per level, with five levels, resulting in a single categorization schema having approximately 5^5 items and a possible limit of human storage equivalent to $(5^5)^5$, or approximately 10^{17} items.

Apart from the more extravagant flights of fancy this implies, the notion of a hierarchical storage suggests a replication and further extension of the work of Bousfield and Sedgewick (1944). We assume that when subjects emit single words freely, this spilling out of storage reflects to some extent the structure of storage. Temporal ordering of the emission of words should reflect the organization, such that words that are structurally related in the storage system should appear together in response to such instructions as "Name all the animals you can." Pollio (1964) has shown that the differences in the *rate* of emission also reflect this organization. Thus, a fluctuation in the rate of response as indicated by inter-response times (IRTs) between successive words should reflect organizational aspects as indicated by clusters of interrelated words. Pollio has shown that the changes of rate of responding were correlated with the presence or absence of "associative clusters." He concluded that there was a greater "intra-cluster associative cohesiveness," as well as smaller "semantic distances" in fast sequences relative to slow sequences of emitted words. He demonstrated a relationship between the appearance of words in the "fast sequences" and the organization of such words into clusters. The experiment on free emission discussed below explores this aspect of the storage.

We have noted a limit of about 5 ± 2 words in recovery from storage. In those cases where categories have more than five words in them, the larger amount of material that can be recovered from these large categories is due, at least in part, to the subcategorization of these large categories. As part of our free emission study we noted that when subjects are given instructions to emit words freely without additional instructions, the number of words within any one category that is emitted before the subject changes categories is also about five. This suggests that the limited capacity of the organism to process about five words in any single category is also reflected in the emission from storage.

EXPERIMENT. A fairly large number of pilot subjects was run in this experiment. but the data to be discussed briefly here were obtained from seven subjects.[6] In order to familiarize them with the procedure, the subjects

---

[6] The experiment and the analyses reported here were carried out by Mr. Peter J. Dean.

119

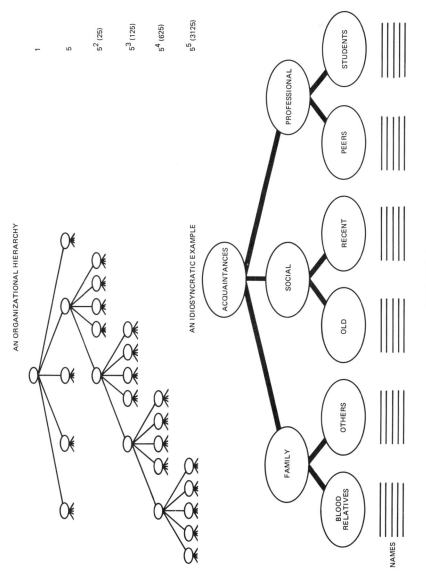

FIGURE 2

were asked to give as many names of cities in the United States as they could. This session lasted approximately two minutes and was not analyzed. Each of the seven subjects was then asked to give verbally as many names of animals as he could think of, proceeding as quickly as possible. He was instructed to try to avoid repetition of words if at all possible. The subject continued to emit words until he indicated a desire to stop or until ten to fifteen minutes had elapsed. With this procedure subjects were approaching the maximum of immediately available words. The animal category was chosen because it contained a sufficient number of members while still enabling the limit to be reached. The subjects' output was then transcribed to IBM cards with one word per card. The subjects returned at a later date and were given the cards, with their emitted words on them, in a random order and were asked to sort the cards into categories, placing words that they felt belonged together in the same category. They were allowed to use as many categories as they wished and were given as long as they desired to sort the words. Each card was then coded to indicate the category into which it had been sorted. The tape recordings of the subjects' emissions were played back through a voice key which, when activated by a word on the tape, deflected a pen on a pen recorder. Interresponse times (IRTs) were obtained by measuring the distance between the end of the previous word and the beginning of the next. Accuracy of the IRT measurements was approximately ± 0.1 seconds.

Individual data plots for the subjects, plotting cumulative number of words against time, were reasonably well fitted by the growth curves suggested by Bousfield and Sedgewick, with individual differences reflected primarily in the limit parameter or the number of total available responses.

After subjects had sorted their words into categories, the words were arranged into the original output order, and sequences of adjacent words in the original emission output that belonged to the same category were determined. Such a sequence defined a cluster emission. In addition, to determine the amount of clustering in each subject's emission, relative ratios of repetition (RRR) based on the formula for ratios of repetition (RR) (Cohen, Sakoda, and Bousfield, 1954) were obtained. RRR relates the ratio of repetition to the maximum and minimum possible for any set of categorized words.

Table 2 shows these RRR values for each of the seven subjects. Note that 0.0 on this measure reflects the degree of clustering that would be expected on the basis of a purely random order, while 1.0 reflects perfect clustering. It is evident that there was a substantial degree of organization in the emission of these words. The result agrees with Pollio (1964) that the sequences of words during emission are organized. It should be noted that these analyses probably underestimate actual organization when subjects do not use the same "frame of reference" during sorting that they use during emission, and secondly, because the sorting procedure is insensitive to momentary idiosyncratic relations between words that exist during production but not during sorting.

TABLE 2

Number of words emitted, relative ratio of repetition (RRR) and conditional probabilities of a word being in a cluster given that it was in a fast sequence, P(C/FS), and of a word being in a fast sequence given that it was in a cluster, P(FS/C), for each S.

Subject	Words Emitted	RRR	P(C/FS)	P(FS/C)
LL	61	.613	.875	.700
GB	84	.431	.714	.577
US	76	.681	.915	.705
LD	102	.504	.889	.746
JP	165	.645	.874	.816
PC	82	.460	.902	.688
RF	87	.547	.958	.605

In order to relate clusters to fast sequences of responding, frequency distributions of IRT classes were obtained for each subject. These distributions were divided into quartiles, and the IRT classes which bounded the first quartile (the one with the fastest IRTs) were noted. Fast sequences were obtained by finding all sequences of words where the IRTs fell into this first quartile. Table 2 shows the relation between clusters and fast sequences. The probability of a word being emitted in a cluster, given that it was in a fast sequence, and the probability of a word being in a fast sequence, given that it was emitted in a category cluster, are very high. The fact that in every case the probability of being in a fast sequence, given that a word was in the cluster, is lower than the probability of the alternative situation is probably due to the fact that an arbitrary definition of a fast sequence was chosen because of the inherent "noise" in the cluster analysis. In any case, fast sequences contain highly related items, and highly related items occur in fast output sequences.

If log IRT is plotted against the ordinal emission number of words, we find a characteristic triangular shape, such that as the ordinal number of words increases, there is an increasing variability in IRTs. Very early in the emission sequence, IRTs are relatively short. Late in the sequence, they can be both short and long. An analysis of the specific words producing long IRTs shows that most of the IRTs that produce the increase in latencies with increasing ordinal number are for first words of a cluster or of a fast sequence. Thus, as the emission proceeds, the time before the emission of a cluster increases. On the other hand, the IRTs that remain relatively constant across ordinal number of words tend to represent words within a cluster.

In general, our response records agree with the results of Bousfield and Sedgewick (1944). There is a decrease in frequency of response as a function of time, but also fluctuation in rate of responding which these authors did not investigate as fully as might be expected in light of subsequent attention to cluster analyses. The appearance of clusters during rapid sequences suggests that the hypothetical search mechanism does not search for words but for groups of words. When it finds a cluster of related words, it emits these as a group, usually of five words or less, and then continues its search.

Consensual Semantic Organization in Categorization

In our sorting studies, subjects categorize 100 words into anywhere from two to seven categories. The basis of their judgment is essentially one of similarity, deciding which words belong to the same category, the category name or concept being of the subjects' own choosing. Given this free conceptualization or categorization of words, it is reasonable to ask to what extent this sorting behavior demonstrates semantic similarity across subjects. In other words, do different subjects tend to sort the same words together, and when they do, does this behavior exhibit any reasonable semantic structure?

Miller (1967) has recently examined semantic structure from a similar point of view, investigating consensus across subjects as to the belongingness of different words. We used the same method used by Miller in the following analysis.[7]

DATA ANALYSIS. The data were those from 40 subjects in Experiments RR and RC1 discussed above. After the sorting, a 100 x 100 word matrix was constructed by entering in the ij-th cell the number of subjects who sorted the i-th word into the same category as the j-th word. If the assumption is made that the more similar a pair of items is, the more frequently that pair will be sorted into the same category, this matrix can be considered a matrix of similarities.

A clustering analysis developed by Johnson (1967) was used to ascertain the structure underlying the matrix.[8] This method determines homogeneous groups of items on the basis of similarity measured by the sorting task and organizes these groups or clusters into a hierarchical structure which can be represented graphically in the form of a tree diagram or dendrogram.

The method is used recursively on the matrix by first looking for groups of words that are always sorted together (all subjects sort these particular words into the same categories). Each of these groups is defined as a cluster at this

---

[7] The analyses were performed by Mr. Peter J. Dean.
[8] I wish to acknowledge the help received from S. C. Johnson and the Bell Telephone Laboratories in providing the computer program for these analyses.

particular level—in this case, Level 40. The criterion is then relaxed, and new groups that are sorted by n-1 subjects into similar categories are determined. At this level, new clusters are uncovered and other clusters or items are merged with old clusters. The process is continued until all words are grouped into one large cluster, or until the '0' level has been reached. The clusters can now be organized into graphical representations as in Figures 3 and 4.

The scale at the top of the figures represents number of subjects who agree on sorting the particular words into the same category—regardless of the name or meaning of the categories used by the individual subjects. For example, in Figure 3 at the bottom, it can be seen that 31 subjects sorted *lake* and *hole* into the same category, while 27 sorted *lake, hole,* and *camp* into the same category.

The main property of these dendograms is the identification on the horizontal dimension of similarity or belongingness for sets of words. The farther to the right a particular node appears, the more similar are the words that it subsumes. The vertical dimension contains no information since it is generated by the order in which words are processed.

Figure 3 shows the structure of the 100 words on the first sorting trial while Figure 4 shows the last or criterion trial. The mean number of trials for the 40 subjects was 4.4 with a range of 2 - 8.

It should be noted that this representation of semantic structure does not produce the kind of hierarchies which we described earlier (p.118) and have shown in Figure 2. Rather it represents the consensual aspect of the semantic structure and reflects only part of the total storage structure. Thus, the scale in Figures 3 and 4 shows the increasing likelihood that particular words belong to the same subcategory, but items to the left of a particular set are not superordinates; they are farther removed, but on the same level of the hierarchical structure. On the other hand, unconnected, independent clusters of the structure probably do represent independent clusters from our hierarchical organization.

Figures 3 and 4 show a high degree of intersubjective agreement on semantic structure. It should be recalled that the sorting exhibited in Trial 1 (Figure 3) takes place at a time when the subjects have not seen the total set of words. They only inspect and make similarity decisions relative to each word at a time as it appears in the deck. The major change from Trial 1 to the criterion trial is an increase in consensus, (word sets move to the right), and a decrease in reticulation (an increase in agreement as to the suborganization of the set of words).

In general, an inspection of the two figures shows that this sorting method produces a reasonable picture of the semantic organization of the set of words used. Five major categories, or subdivisions, can be seen in Figure 4, which adequately account for the organization of the 100 words.

124

Dendrogram obtained from 40 subjects sorting 100 words
into two to seven categories on the first trial of the sorting task.

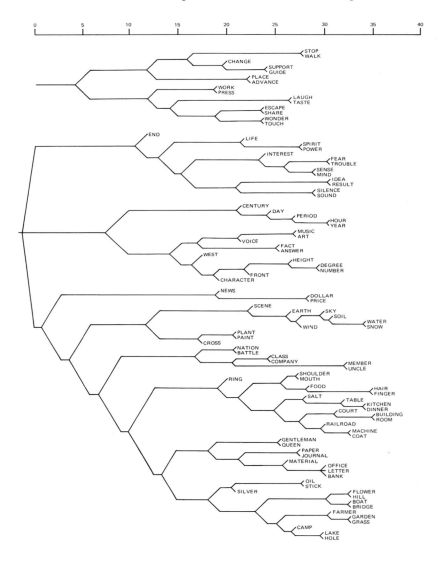

FIGURE 3

Dendrogram obtained from 40 subjects sorting 100 words into two to seven categories on the last (criterion) trial of the sorting task.

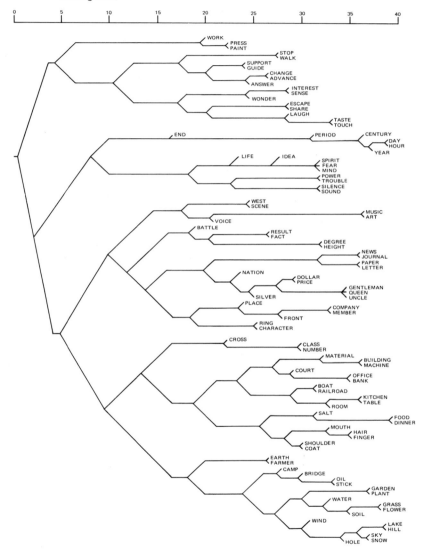

FIGURE 4

One difficulty in our use of this clustering analysis arises from the fact that subjects were forced to use no more than seven categories. They were thus probably somewhat restricted in generating fine semantic distinctions. Another problem in this example is that some of the words may have more than one common meaning. For example, *place* may be used both as a verb and as a noun. There was no way to determine which meaning a subject was using at any particular time.

RELATIONAL IMAGERY

In a sense, all mechanisms discussed in this chapter could be subsumed under the heading "Relational Imagery." Both seriation and categorization involve relational processes, either in terms of serial ordering or categorical organization. The notion that some superordinate conception of order is necessary for seriation, as Lashley has suggested, and the idea that the processing mechanism has access to information about levels within a hierarchical organization suggest similar "cognitive" mechanisms. Thus, we are in a larger sense dealing with relational imagery whenever we deal with organized information processing in memory.

However, some category of mechanisms is needed to account for memory retrieval that involves neither seriation nor categorization. Particularly, those retrieval mechanisms involving about two or three items need to be segregated. I have reserved the term "relational imagery" for such mechanisms.

Unfortunately there is shamefully little to say about this aspect of mnemonic rules. It is probably the aspect that is intuitively most obvious and on which least has been done by the experimental psychologist. The aid to memory which the forming and elaboration of complex mental images can give has been known for several millenia (cf. Yates, 1966). The "One is a bun . . ." jingle mentioned earlier is widely known, though little used. But the investigation of visual imagery and its function in memory and thought has been proscribed too long in American psychology to be the subject of a lengthy disquisition here. We do know that the use of visual imagery significantly helps the memory of word or thought pairs. (Our hypothetical husband used it to remember iceberg lettuce.) These images are usually visual and idiosyncratic—practically nothing is known about auditory or other sensory imagery and their relation to memory and storage. Between Galton and the mid-twentieth century, the evidence is either repetitious or absent.

Some recent work, however, does deserve mention. In an extended series of studies, Paivio (e.g. 1965) has shown the advantage of imagery and vividness in the recall and acquisition of word lists and pairs. Bugelski's (1962) data strongly support the notion that the reported presence of imagery may be a necessary condition for the pairwise acquisition of words.

Bower (1968) has shown dramatic effects of imagery through demonstration of superior acquisition of word pairs when subjects are instructed to form mental images.

In our laboratory, Kuhlman showed some years ago (1960) that children with a high level of visual imagery learn word pairs faster than children with low imagery. Following up these results with adult subjects, Stewart (1965) showed that lists of pictures are generally learned more rapidly than lists of words and that subjects with a high level of imagery do particularly well in storing lists of pictures. Her study also suggests that subjects with a low level of imagery tend to use nonvisual mnemonic strategies in the organization of lists of words. Thus, while visual imagery seems to have a generally beneficial effect in memory experiments, it is of special advantage for subjects better equipped to use relational imagery as a strategy.

In conclusion, all we really know is that visual imagery, particularly when it is used as a relational device, is an important cognitive strategy. We do not know why and how it works. With the decline of behavioristic dicta about what psychologists may or may not study, we can look forward to some insight into these problems over the next decade.

SOME DIFFICULTIES WITH ASSOCIATION THEORIES

Given these experimental characteristics of organized memory, it is necessary to consider the way traditional associationistic thought might be adequate to handle these phenomena. The British empiricists and the modern associationists, whether distinguishable or not, have been flayed privately and publicly in the recent psychological literature. Having contributed to this public exhibition myself (Mandler and Mandler, 1964), I shall not dwell at length here on the inadequacies of association theories or upon the question of whether they are theories at all (Mandler, 1968).

Suffice it to point out that the kind of phenomena we are discussing here is by definition beyond the ken of a theory that relies on the strength of associative bonds and on laws of contiguity, similarity, or contrast, to produce these bonds (cf. Aristotle or any contemporary writer). The schema of seriation is beyond associative strength, and the notion that memory depends on sheer number of categories used to order a list seems also unamenable to a theory of memory which relies on contiguities of input or output to produce an ordering of elements in the mind.

What is more relevant to the present discussion is the quicksand of empirical associationism, the attempt to make any theoretical sense of production or reproduction on the basis of empirical associative norms. To say that the probability of association between two words orders their relation in storage is patently false, and has been shown to be false ever since the days of the Würzburg School some sixty years ago. Whether the word *table* will elicit the response *plate* or the response *figure* depends on whether we imply the question "What is on the *table*?" or the question "What is in the *table*?" The notion that context sets up independent distributions of probabilities that summate to produce the different responses was destroyed by Otto Selz some fifty years ago (cf. Mandler and Mandler, 1964).

An empirical distribution of associative probabilities fails to take into account that the high probability of some particular response to some particular stimulus may be due to synonymity, antonymity, categorization, syntactic factors, or several other variables. To say that both *black* and *knight* have a high probability of elicitation by *white* says nothing at all about any useful ordering or relation between *knight* and *black*. So much for association theories.

PROSPECT AND RETROSPECT

We have presented some evidence here for the power of the three processes that we consider central to the organization of long-term memory or storage—seriation, categorization, and relational imagery. Such a listing of processes is theoretically somewhat inelegant and unsatisfying. However, if this endeavor does nothing but encourage the search for other such basic processes or even leads to their rejection in favor of a more general—and therefore more satisfying—formulation, I would consider it a major success.

An understanding of the structure of human thought requires as one of its constituents a reasonable view of the way the human mind stores information—in particular linguistic information. The dissatisfaction with traditional views which have given us little in the way of information on such a structure has led me to the kind of formulations presented here. They are preliminary and have no claim to lasting fame; they do seem to be a reasonable beginning for an eventual theory of mental storage.

Clearly such a theory will be far more complex than the beginnings made here and elsewhere during the past decade. Long-term storage cannot be a simple analysis of a word, its assignment to a single location, and a linear output from that location. No such view is being defended here. In particular, we are essentially ignorant of the analytic process that precedes many of the phenomena discussed here. When a series of sounds impinges on the human ear, or a fleeting black and white impression from a page is registered on the retina, and we say that that event was such and such a word, the system has already engaged in an analytic endeavor which dwarfs the simple categorization that follows such registration.

A series of rapid and very precise decisions is made by the system as such a "stimulus" travels through the processing chain. Initial decisions are quite clearly made on a purely phonetic basis: phonemic decision chains shunt the input to one or another part of the storage, and semantic or structural decisions of the order explicated here can only follow this initial analytic process.

How such analysis proceeds needs detailed investigation and such investigation and theory are already in the process of formulation in various laboratories. For our purposes it is relevant to note that quasi-semantic decisions must be made by the system during and not just at the conclusion of this analytic process. Thus a phonetic analysis may decide very early in the chain that a particular input is nonsense, i.e., not English, on the basis of the occurrence of particular visual or phonemic information, e.g., the occurrence of the letters Q and L in sequence, or phonemic analysis may decide that a word is not English long before it assigns some semantic place to it. As an example, the system may decide that the word *MISSerfolg* is not English before it decides —incorrectly—that it has something to do with being female. Similarly, it can make decisions about familiarity on the basis of letter and phoneme frequencies before making decisions about semantic location. All such decisions made during the analysis in turn feed into semantic analysis. Most important, of course, are contextual and syntactic markers which we have not even considered here. Once a location on these generally phonetic grounds is made and the item is located, the system can proceed to a semantic analysis in terms of the kind of hierarchic organization we have proposed.

Essentially we have described a program of further research. Such a description implies that we know the right kinds of questions a psychologist of thought, memory, and language must ask. It is essentially this conviction that motivates this chapter—namely that we are finally asking the proper questions. And questions are still the easier part of the scientific endeavor; answers are more difficult.

REFERENCES

Bousfield, W. A. & Sedgewick, C. H. W., 1944. An Analysis of Sequences of Restricted Associative Responses. *J. Gen. Psychol., 30,* 149-165.

Bower, G. H., 1968. Organization in Human Memory. Address given at meetings of Western Psychological Association, San Diego.

Bugelski, B. R., 1962. Presentation Time, Total Time, and Mediation in Paired-Associate Learning. *J. Exp. Psychol., 63,* 409-412.

Cohen, B. H., 1963. Recall of Categorized Word Lists. *J. Exp. Psychol., 66,* 227-234.

Cohen, B. H., Sakoda, J. M., and Bousfield, W. A., 1954. The Statistical Analysis of the Incidence of Clustering in the Recall of Randomly Arranged Associates. TR No. 10, ONR Contract Nonr-631(oo), University of Connecticut.

Earhard, M., 1967. The Facilitation of Memorization by Alphabetic Instructions. *Canad. J. Psychol., 21,* 15-24.

Garner, W. R., 1962. *Uncertainty and Structure as Psychological Concepts.* New York: Wiley.

Green, D. M., and Swets, J. A., 1966. *Signal Detection Theory and Psychophysics.* New York: Wiley.

Jensen, A. R., 1962. Transfer between Paired-Associate and Serial Learning. *J. Verb. Learn. Verb. Behav., 1,* 269-280.

Johnson, N. F., 1968. Sequential Verbal Behavior. *Verbal Behavior and General Behavior Theory,* ed. T. R. Dixon and D. L. Horton, Englewood Cliffs, N.J.: Prentice-Hall.

Johnson, S. C., 1968. Hierarchical Clustering Schemes. *Psychometrika, 32,* 241-254.

Katona, G., 1940. *Organizing and Memorizing.* New York: Columbia University Press.

Kuhlman, C. K., 1960. Visual Imagery in Children. Doctoral dissertation, Harvard University.

Lashley, K. S., 1951. The Problem of Serial Order in Behavior. In *Cerebral Mechanisms in Behavior,* ed. L. A. Jeffress, New York, Wiley.

Mandler, G., 1954. Response Factors in Human Learning. *Psychol. Rev., 61,* 235-244.

Mandler, G., 1962. From Association to Structure. *Psychol. Rev., 69,* 415-427.

Mandler, G., 1967a. Verbal Learning. In *New Directions in Psychology III,* ed. G. Mandler, P. Mussen, N. Kogan and M. A. Wallach, New York: Holt, Rinehart and Winston, pp. 1-50.

Mandler, G., 1967b. Organization and Memory. In *The Psychology of Learning and Motivation,* ed. K. W. Spence and J. T. Spence. Vol. 1. New York: Academic Press, pp. 327-372.

Mandler, G., 1968. Association and Organization: Facts, Fancies, and Theories. In *Verbal Behavior and General Behavior Theory,* ed. T. R. Dixon and D. L. Horton. Englewood Cliffs, N.J.: Prentice Hall.

Mandler, G. and Dean, P. J., 1969. Seriation: The Development of Serial Order in Free Recall. *J. Exp. Psychol., 81,* 207-215.

Mandler, G. and Pearlstone, Z., 1966. Free and Constrained Concept Learning and Subsequent Recall. *J. Verb. Learn. Verb. Behav., 5,* 126-131.

Mandler, G., Pearlstone, Z., and Koopmans, H. J., 1969. Effects of Organization and Semantic Similarity on Recall and Recognition. *J. Verb. Learn. Verb. Behav., 8,* 410-423.

Mandler, J. M. and Mandler, G., 1964. *Thinking: From Association to Gestalt.* New York: Wiley.

Melton, A. W., 1963. Implications of Short-Term Memory for a General Theory of Memory. *J. Verb. Learn. Verb. Behav., 2,* 1-21.

Miller, G. A., 1956. The Magical Number Seven, Plus or Minus Two: Some Limits on our Capacity for Processing Information. *Psychol. Rev., 63,* 81-96.

Miller, G. A., 1967. Psycholinguistic Approaches to the Study of Communication. In *Journeys in Science: Small Steps—Great Strides,* ed. D. L. Arms. Albuquerque: University of New Mexico Press.

Norman, D. A., 1968. Toward a Theory of Memory and Attention. *Psychol. Rev., 75*, 522-536.

Paivio, A., 1965. Abstractness, Imagery, and Meaningfulness in Paired-Associate Learning. *J. Verb. Learn. Verb. Behav., 4,* 32-38.

Parks, T. E., 1966. Signal-Detectability Theory of Recognition Memory Performance. *Psychol. Rev.,* 1966, *73,* 44-58.

Pollio, H. R., 1964. Composition of Associative Clusters. *J. Exp. Psychol., 67,* 199-208.

Seibel, R., 1964. An Experimental Paradigm for Studying the Organization and Strategies Utilized by Individual Ss in Human Learning and Experimental Evaluation of It. Paper presented Psychonomic Society meetings, October.

Sperling, G., 1967. Successive Approximations to a Model for Short-Term Memory. *Acta Psychologica, 27,* 285-292.

Stewart, Joan C., 1965. An Experimental Investigation of Imagery. Doctoral dissertation, University of Toronto, 1965.

Tulving, E., 1962. Subjective Organization in Free Recall of "Unrelated" Words. *Psychol. Rev., 69,* 344-354.

Tulving, E., 1964. Intratrial and Intertrial Retention: Notes Towards a Theory of Free Recall Verbal Learning. *Psychol. Rev., 71,* 219-237.

Waugh, N. C., 1961. Free Versus Serial Recall. *J. Exp. Psychol., 62,* 496-502.

Waugh, N. C. and Norman, D. A., 1965. Primary Memory. *Psychol. Rev., 72,* 89-104.

Wertheimer, M., 1921. Untersuchungen zur Lehre von der Gestalt: I. *Psychol. Forsch., 1,* 47-58.

Young, R. K., 1968. Serial Learning. In *Verbal Behavior and General Behavior Theory,* ed. T. R. Dixon and D. L. Horton. Englewood Cliffs, N.J.: Prentice-Hall.

Yates, F. A., 1966. *The Art of Memory.* University of Chicago Press.

6

Interpersonal Verbs and
Interpersonal Behavior
Charles E. Osgood

This paper is my attempt to summarize and interpret some four years of research on the semantics of interpersonal verbs in relation to the norms of interpersonal behavior. Quite a number of colleagues and graduate students in the Center for Comparative Psycholinguistics at the University of Illinois have contributed to this research.[1] Some of their studies, and mine, have already been published, some others will be in the near future, and some will never be published because we were thoroughly dissatisfied with them. Nor are we at this point satisfied that we have solved the central problem of specifying a theoretically principled and empirically rigorous procedure for discovering the semantic features of word forms. Nevertheless, in the patterning of failures and partial successes we are beginning to see some sense and some relationships to the approaches of others.

The schema of this paper will be as follows: After some introductory comments on relations between language, thought and behavior, and a brief review of earlier work with the semantic differential technique, I will describe an approach to the measurement of meaning which employs the rules of usage of words in combination as a means of discovering the semantic features of the words thus combined. I believe that this approach, while designed to be empirical rather than intuitive, will be found to be not inconsistent with those of some contemporary linguists (e.g., Chomsky, 1965;

---

[1] Contributors to particular studies will be cited in course, but I want to express special gratitude to Dr. Kenneth Forster, with whom I first explored some new directions in semantic feature analysis while on sabbatical in 1964-65 at the University of Hawaii, and to Dr. Marilyn Wilkins, with whom I have worked closely since returning to the University of Illinois. Both have served as intellectual goads and sophisticated critics throughout.

Fillmore, 1967). An a priori analysis of the features of interpersonal verbs, designed to serve as a rough guide for interpreting and evaluating subsequent research, will be followed by a variety of empirical studies on discovery procedures and validity studies on what was discovered. Then we will turn to the interpersonal behavior side of the coin, reporting studies which use what has come to be called "a role differential" and studies of a cross-linguistic and cross-cultural design which enliven the possibility of discovering universal semantic features. I will conclude with a few notes concerning a semantic performance model and a critique of our own work to date.

LANGUAGE, THOUGHT AND BEHAVIOR

Put in most general terms, I conceive of *thought* (meaning, significance-intention) as an intervening variable mediating between antecedent *signs* (perceptual or linguistic) and subsequent *behaviors* (non-verbal or verbal). Interpersonal behavior is merely a special case, albeit a very interesting one, of this more general paradigm. The sequences of events may be completely non-verbal, as when **person A** *beckons to* **person B** (perceptual sign for B), and when B fails to respond, we infer an interpersonal intention (thought) on the part of B which might be characterized as *To Disregard*. The sequence may be entirely verbal, as, when on the telephone, **person A** says *"You ought to be ashamed of yourself"* (linguistic signs), **person B** replies *"I'm sorry I did it"* (linguistic responses), and we infer the intention of A *To Criticize* B and of B *To Apologize To* A. (Throughout this study I shall try to adhere to the conventions of using bold face lower case to indicate roles [e.g., **father to son**], italic lower case for non-linguistic signs and behaviors [e.g., A *beckons* and B *approaches*], italic lower case in quotes for linguistic signs and behaviors [e.g., A *"You clumsy ox"* to B *"I'm terribly sorry"*], and italics with initial caps for interpersonal significances or intentions [e.g., **person A** *To Help* **person B**].)

It might be noted in passing that the interpersonal verbs of English fail to make any obvious distinction between overt behaviors and the intentions behind them. For instance, whereas the sentence Sally *beckons to* John refers to interpersonal behavior, the sentence Sally *helps* John refers to an interpersonal intention, for Sally may be expressing the intention *To Help* John *by handing him tools, by typing his term paper*, and so on nearly ad infinitum. Indeed, the distinctions between verbs describing concrete actions (*beckoning*), classes of actions (*typing*) and intentions (*Helping*) are very difficult to specify.

A Generalized Mediation Model

Figure 1 describes a generalized mediation model for interpersonal perception and behavior. I assume that mature and participating members of any language-culture community have developed an elaborate set of symbolic processes (r - - - - s) for which the antecedents are the perceived interpersonal behaviors of others (B's) in certain situational contexts (S's) and for which the subsequents are interpersonal behaviors of the individual himself, also dependent upon situational contexts. As dependent events, these symbolic processes (thoughts) will be termed *significances* (interpretations of the behaviors of others). As antecedent events, the same symbolic processes (thoughts) will be termed *intentions* (motivations of behaviors toward others). It is apparent that the significance attributed by A to the perceived behavior of B is A's *inference* about the intention of B — and, of course, such inference may be quite wrong, particularly in the interactions of people from different cultures.

Like other semantic processes or meanings, it is assumed that each significance/intention (r - - - - s) can be characterized as a simultaneous bundle of distinctive semantic features (A, B, C . . . . N in Figure 1). I conceive of these features behaviorally as a simultaneous set of events in N reciprocally antagonistic reaction systems.[2] They may also be represented by a code-strip, as in Figure 1. For convenience in exposition, it is here assumed that coding

FIGURE 1

A Mediation Model of Interpersonal Behavior

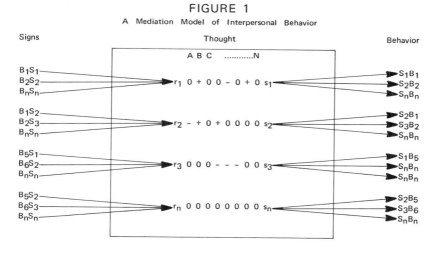

---

[2] Although this behavioristic identification is not essential to much of the quantitative research to be described—many other models could be used—it is my conviction that since (a) language behavior must ultimately be treated as part of behavior-in-general, (b) interpersonal behavior involves non-linguistic, perceptual as well as linguistic signs (and purely linguistic constructs make no contact here), and (c) interpersonal norms can be established in the absence of language (e.g., in congenital deaf-mutes), maintaining linkage with behavioristic conceptions is fruitful. It also leads to some unique predictions.

on features is discrete (+, 0, or − coding as opposed to continuous coding such as +3 through 0 to −3). The probability of the matter is that continuous coding is the general case and discrete coding the special case.

A componential system of this sort is extraordinarily efficient: although the number of distinctive features will (hopefully) be quite small, the number of significance-intention processes that can be generated from their combinations will be large. These mediational processes can render many diverse overt behaviors functionally equivalent, both as significances and as intentions (as suggested by the convergent and divergent arrows in Figure 1). Add the notion of mediated generalization (or rule, if you prefer), and a potentially infinite set of interpersonal perceptions and behaviors can be identified with a limited set of mediation processes which, in turn, can be differentiated in terms of a relatively small set of semantic componential features.

Language as a Mirror of Thought

As has already been implied, I make the further assumption that in any language the words used to talk about interpersonal behaviors will be coded on the same semantic features as the perceived behaviors themselves. Thus, the interpersonal verb *To Console* as a linguistic sign will evoke in a listener a pattern of semantic features similar to that which the perceptual sign in the observer produces (e.g., seeing a mother stroking the face of a frightened child). This assumption − if justified − provides an entrée to the structure of interpersonal behavior in a culture. Appropriate analysis of the *semantics* of interpersonal verbs may illuminate the rules which govern the *norms* of interpersonal behavior in that culture.

This procedure does *not* assume that language is a perfect mirror of thought or that it maps all of the subtleties of interpersonal behavior. Not only are there many intentions for which a language fails to provide adequate expression (translation difficulties across even closely related languages like English and French testify to this), but the semantic codings of words must inevitably constitute a reduction, an abstraction, from the potential codings of things-as-perceived. The sight of a mother stroking the face of a frightened child is at once more unique and more rich in meaning than the hearing of the word *console*. Words sacrifice semantic richness to achieve generality of usage. However, a perfect mapping is not essential for present purposes. If the meanings of words and the meanings of things-as-perceived share the same semantic features, and if the mapping of the one into the other is at least roughly co-extensive, then it should be possible to use the rules governing the one as an indicator of the rules governing the other.

Cross-cultural Comparison

In order to make comparisons across languages and cultures in any domain, it is necessary that they have something in common. If the items of subjective culture — values, attitudes, meanings, and norms of interpersonal behavior — were in truth completely unique, they would be completely incomparable. The reduction of the complexities of interpersonal behaviors to sets of mediating intentions, and these in turn to a limited set of componential semantic features, enlivens the possibility of discovering universals, without, of course, guaranteeing it.

What might we expect to be shared across human groups in the domain of interpersonal relations? Certainly not the overt expressions of intentions. Certainly not the appropriateness of particular intentions for particular role-pairs — the intent *To Obey* may be quite appropriate for a mature son toward his father in one place but quite inappropriate in another. Probably not the exact set of intentions themselves, for as culturally defined roles vary, so may the types of intentions. The most likely constant in this domain would seem to be the dimensional feature structure of the intentions themselves. Thus we might expect all human groups to distinguish between such opposites as Associative and Dissociative intentions (*Helping* vs. *Hindering*), and Supraordinate and Subordinate intentions (*Dominating* vs. *Submitting*) simply because they *are* human. If such a common feature system could be demonstrated, then comparisons across groups could be made in a reasonably rigorous way.

If A and B are members of different cultures, we might (in theory) expect them to use the same distinguishing features, to vary somewhat in the set of intentions they employ, to differ considerably in codings and weights given to translation-equivalent intentions, to differ considerably in the exact overt behaviors by which they express these translation-equivalent intentions, and to differ markedly in the rules governing the appropriateness of having and expressing certain intentions in certain role relations. Assume that **American business man** *slaps on the back* **Japanese business man** when *meeting by surprise on a street corner in Tokyo.* If the nearest equivalent of the intent *To Express Friendship* in the Japanese system includes a negative coding on the Supraordinate-Subordinate feature, the Japanese may correctly interpret the American's behavior, yet respond in a deferential manner that surprises the American. Or, if the intent *To Express Friendship* is inappropriate between businessmen role-pairs, the Japanese may correctly interpret the action but privately think the American is a fool. Or, if *slapping on the back* between adult males signifies the intent *To Insult*, our Japanese friend is most likely *to turn away abruptly* and the American might conclude that Japanese are unfriendly! Needless to say, this illustration is thoroughly hypothetical.

In order for a person to assimilate the norms of another culture, he presumably must experience a sample of interpersonal behaviors in that culture involving various roles and overt expressions, and gradually establish a set of inferences about the significance-intention mediators that are operating. The test of his assimilation is the success with which he can project this "knowledge" into novel interpersonal situations. The term 'knowledge' is used here in much the same sense that one may be said to have "knowledge" of the rules of his grammar — by following the rules but not necessarily being able to verbalize them. There is probably more than just an analogy between "knowing" the rules of a grammar and "knowing" the norms of a system of interpersonal behavior. In both cases, a sure intuitive feeling is a better guarantee of fluency than an ability to verbalize the abstract rules. And in both cases induction of the semantic features operating and their "deep structure" is essential if one is to make successful projections into new instances.

THE PROBLEM OF CHARACTERIZING MEANING

There appears to be fairly general agreement among psycholinguists, regardless of their disciplinary origins, that meanings can be characterized as "simultaneous bundles of distinctive semantic features," in much the same way that Jakobson and Halle (1956) and others after them have characterized phonemes as simultaneous bundles of distinctive phonetic features. There is disagreement about whether all, most or only some of the features known to be operating are properly called 'semantic' rather than 'syntactic,' but this issue will not concern us at the moment. The efficiency with which a relatively small number of features can generate an extraordinarily large number of distinctive meanings makes such a componential system very appealing. The problem, of course, is to devise a principled basis for discovering these features. An ideal discovery procedure would meet the usual scientific criteria of objectivity (comparability of features discovered across observers), reliability (yielding the same features in repeated, independent observations), validity (yielding features that correspond to those discovered by other methods) and generality (applicability of the procedures to the discovery of features of all types). This is a large order, and no ideal discovery procedure may be attainable.

Alternative Discovery Procedures

It is possible to distinguish two grossly different discovery procedures at the outset, and these do reflect the disciplinary backgrounds of those who use them. The first involves intuitive methods. Here the investigator utilizes his intimate knowledge of (usually) his own language as a native speaker. Semantic features are discovered by the same strategies of substitution and contrast that have proven so successful at the phonemic level. The criteria of objectivity, reliability and validity are sought, typically, by the use of compelling demonstrations that appeal to the intuitions of other (scholarly) native speakers. For example, it might be shown that in the sentence *John is eager to please, John* is obviously coded for subject whereas in the superficially similar sentence *John is easy to please, John* is obviously coded for object (appropriately chosen paraphrases reinforce the appeal). Generality of application is not a problem.

The second type of discovery procedure uses empirical methods. Here the investigator may also employ his own intuition as a native speaker (indeed, he should), but his intuition is used in devising appropriate linguistic measures to be applied to *other* native speakers and for interpreting the results. Here the strategies of substitution and contrast take the form of quantitative similarities and differences which appear in the judgments about, or usages of, selected language items by these other native speakers. Objectivity (across investigators) and reliability (across repetitions) are tested statistically; validity is sought by checking features against those obtained by other methods (where available) or against the linguistic intuitions of other investigators. But here generality becomes a significant problem: a method that works for certain types of features or for certain form classes may not work for others.

Intuitive or rational methods are typically used by linguists, semanticists, lexicographers and philosophers; they are part of their tradition. Empirical methods are typically used by psychologists; these are part of *their* tradition. Intuitive methods have the advantages of obvious generality and full utilization of the competence of sophisticated native speakers, but they also have certain disadvantages — what may be compelling demonstrations to one native speaker may not appeal at all to another, as the many delightful bickerings at linguistic symposia testify, and what may be easy to intuit in one's own language may be difficult if not impossible to intuit in a foreign language, particularly an "exotic" one.

Empircal methods have the advantages of scientific objectivity and quantification, as well as the potential for application to languages of which the investigator is not a native speaker; they also have certain disadvantages — beyond the problem of generality, there are questions about the fruitfulness of using ordinary native speakers, about the appropriateness of statistical determinations in an area like this, and about the sensitivity of such procedures in discovering the subtle distinctions made in semantics.

Semantic Differential Technique: Its Successes and Limitations

The semantic differential technique is one empirical approach to the measurement of meaning, and it will illustrate nicely both the potential powers and potential limitations of empirical approaches generally. This particular discovery procedure, on which we started working almost twenty years ago at Illinois, takes off from the theoretical notion that the meaning of any concept can be represented as a point in an n-dimensional space. The origin of this space is defined as "meaninglessness," and the vector from the origin to any concept-point represents by its length the degree of "meaningfulness" and by its direction the "quality of meaning" of the concept. The dimensions of this space, represented geometrically by straight lines through its origin, are defined by polar qualifiers (adjectives in English), and it is the clusterings among these qualifiers, as determined from the similarities of their usage in rating substantives (nouns in English), that characterize the underlying semantic structure.

There are several things to be noted about this model: First, it lends itself readily to the powerful mathematical procedures of multivariate statistics, including factor analysis (feature discovery) and distance analysis (similarity and difference in meaning). Second, it is a componential model and gains all the efficiency of such models, but unlike those familiar to linguists, its features (factors) are continuous rather than discrete in coding and linear rather than hierarchical in organization. Third, the data which fit the model and are analysed by multivariate procedures can be viewed as a sampling of linguistic frames — a "corpus" if you will — but as a highly selective rather than a random sample.

This third point requires a bit of elucidation. When a sample of subjects (native speakers) rates a sample of concepts (substantives) against a sample of bi-polar scales (qualifiers and quantifiers), a three-dimensional cube of data is generated. Each cell in this cube represents the discriminative usage of a particular substantive with respect to a particular mode of qualification by a particular speaker. In the usual format, every concept is rated against every scale, with each item appearing as in this example:

TORNADOS

fair _____:_____:_____:_____:_____:_____:__X__unfair
       +3   +2   +1   0   −1   −2   −3

The subject is instructed to check the appropriate position. The spaces in both directions from the center are defined by the adverbial quantifiers, 'slightly,' 'quite,' and 'extremely' — quantifiers which happen in English to yield approximately equal increments in intensity. Each item as checked may be viewed as a standardized type of sentence in the corpus — in the present case, the sentence *Tornados are extremely unfair*.[3] Other sentences in the speaker's corpus might be *My mother is slightly cold, Sponges are neither*

---

[3] Of course, it can be legitimately argued that it is semantically anomalous to speak of tornados as being *either* fair or unfair, but this is precisely the nub of the issue, as will become apparent.

honest nor dishonest, Defeat is quite ugly, and so forth. The representativeness of the corpus — within the limitations of this standard "syntactic" frame — depends upon the adequacy with which both concepts (sentence subjects) and scales (sentence predicates) are sampled.

Working first with various groups of American English speakers and more recently with native speakers in some twenty language-culture communities around the world,[4] both indigenous factor analyses (interpretable by translation of scales loading high on factors) and what we call pan-cultural factor analyses (interpretable directly, mathematically, in terms of scales having similar discriminating functions across 100 translation-equivalent concepts) have regularly yielded the same 3 dominant factors or features. The first is a generalized Evaluation Factor (defined by scales translating to such pairs as *good-bad, kind-cruel, pleasant-unpleasant*); the second is a generalized Potency Factor (defined by scales like *strong-weak, hard-soft, big-little*); and the third is a generalized Activity Factor (defined by scales like *active-passive, quick-slow, excitable-calm*). From this point on I shall refer to this as the E-P-A system. Factors beyond these three are nearly always small in magnitude and usually defy interpretation. If we consider the various analyses of American English data and the twenty or so analyses involving other languages and cultures to be replications in the experimental test of an hypothesis, then we can certainly conclude that E-P-A is a reliable and valid characterization of at least part of the human semantic system — a universal set of features, if you will.[5]

But it will also be evident to the reader, as it was to us early in the game, that the semantic differential technique as usually employed does not have generality as a discovery procedure. The three features identified as E, P and A — universal and significant in human behavior though they may be — obviously do not provide a sufficient characterization of meaning. Not only are these features quite unlike those discovered by intuitive methods (e.g., Abstract/Concrete, Animate/Inanimate, Human/Non-human, and the like), but it can be readily demonstrated that word forms having near-identical E-P-A codings rarely meet the substitution criterion of synonymity. *Nurse/-sincere* and *hero/success* are two such pairs: I can say *She's a cute nurse,* but not **She's a cute sincere*; I can say *Our hero defied them,* but I can't say, **Our success defied them.* I once carried around a little notebook and jotted

---

[4] Space does not permit any detailing of the procedures followed in our cross-cultural studies. Interested readers are referred to Osgood, C. E., Semantic Differential Technique in the Comparative Study of Cultures, *Amer. Anthr., 66,* 3, 1964.

[5] Of course, there will be some who will argue that E-P-A are not semantic features at all, but have something to do with emotional reactions. But proponents of this view must then explain the significant role of the E-P-A system in strictly linguistic behaviors. I will return to this question.

down my own "aphasic" slips; they were all denotative in nature, quite unrelated to the E-P-A system — like saying *Bring me the pliers* when I intended *Bring me the nail-clippers* and saying *Where is the mushroom?* when I intended *Where is the marshmallow?* (usually served in my hot chocolate).

I think the answer to why the E-P-A system of features is so universal and so obviously affective in nature is simultaneously the answer to why the semantic differential technique, as usually employed, is insufficient as a discovery procedure. The E-P-A features only appear dominantly and clearly when a large and diversified set of concepts is rated against a large and diversified set of scales. Let us ask ourselves what must happen to particular scales in this situation, taking as examples *hot-cold* and *hard-soft*. For only a few concepts in our typical set of 100 will *hot-cold* be denotatively relevant (e.g., *Fire, Stone, Hand, River*) or *hard-soft* be denotatively relevant (e.g., *Stone, Bread, Tooth, Chair*). For all other concepts, since we require every concept to be rated on every scale, *hot-cold* and *hard-soft* must be used metaphorically (e.g., for concepts like *Defeat, Anger, Power, Mother, Music, Crime* and *Peace*).

Perhaps the most important general principle of human language behavior we have found in our work is that *affective meaning is the common coin of metaphor*. When substantives and qualifiers that are literally anomalous are forced into syntactic confrontation — as in *hard power* vs. *soft power* or *hot defeat* vs. *cold defeat* — it is the common affective features (E-P-A) which determine the semantic resolution. In effect, each scale tends to *rotate* in the semantic space toward that basic affective factor on which it has some loading — *hot-cold* toward A (Active-Passive), *hard-soft* toward P (Potent-Impotent), *sweet-sour* toward E (Good-Bad), and so forth. And since, in multivariate analysis, the factors run through the regions of highest density (correlations among scales), massive E, P and A features appear while other semantic features are obscured.

AN A PRIORI SEMANTIC ANALYSIS OF INTERPERSONAL VERBS

It appears that some judicial combination of intuitive and empirical methods is in order. An a priori, rational analysis of the semantics of interpersonal verbs could serve several functions. First, it could provide a kind of short-cut into the major features which differentiate words in the interpersonal domain. Second, an intuitively satisfying set of a priori features could serve as a criterion against which to evaluate the validity of empirical discovery procedures. I decided to work with interpersonal verbs drawn from categories in Roget's *Thesaurus,* using myself as the sole informant — a reasonably sophisticated native speaker as well as native "behaver." A large number of interpersonal verbs were coded on a small number of intuited features, to determine how small a set of features could satisfactorily differentiate all of the verbs.[6] I assume that in many respects the approach I took here is similar in principle to that employed by lexicographers, particularly in its use of minimal contrasts in meaning as a discovery procedure. It probably differs in the source of intuitions about features (an informant with a behavioral science background), in the systematic comparisons within a semantic area (interpersonal verbs), and in its validation procedures (statistical contingency and distribution considerations).

Procedures

On the basis of discussions with Harry Triandis and Evelyn Katz about the development of a "Behavioral Differential,"[7] six a priori features were selected which it was thought differentiated significantly among interpersonal intentions and hence, by inference, should differentiate semantically among interpersonal verbs. Feature A: Associative/Dissociative (*To Help/To Hinder, To Guide/To Corrupt*); Feature B: Initiating/Reacting (*To Cheer Up/To Congratulate, To Persuade/To Disuade*); Feature C: Directive/Non-directive (*To Guide/To Set Free, To Command/To Disregard*); Feature D: Tension-increasing/Tension-decreasing (*To Stimulate/To Placate, To Irritate/To Calm*); Feature E: Ego-oriented/Alter-oriented (*To Confide In/To Cheer Up, To Exploit/To Corrupt*); and Feature F: Supraordinate/Subordinate (*To Lead/To Follow, To Indulge/To Appease*). These contrastive intentions were defined as carefully as possible to facilitate the coding process.[8] Search of all *Thesaurus* categories for verbs expressing interpersonal intentions (that is, verbs acceptable in appropriate PN_1————PN_2 sentences [he *Courted* her] and referring to abstracted intentions rather than concrete behaviors [*To Punish* but not *to strike with a whip*]) and selection of only the most familiar in each category yielded a sample of 210 verbs.

Each verb was coded on each feature according to the following system: plus (+) signifies that the intention includes the feature in its positive aspect and not its negative; minus (−) signifies that the intention includes the feature in its negative aspect and not its positive; zero (0) signifies that the

<hr>

[6] The reader may be wondering just why interpersonal verbs have been the focus of our attention rather than some other word category. It is because, beginning in 1963, the author became involved in a project titled "Communication, Cooperation, and Negotiation in Culturally Heterogeneous Groups" (F. E. Fiedler, L. M. Stolurow, and H. C. Triandis, principal investigators), and the research reported here was supported in part by the Advanced Research Projects Agency, ARPA Order No. 454, under Office of Naval Research Contract NR 177-472, Nonr 1834 (36). The combination of purely psycholinguistic and cross-cultural interests seemed a natural one.

[7] Dr. Katz was developing a system for coding interpersonal behaviors in the content analysis of short stories (Katz, 1964).

[8] Details of these procedures may be found in a paper titled "Speculation on the Structure of Interpersonal Verbs" (Osgood, in press).

intention is not distinguished by the feature (it includes the feature in neither its positive nor its negative aspect *or* it is capable of including either).

Each interpersonal verb was first coded globally on the six features. Next the codings of all verbs on each feature separately were checked, and final adjustments were made for consistency in application.

Validity Tests for Six A Priori Features

Several questions of intuitive validity were put to this initial a priori analysis. (1) Are the clusters of words having identical feature code-strips closely synonymous in meaning? All such sets of verbs were tabulated and inspected; in some cases they did seem practically synonymous (e.g., +A -B -C -D -E +F, *Forgive, Pardon, Excuse*), but in others they were clearly not synonymous (e.g., -A -B +C +D -E +F, *Punish, Condemn, Ridicule*). Non-synonymous clusters imply either faulty coding or insufficient features.

(2) Are words with opposed coding on only one feature and identical coding on all others minimally contrastive and contrastive on the appropriate feature? All verb pairs with codings satisfying this condition were tabulated and evaluated. In many cases the sense of minimal contrast was compelling (e.g., *Inspire* vs. *Shame* on Associative/Dissociative, *Impress* vs. *Inform* on Ego-oriented/Alter-oriented, *Indulge* vs. *Appease* on Supraordinate/-Subordinate), but in many others it was lacking (e.g., *Court* vs. *Retard* on Associative/Dissociative, *Confuse* vs. *Shame* on Ego-oriented/Alter-oriented, and *Tolerate* vs. *Follow* on Supraordinate/Subordinate). Again assuming perfect coding, failures on this test imply that there are additional features besides the one in question on which the verbs are also differentiated.[9]

(3) Are the features reasonably independent of each other in coding across the verb sample, and do they distribute the verbs reasonably among plus, zero and minus categories? Contingency tables of codings for each feature against every other feature were prepared and tested for significance. Table 1 presents only two of these tables for illustrative purposes, A/D and E/F. In the A/D table (Associativeness and Tension) note first the high negative correlation, corresponding to a Chi Square significant at the .001 level, with Associative behaviors being Tension-reducing and Dissociative behaviors being Tension-increasing; note second that, while Associativeness distributes the verbs reasonably well among plus, zero and minus categories, Tension codings have a very high proportion of zeros. For the E/F table (Ego-

---

[9] It may be worth noting in passing that verbs diametrically opposed on all non-zero features do *not* have the feel of natural "opposites" (e.g., *Guide* vs. *Evade, Flatter* vs. *Repudiate, Serve* vs. *Molest*), although they do give one the impression of complete reciprocity; the familiar opposites in my sample (e.g., *Defend/Attack, Reward/Punish, Lead/Follow*) characteristically display both some shared features and some opposed features. *Reward* and *Punish*, for example, share Reactiveness, Alter-orientation and Supraordinateness, while they are opposing on Associativeness and Tension-production.

TABLE 1

Illustrative Contingency Tables for Features A/D and E/F

Tension-increasing/Tension-decreasing (D)

		+	0	−	
Associative/	+	1	37	32	70
Dissociative (A)	0	11	40	3	54
C = .52 .001	−	33	53	0	86
		45	130	35	210

Supraordinate/Subordinate (F)

		+	0	−	
Ego-oriented/	+	19	17	10	46
Alter-oriented (E)	0	26	31	8	65
C = .17, n. s.	−	54	33	12	99
		99	81	30	210

vs. Alter-orientation and Supra- vs. Subordinateness), on the other hand, there is reasonable independence between the features, although both tend to be somewhat biased in distribution with more Alter-oriented than Ego-oriented and more Supraordinate than Subordinate interpersonal verbs. This biased distribution may, of course, faithfully reflect human relationships.

Modification of the A Priori Feature System

Because the total evidence revealed several difficulties in the a priori feature system as we were using it (difficulty in coding, failure to yield many minimal contrasts, redundancy with other features and extreme biases in distributions), it was decided to eliminate original features C (Directive/Non-directive) and D (Tension-increasing/Tension-decreasing). When classified by the remaining four features, of course, verb categories collapsed together and the sets of quasi-synonyms became larger. These sets were searched for additional features which would do a maximum amount of work: a Terminal/Interminal feature was suggested by contrasts within sets like *Unite With/Associate With, Inform/Supervise*; a Future-oriented/Past-oriented feature was suggested within sets like *Promise/Apologize, Compete With/Profit From, Frustrate/Disappoint*; and a Deliberate/Impulsive feature was suggested by contrasts like *Guide/Inspire* and *Congratulate/Praise*. Finally, the three affective features (E, P, A) found so regularly in our cross-cultural work were included, not because they do as much "work" in this domain as in others (e.g., with emotion nouns), but because they seem to be part of the total semantic picture.

With all interpersonal verbs coded on all ten final features, as illustrated in Table 2 by a small sub-set, the same tests of intuitive validity which had been previously used were applied. The few clusters of verbs which retained identical features do seem closely synonymous (e.g., *Soothe* and *Comfort; Concede* and *Acquiesce; Stimulate* and *Arouse; Confuse* and *Mystify; Shame, Embarrass,* and *Humiliate*). The distinctions made between otherwise very similar interpersonal verbs are also intuitively satisfying: *Greet* is distinguished from *Charm* by being more Terminal but less Future-oriented; *Pay Homage To* differs from *Show Respect For* by being both more Potent and more Terminal; *Forgive* is distinguished from both *Pardon* and *Excuse* by its more Moral tone; *Command* differs from *Lead* only by its more Terminal character; and *Advise* is distinguished from *Convert* only by its more Deliberate (or cognitive) character.

In the contingency analyses, only one of the three added "denotative" features showed significant relations with others — Feature I (Future/Past) is somewhat correlated positively with E (Initiating/Reacting) and negatively with H (Terminal/Interminal), relations which are not unreasonable. The E-P-A affective factors (here, Features A, B and C) seem to operate on a different level; their contingencies with other types of features (Moral/-Immoral with Associative/Dissociative, Potency with Supraordinateness, and Activity with Initiating) suggest that they typically serve to add an affective "feeling tone" to verbs already differentiated on other features.

This was an intuitively satisfying conclusion, and one might be content to let the matter rest here. The same systematic use of linguistic intuition could be applied in any semantic domain — human role-nouns, emotion nouns, personality adjectives, and so on. But, for one thing, this is a soft methodology; the coding of words on a priori features is a rather slippery business, and, as many animated discussions with my colleagues revealed, codings can shift when words are placed in different frames (i.e., given different senses). We were aiming for a more powerful and objective methodology, one that could employ ordinary native speakers who had no semantic axe to grind. For another thing, the semantic features intuited for one doman (here, interpersonal verbs) might prove to be unique to that domain and not readily relatable to features intuited in another (role-nouns or verb-modifying adverbs, for example). But just as the E-P-A system can be demonstrated in all lexical form classes (nouns, verbs, adjectives, adverbs), so it might be expected that more denotative features would also have generalized linguistic functions.

FROM RULES TO FEATURES

In 1964-65, with a sabbatical in Hawaii, time to do some much needed reading, and a young colleague, Kenneth Forster, to debate with more or less

TABLE 2
A Priori Coding of Selected Interpersonal Verbs on Ten Features

	A Moral Immoral	B Potent Impotent	C Active Passive	D Associative Dissociative	E Initiating Reacting	F Ego- Alter	G Supra Sub	H Terminal Interminal	I Future Past	J Deliberate Impulsive
To Greet	0	0	0	+	+	0	0	+	0	0
To Charm	0	0	0	+	+	0	0	0	+	0
To Show Respect for	0	0	–	+	0	–	–	0	–	–
To Pay Homage to	0	+	0	+	0	–	–	+	–	–
To Forgive	+	0	0	+	–	–	+	+	–	+
To Pardon	0	0	0	+	–	–	+	+	–	+
To Excuse	0	–	0	+	–	–	+	+	–	+
To Soothe	+	0	0	+	–	–	0	0	0	–
To Comfort	+	0	0	+	–	–	0	0	0	–
To Concede to	0	–	–	+	–	–	–	+	–	+
To Acquiesce	0	–	–	+	–	–	–	+	–	+
To Command	0	+	+	0	+	0	+	+	0	+
To Lead	0	+	+	0	+	0	+	0	0	0
To Advise	0	0	0	0	+	–	+	+	+	+
To Convert	0	0	0	0	+	–	+	+	+	0
To Stimulate	0	0	+	0	+	–	+	+	0	–
To Arouse	0	0	+	0	+	–	+	+	0	–
To Confuse	0	0	0	0	0	–	+	0	0	0
To Mystify	0	0	0	0	0	–	+	0	0	0
To Shame	0	0	0	–	+	–	+	+	–	–
To Embarrass	0	0	0	–	+	–	+	+	–	–
To Humiliate	0	0	0	–	+	–	+	+	–	–

continuously, a quite different approach to the discovery of semantic features began to take form. The general notion that motivated our thinking was that the rules which govern usage of words in sentences and phrases are themselves based upon semantic distinctions.[10] This meant, in the first place, that we should study the meanings of words in combination rather than in isolation. It also implied a return to the linguistic notion that similarity of meaning varies with the extent to which speakers use forms in the same or different contexts or frames (e.g., Harris, 1954). If acceptability of utterances depends on both grammatical and semantic congruence among their parts — and if purely grammatical congruences are assured — then differences in acceptability should become direct functions of semantic congruences. But what syntactical frames are appropriate, and can the task be adapted to ordinary speakers?

An Assist from Gilbert Ryle

In reading and discussing some of Ryle's papers on philosophy and ordinary language, we came across the following illustration. Ryle claimed that one could not say significantly in ordinary English *He hit the target unsuccessfully*. Why? Although he does not put it exactly this way, it is because the verb phrase *hit the target* is coded for what might be called "goal achievement" whereas the modifying adverb is explicitly coded for "goal non-achievement"; therefore the sentence is, in Ryle's terms, "absurd." It occurred to us that, rather than merely using such examples as compelling arguments in philosophical debate, one might systematically explore the compatabilities of verb/adverb phrases as a discovery procedure in experimental semantics. In other words, our purposes were a bit different from those of philosophers identified with the Oxford School.

There was also a difference in stress. Whereas the Oxford philosophers repeatedly emphasize that sentences have meanings and words only uses (the analogy of words with the moves of pieces in a chess game is offered), it seemed to us that there were two sides to this coin. If certain sentence frames can be said to accept certain words and reject others as creating absurdity, then the words so accepted or rejected can be said to share certain features which are either compatible or incompatible with the remainder of the sentence.

It was interesting to discover that, in one of his earlier papers (1938), Ryle seems to accept the two-sidedness of this coin:[11]

---

[10] This notion was not new then (cf., Jakobson's paper in memory of Franz Boaz, 1959) and is even more familiar today after the publication of Chomsky's *Aspects of a Theory of Syntax* (1965), in which he indicates that "selectional rules" may well belong in the lexicon. It was, however, still a rather novel notion to us in 1964.

[11] I am grateful to John Limber for bringing this article to my attention.

"So *Saturday is in bed* breaks no rule of grammar. Yet the sentence is absurd. Consequently the possible complements must not only be of certain grammatical types, they must also express proposition-factors of certain logical types. The several factors in a non-absurd sentence are typically suited to each other; those in an absurd sentence or some of them are typically unsuitable to each other." (Ryle, 1938, p. 194)

Compare the following:

*(1) sleep ideas green furiously colorless
*(2) colorless green ideas sleep furiously
?(3) colorless grey misery weeps ponderously
 (4) colorful green lanterns burn brightly

String 1 breaks both grammatical and semantic rules and must be read as a word list. String 2, Chomsky's classic, is not agrammatical but "asemantical," clashing semantically at every joint and for different reasons.[12] String 3 breaks many of the same rules as string 2, but by maintaining congruence of certain semantic features it creates a quasi-poetic meaning. String 4 is an entirely acceptable sentence, even if less interesting than 3.

Returning to the early Ryle paper (1938), we find him saying, quite appropriately: "We say that (a sentence) is absurd because at least one ingredient expression in it is not of the right type to be coupled or to be coupled in that way with the other ingredient expression or expressions in it. Such sentences, we may say, commit type-trespasses or break type-rules. (1938, p. 200)

It was our own insight,[13] and I hope a felicitous one, that if indeed this is a two-sided coin, then it should be possible to infer the semantic features of word forms from their rules of usage in combination with other words in appropriate syntactical frames. Let us take some verbs and try them in some frames: using the frame *It verbed.* vs. the frame *I verbed.*, one can make an acceptable sentence by inserting *fastened* in the first but not in the second and by inserting *prayed* in the second but not the first; thus we may infer that *it* and *pray* contrast on some feature(s) as do *I* and *fasten*. (Although we need not worry about naming features at this point, it would appear that Human/Non-Human and Transitive/Intransitive features are involved.) Or take the alternative frames *He verbed her successfully* vs. *He verbed her unsuccessfully*. The interpersonal verbs *Plead With* and *Courted* will go in

---

[12] Many would call some of these clashes grammatical, in the sense of breaking selectional rules (*green ideas*), and others really semantic, in the sense of breaking lexical rules (*sleep furiously*). It seems to me that we have a continuum rather than a dichotomy here. I shall return to this matter.

[13] I realize that the word *insight* is also coded for goal-achievement, and we are far from it!

either frame (implying that on whatever features distinguish *successfully* from *unsuccessfully,* here presumably Goal-achievement, *Plead With* and *Courted* are not coded). On the other hand, the verbs *Confided In* and *Reminded* fit easily in neither frame (implying that they contrast on some feature which *successfully* and *unsuccessfully* share, perhaps a Striving feature). Examples like these make it seem reasonable that regularities in the acceptability vs. absurdity judgments of speakers about sets of interpersonal verbs in sets of adverbial frames could be used to infer the semantic features of both sets. But some theory about how semantic features interact in the production of such judgments is required, both for asking native speakers the right questions and for interpreting their responses.

Fragment of a Theory of Semantic Interaction

I start from the notion that the meaning of a word can be characterized as a simultaneous bundle of distinctive semantic features. I assume that each of these features represents the momentary state of a single, reciprocally antagonistic representational system; this means that a word cannot be simultaneously coded in opposed directions on the same feature — it must be *either* "positive", *or* "negative" *or* neither. Whether or not these features are independent of each other, with the coding of a word on one feature not restricting the coding of the same word on any other feature, is left open at this point. The simultaneous bundle of features characterizing the meaning of a word form can be represented by a code-strip without anything being implied as yet about the form of the coding or, for that matter, about the psychological nature of the features. I do assume that the features would be ordered according to some linguistic principle.

The meaning of a grammatical string of words (phrase, acceptable sentence, absurd or anomalous sentence) is assumed to be the momentary resolution of the codings on shared features when words are forced into interaction within syntactic frames. This is required by the previous assumption that the system of any single feature can only be in one state, can only assume one "posture," at a given time. Thus if one is to understand the meaning of *He's a lazy athlete,* the simultaneous pattern of semantic features generated cannot be only that associated with *athlete* or only that associated with *lazy,* but must be some compromise. This semantic interaction can be represented as the fusion of two or more word code-strips, according to some set of rules. Going back to Ryle's example, and assuming the simplest kind of rules, the phrase *hit the target unsuccessfully* might be represented by,

	A	B	C	D	E	F					features
hit the target	0	−	0	+	0	+	.	.	.	.	
unsuccessfully	+	0	0	−	0	+	.	.	.	.	
	+	−	0	X	0	+	.	.	.	.	fusion,

A, B, etc. representing features, X representing antagonism on a goal-achievement feature (signal for absurdity judgment) and the + 0, or — representing simple coding directions.

When we come to the nature of the coding on features, the kind of interaction within features and the mode of combining influences across features, we must simply admit to alternative models and seek empirical answers. Coding on features could be *discrete* (+, 0, or —) or *continuous* (e.g., +3 through 0 to −3, as in semantic differential scaling); interactions within features could be *all-or-nothing* (the fusion must be antagonistic, represent the dominant sign, or be zero) or *algebraic* (same signs summate and opposed signs cancel); relations between features could be *segregate* (numbers of shared or antagonistic codings being irrelevant) or *aggregate* (final resolution depending upon, for example, the ratio of shared to antagonistic codings across the entire strip). Almost any combination of these possibilities is at least conceivable, and it is even conceivable that different levels of features operate according to different types of rules.[14] The kinds of rules assumed will influence both the kinds of judgments required from speakers and the kinds of statistical treatments that are appropriate.

We were already familiar with a general cognitive interaction model which assumed continuous coding on features (factors), segregation between features and a special type of weighted interaction within features. This was the Congruity Hypothesis. Applied to semantic differential type data and hence affective features, it was used to predict attitude change (Osgood and Tannenbaum, 1955) and semantic fusion under conditions of combining adjective-noun pairs, like *shy secretary, breezy husband, sincere prostitute* (as reported in Osgood, Suci and Tannenbaum 1957, pp. 275-284).

Using the geometric model discussed here on p. 140, the projections of the vectors representing the two words to be combined (e.g., *shy* and *secretary* as components) onto each factor were independently entered into a formula which, in effect, predicted a resolution point which was inversely proportional to the semantic intensities of the words combined (e.g., +3 with 0 on a factor yields +3, +2 with −2 yields 0, +2 with − 1 yields +1, etc.). It was noted at the time that opposed codings (directions) on the same factor yielded what was termed "incredulity" (e.g., for *sincere prostitute* on the E-factor). However, the model yields compromise rather than intensification when words having codings of the same sign but different magnitude are combined, and this has been a matter of experimental debate in recent years.

On the ground that denotative features, as compared with affective E-P-A features, might well be discretely coded, Forster and I devised a model which

---

[14] For example, "grammatical" features might be discretely coded, all-or-nothing in fusion and segregate in combination across features, whereas "semantic" features might be continuously coded, algebraic in fusion and aggregate in combination across features.

assumed discrete (+, 0, −) coding on features, all-or-nothing rather than algebraic interaction within features and, like the Congruity Model, segregation across features. We assumed an ordered set of rules and tried to relate them to potential judgments of combinations by speakers:

Rule I. If the strip-codes for words to be combined in a syntactic frame have opposed signs on any shared feature, then the combination will be judged semantically anomalous (e.g., *happy boulder, the brakes shouted, plead with tolerantly*). In cognitive dynamics more generally, this is the condition for "cognitive dissonance" or "incongruity."

Rule II If Rule I does not apply (if there are no features with opposed signs) and there are the same signs on any features (either ++ or − −), then the combination will be judged semantically apposite or fitting (e.g., *hopeful sign, the brakes shrieked, plead with humbly*). This is the condition for intensification of meaning.

Rule III. If neither Rule I (opposed signs) nor Rule II (same signs) apply and either code-strip contains unsigned (zero) features where the other is signed, then the combination will be judged simply permissable (e.g., *sad face, the brakes worked, plead with sincerely*). This is the condition for ordinary modification of meaning.

Several things should be noted about this model. First, it requires three types of judgment from subjects: anomaly, appositeness and permissiveness criteria. Second, anomaly criteria take precedence over appositeness criteria in determining judgment, and these both take precedence over mere permissiveness. Third, there is no summation or compromise within or across features; several opposed features do not make a combination more anomalous than one opposed feature, and several same features do not override a single opposition.

In a most intriguing paper titled "The Case for Case "[15] Charles Fillmore proposes what he calls a Case Grammar which

> ... is a return, as it were, to the "conceptual framework" interpretation of case systems, but this time with a clear understanding of the difference between deep and surface structure. The sentence in its basic structure consists of a verb and one or more noun phrases, each associated with the verb in a particular case relationship. . . . The arrays of cases defining the sentence types have the effect of imposing a classification on the verbs in the language (according to the sentence types into which they may be inserted), and it is very likely that many aspects of this classification will be of universal validity. (1967, pp. 29-30)

The case relationships which Fillmore assigns to noun phrases (subjects or objects) and verb phrases, and the uses to which he puts them, are clearly

---

[15] As of the time of this writing, to the best of my knowledge, this paper had not been published. I borrowed a dittoed version from Professor Robert Lees; it was dated April 13, 1967, from Austin, Texas.

semantic in nature and generally similar to the approach we have been taking. The Agentive (A) Case is "the case of the animate responsible source of the action identified by the verb; Instrumental (I), the case of the inanimate force or object which contributes to the action or state identified by the verb; Dative (D), the case of the animate being affected by the action or state identified by the verb . . ." (1967, p. 32), and so forth.

There is one significant difference between Fillmore's approach and ours: whereas he assigns what he calls 'frame features' to verbs, which represent case relations between verbs and noun phrases which he believes simplify the lexicon, we assign codings to common features in each of the form classes, in the belief that this is a more generally applicable procedure. Thus, he expresses the frame feature for the verb *cook* as +[_____ (O) (A)] , where either O (Objective Case) or A (Agentive Case), or both, may occur. If both occur, we have sentences like *Mother is cooking the potatoes*; if only O, then we have sentences like *The potatoes are cooking;* and if only A, then we have sentences like *Mother is cooking* — and he notes that the last is potentially ambiguous only because we are familiar with the diversity of customs in human societies.

Our procedure would probably break "case" down into semantic features like ± A (animate), ± H (human), ± C (concrete) and assign them to nouns and verbs separately, letting the interactions within features thus assigned determine acceptability. But, admittedly, in this case we would have to include "semantic" features specifying subjects versus objects as well as form-classes more generally.

It might be noted that all *interpersonal* verbs must be marked +A (Agentive) in relation to subject noun phrases and +D (dative) in relation to object noun phrases, or perhaps better, they cannot be marked −A or −D in relation to these noun phrases. This means that features associated with case relations will *not* be discoverable in the rules of combination of IPV's (interpersonal verbs) with AV's (adverbs) — case features being, in effect, held constant — but rather features "further down the line" in generality, so to speak, will have a chance of appearing. This relationship between type of linguistic sampling and level of features discoverable will become clearer in the next section.

OUR SEARCH FOR EMPIRICAL DISCOVERY PROCEDURES

A theory about meanings of word forms as componential patterns of features, about how codings on shared features interact to yield the meanings of words in combination — and so on — is all very fine, but there is very little one can do with it until he can specify what the significant semantic features are. In the domain of interpersonal behavior, for example, there is little one can do about predicting similarities and differences across cultures from their usage of interpersonal verbs until one can code such verbs on a sufficient set of valid features. As already noted, intuitive discovery procedures are pretty much limited to the language of which one is a native speaker and are of debatable validity even then. The trouble is that one's theory about semantic features is in continuous interaction with the empirical procedures one uses for discovering them. So our search of necessity has been something of a bootstrap operation — and it still is.

Problems of Sampling Linguistic Data

Sampling problems appear in many forms in an endeavor like this. First there is the question of what semantic domain to investigate (in our case this was largely decided by our interest in interpersonal behavior, although we have also worked with emotion nouns[16]) and how openly or restrictively to define this domain. There is the question of what syntactic frames to use as complements for the items in the domain under investigation and what lexical content to give them. Once decisions have been made on these matters there rises the question of what size sample of linguistic data is necessary whether it is to be drawn from natural sources or experimentally induced, whether it is to be random or systematic, and so on. And, of course, there is the usual question of what subjects (speakers) to use.

Early in our explorations at the University of Hawaii, in an attempt to clarify such problems, we took a reasonably random sample of 100 verbs-in-general (the first verbs appearing on the second 100 pages in James Michener's *Hawaii*, appropriately enough!) and subjected them to various tests in comparison with a smaller sample of interpersonal verbs drawn from my own a priori analysis as previously described.

Our general procedure was to make what we termed 'intersections' of the verb class under study with various other form classes or combinations of form classes, the latter being either sentences or phrases. Figure 2 illustrates some of the intersections we tried. The whole circles represent the entire

FIGURE 2
SAMPLE INTERCEPTS OF VERBS AND FRAMES

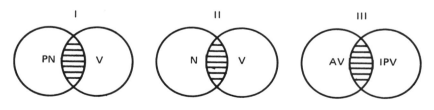

[16.] A report on semantic interactions of emotion nouns and modifying adjectives was in preparation at the time of this writing by Dr. Marilyn Wilkins and myself.

(hypothetical) sets of the classes in question and the shaded regions of intersection represent those sub-sets of each class which are actually brought into syntactical relation. Within these intersections, *all possible combinations of the two sub-sets* (e.g., all PN frames with all V's in intersection I) *are created and judged for acceptability or anomaly in ordinary English.* Kenneth Forster and myself were the only native speakers involved in these preliminary tests, and by no means did we always agree. The linguistic data generated by this means were sometimes submitted to a computer program which categorized elements of either sub-set into hierarchical "trees" in terms of similarity of usage over the other sub-set.[17]

Before making some general observations about sampling let me note briefly what happens in some of the intersections illustrated in Figure 2. Intersection I related the sample of 100 verbs-in-general (V) to simple sentence frames of three types, all composed of pronouns (PN): Type I, intransitive: *I, We, It,* or *They____(V)___;* Type II, *transitive: They ___(V)__ me, us, it* or *them*; Type III, reflexive: *I, We, It* or *They ___(V)___ PN-self.* Beyond the gross transitive and reflexive relations for verbs, there are finer distinctions in terms of which pronouns in these frames, as subjects or objects, will accept which verbs. Figure 3 displays the pronoun categorizations based upon this intersection — nine sentence frames in all. As

FIGURE 3
PRONOUN CATEGORIZATIONS BASED ON VERB INTERSECTION

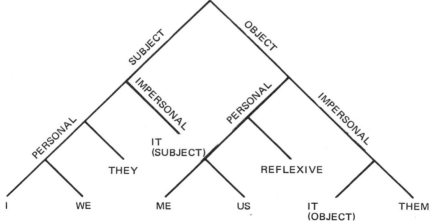

---

[17] This program creates similarity trees "from the ground up", so to speak. All elements are searched for the ones most similar in usage, and these are linked under a node; then the mean of these plus all remaining elements are searched and another node is established. When a previously linked set becomes most similar to another element or set, a higher node connects them, and so on. This program seems very much like a categorizing procedure developed by S. C. Johnson of the Bell Telephone Laboratories and used by G. A. Miller and his associates (1967) for similar purposes.

expected, we find Subject vs. Object, Personal vs. Impersonal, and Singular vs. Plural categories. Perhaps less expected is the fact that *they* (subject) is more Personal than *them* (object), where both should be coded zero on this feature, and the fact the reflexive seems more Personal than Impersonal — this latter situation perhaps reflecting a tendency for reflexive verbs to require Animate subjects.

Figure 4 presents the categorization of verbs resulting from the inter-section with pronouns, or the inverse of the pronoun categorization. Not only is this "tree" much more complex, but it must be kept in mind that it is based on the (to some degree) fallible judgments of one English speaker (myself). As to the major categories: verbs under node 1 are characterized by taking personal subjects (*I, we, they*) but not personal objects (*me* or *us*); verbs under node 2 are marked in common as being necessarily transitive, i.e., they are not acceptable in frames of Type I above, verbs under node 3 have in common only the fact that they will take both *they* as a subject and *them* as an object, but what this signifies, if anything, is obscure. Finer distinctions

FIGURE 4

VERB CATEGORIZATIONS BASED ON PRONOUN INTERSECTION

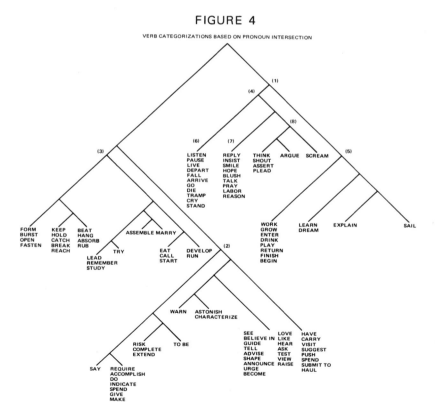

are made beneath these major nodes. Nodes 4 and 5 are distinguished by the fact that the latter will accept both *them* and *it* as objects while the former will accept only *it*, if any object. Within node 4, nodes 6 and 7 are completely intransitive, the former taking *it* as a subject and the latter not (*Reply, Insist, Hope,* etc.; can these be called Human coded?), whereas node 8 verbs will take *it* as object. Even finer distinctions appear among the "twigs": Personal/Impersonal (*Marry me* but not *Assemble me, Assemble it* but not *Marry it*), Reflexive/Non-reflexive (*Study themselves* but not *Try themselves*), for example.

In the sense of revealing features previously undiscovered, of course, these results are trivial. But in the sense of testing the adequacy of a procedure, they are not. If, under appropriate sampling conditions for an intersection, such basic grammatical distinctions as Transitive/Intransitive, Personal/-Impersonal, Subject/Object and the like can be obtained, then it implies both generality for the method and its potential validity in less familiar (or perhaps better, less open) semantic domains. The categories of verbs established by Fillmore via his case frames appear similar to our PN/V intersection results, but I have not been able to make a successful analysis in his terms. The use of an appropriate set of subject nouns and object nouns, drawn from his examples, might yield a closer relationship between his intuitive and our empirical methods. But this remains to be done systematically.

We did try an intersection of 14 plural nouns with the set of 100 random verbs, using the nouns in both a subject frame *N___(V)___PN* (or *zero*), e.g., *Dogs___(V)___them* and an object frame *PN (I, they, it)___(V)___(PP) N*, e.g., *They___(V)___doctors*. Because at that time we considered the noun set too small for such a large category, we did not submit the data to the "tree" categorizing analysis – which I realize, after reading Fillmore, may have been a mistake. Informal inspection of the data, however, indicates expected noun categories (in terms of Concrete/Abstract, Animate/Inanimate, Human/Non-human). With *women* and *doctors* in the subject frame, every verb is accepted, and for these nouns in the object frame the largest numbers of verbs are accepted (76/100 and 74/100) – suggesting that human languages were designed primarily to enable humans to talk about humans! What verbs will not accept *women* and *doctors* as objects? One set includes verbs like *form, complete, accomplish, finish* and *begin* (verbs requiring non-animate objects?); another includes *say, learn, explain, indicate* and *reason* (verbs requiring abstract objects?); another includes *die, arrive, fall,* and *live* (intransitive verbs?). What verbs fall out when *dogs* rather than humans are subjects? Exclusively human-coded cognitive processes (*say, reply, insist, advise, explain,* etc.), emotive processes (*smile, blush, hope, pray*) and activities (*sail, hang, spend,* and *marry*). Abstract nouns like *anger* and *respect* as subjects, accept relatively few verbs (mostly spatio-temporal generalizations like *develop, grow, hold, start, begin, return,* but also reference to an observer like *astonish* and *urge*). Let me now return to problems of sampling.

The first general observation I have concerns the effect of restricting the domain of forms analysed: When we compare the types of features obtained from open classes (randomly selected verbs) with those obtained from more restricted classes (interpersonal verbs),[18] the more open domains yield more general, "grammatical" features and the more restricted domains yield more specific, "semantic" features. The primary reason for this is that restricting the semantic domain, in effect, holds features shared by items in that domain constant and hence "undiscoverable." If we assume that the semantic component is an ordered system, with those features doing the most "work" (e.g., Abstract/Concrete) being in some way prior to those doing the least (e.g., Moral/Immoral), then this makes sense — an efficient algorithm would look first for the distinctions that are most likely to make a difference.

My second observation concerns the nature of the syntactic frames to be used in empirical analyses. Within sentences there are what might be called "intimate" syntactic relations and more "remote" syntactic relations. In the sentence, *The tall boy leaped eagerly to the side of the fainting woman,* it is obvious intuitively (as well as from immediate constituent analysis) that *tall* is more intimately interactive with *boy* than with *side,* that *eagerly* is more intimately interreactive with *leaped* than with *woman,* that *boy* is more intimately related to *leaped* than to *fainting,* and so forth. The more remote the syntactic relation, the weaker should be the syntactical constraints upon semantic interaction. Therefore, it would seem that semantic features would be most clearly revealed in intersections of intimate form classes. It is also the case that the greater the complexity of syntactic frames, the greater the number of interactions that must be involved; if we change the last two words of the sentence above to *decadent dictatorship,* whole sets of semantic relations fall into confusion. Of course, one may deliberately vary several elements of sentences simultaneously, but this complicates matters.[19]

The effect of size of sample upon discovery of semantic features seems to be relatively straight-forward. Given that one is working within a particular syntactic frame (or specifiable set of frames) there should be a negatively accelerated increase in the number of features discovered as the number of items in the sample increased — that is, the features found to determine

---

[18] Compare the types of features yielded by the PN/V intersection and by the IPV/AV intersections displayed in Figures 5 - 8.

[19] For example, in his dissertation John Limber simultaneously varied 10 nouns, 10 sentence frames, and 50 adjectives (e.g., *N is A about it, it is A of N to do it,* etc.) in an attempt to determine the interactions among these sources of variance in sentence interpretation.

judgments of earlier items should serve to determine later items as well, and the new features required should become progressively fewer. Of course, there is always the possibility of some new distinction being required — such as X being closer or further from Paris than Y — but such distinctions will not be very productive and should not inhibit one's search "in principle."[20]

Finally, as to the source of data: should they come from natural texts or experimentally devised samples, from random or systematic arrays? I think that here we come back to the basic nature of methods. At one extreme we have the purely distributional study of forms-in-contexts, as proposed hypothetically by Harris (1954); although in principle it might be possible to categorize interpersonal verbs in terms of the sharing of linguistic frames in natural texts, it would require miles and miles of text and a very heavy computer to assemble a sufficient sample of shared frames. At the other extreme we have the "compelling examples" of linguists and philosophers; here the "heaviest" computers of all rapidly search their memories and use their projection rules to create apposite examples, but the N is one, or a few, and compulsion is liable to lead to obsession. A middle road is one which decides upon a domain and a type of frame, selects as representative as possible a sample of each, and then literally (experimentally) forces all possible combinations to be evaluated.

As a result of our explorations and debates, we decided upon the following criteria for sampling with respect to the domain of interpersonal verbs: (1) we would use the syntactic frame which most intimately relates interpersonal verbs and some other single form class, that is, intersections of such verbs with modifying adverbs; (2) we would begin with a manageable set of interpersonal verbs and adverbs (30 x 20), try to determine by our methods their distinguishing features, and then expand the sample in subsequent experiments; (3) we would use our a priori analyses of interpersonal verb features as a basis for selecting representative samples of verbs and modifying adverbs (coded on the same features), forcing all possible combinations within the verb/adverb syntactic frame; and (4) we would use first ourselves, as reasonably sophisticated (and undoubtedly biased) English speakers, and then samples of ordinary English speakers (college sophomores) as subjects in judging the linguistic materials created in these procedures.

The Trouble with Trees

George Miller, assisted by Virginia Teller and Herbert Rubenstein, has been carrying on studies designed to test the potential of empirical categorizing methods for determining similarities and differences in the meaning of

---

[20] This is a delayed response to a criticism posed "in principle" by Jerry Fodor several years ago in informal discussions.

words.[21] The verbal items to be classified are sorted into piles by judges, as many piles as are felt required. These sorting data are analysed by a computer program[22] that joins items under nodes progressively — first groups of items that are placed in the same piles by the most subjects and finally those placed in the same piles by the fewest subjects. Application of this procedure to 48 word-forms which could function either as nouns or as verbs in English (e.g., *kill, aid, inch, mother*), but with a set for nouns, yielded the tree shown here as Figure 5. Labelings of the major categories are inferential, of course, but

FIGURE 5

Results of a Cluster Analysis of 48 Nouns
(Miller, Teller, and Rubenstein)

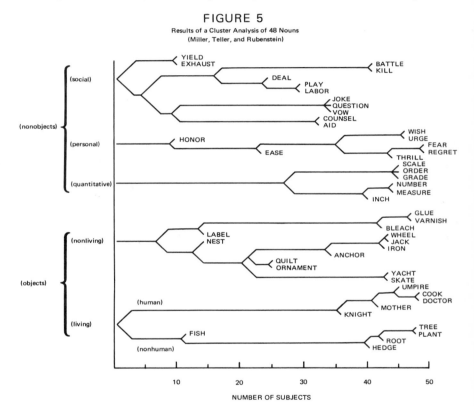

they are similar to what I have referred to as Abstract/Concrete with Animate/Inanimate categories under Concrete and Human/Non-human under Animate. The distinctions within the Abstract category are less familiar (Social/Personal/Quantitative). One advantage of this procedure is that the

---

[21] I have not seen this work reported in detail as yet, but it is summarized in the Seventh Annual Report (1966-67) of the Center for Cognitive Studies at Harvard University and in Miller (1967).

[22] See footnote 17.

hierarchical ordering of features in terms of generality and clarity of usage comes out directly in terms of the numbers of native speakers agreeing on co-assigning items. A disadvantage, as I see it, is that the use of words in isolation rather than in syntactic frames allows this powerful syntactic factor to vary randomly. It is interesting that "when the 48 words . . . were presented *as verbs* in another study, neither the object-concept distinctions appeared nor did anything else that was recognizable." (Miller, 1967, p. 23) I think that this was precisely because the semantic features of verbs depend heavily upon the syntactic frames in which they participate, and this factor does not enter into the Miller, *et al* discovery procedure.

Our own initial approach to the differentiation of interpersonal verbs was also through a categorizing procedure — that described in the preceding section of this paper. It differs from Miller's in that (a) similarities among one set of items (IPV's) depend upon similarities of usage across syntactic frames involving another set of items (AV's) and (b) inter-subject agreement does not enter directly into the process — indeed, single-subject analyses are feasible and are employed. The linguistic data determining the "trees" to be reported in this section were derived from the intersection of 30 IPV's (drawn from my earlier a priori analysis) with 20 AV's (selected to give some representation to the same ten a priori features used for the IPV's). The frame was simply *IPV AV*, in all 600 possible combinations: e.g., *Humiliate firmly, Plead with hopefully, Corrupt excitedly,* and so forth.

Figures 6 and 7 compare the IPV trees generated from the judgments of Kenneth Forster (Figure 6) and myself (Figure 7). The over-all similarities in structure are apparent — for example, in the basic division into Associative (right branch) and Dissociative (left branch) behaviors and the subdivision of the latter into Immoral (*Disable, Corrupt, Humiliate, Bewilder*) and Not-immoral (*Contradict, Punish, Blame, Oppose, Defy*) — but there are many fine differences. Osgood considers *Ridicule* Immoral, while Forster does not; Forster links *Borrow from, Appease, Indulge, Imitate* and *Evade* with clearly Dissociative behaviors — Osgood links them all with Associative behaviors. In discussion between us, it became apparent that some of our differences reflected either errors in our judgments or inadequacies in the method — e.g., KF's *Ridicule* not being Immoral and CO's *Evade* not being Dissociative. On the other hand, there were some real differences in our semantics, in how we thought certain verbs ought to be coded — as when for KF *Indulge, Appease, Imitate* and *Borrow from* were clearly Dissociative and somewhat Immoral interpersonal intentions, whereas for me they were clearly Associative intentions, albeit a bit tinged with immorality. Our differences on **parent** *Indulging* **child** were sharp — clearly immoral for him, clearly not for me. Perhaps it should be in the record that Forster speaks Australian English and I speak American!

162

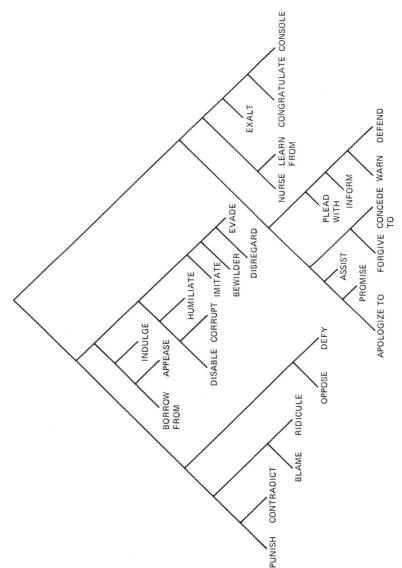

FIGURE 6

IPV TREE BASED ON IPV/AV INTERSECTION (FORSTER DATA)

FIGURE 7

IPV TREE BASED ON IPV/AV INTERSECTION (OSGOOD DATA)

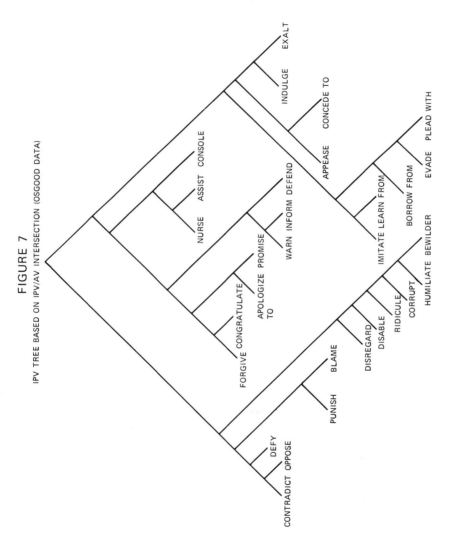

What would a sample of "ordinary" English speakers tell us? We asked the graduate students in my seminar in psycholinguistics at the University of Hawaii (about 20 people) to perform the same task on the same materials. Although they were by no means "ordinary" English speakers (they included Chinese, Fillipinos, Canadians and residents of Hawaii as well as students from the U.S. mainland), they produced a tree more consistent over-all than either Forster or I produced, at least in my opinion. In Figure 8, we may note some of the more interesting items: *Evade* is still Associative as it was for me, for some reason I do not fathom; the students agree with me about *Indulge* being Associative, but also with both KF and CO about *Disregard* and *Bewilder* being Immoral, which seems strange; the fact that the students use *Learn from* in a fashion similar to *Exalt* (rather than like *Nurse* by KF and like *Imitate* by CO) may simply reflect their student status. By checking the limbs, branches and twigs of the student tree against my a priori features for these verbs, it is possible to make some feature assignments: An Alter-oriented/Ego-oriented feature and an Initiating/Reacting feature appear within the Associative set, and a Moral/Immoral feature divides the Dissociative set. A careful inspection of the terminal twigs suggests that a kind of Dynamism feature (Potent and Active/Weak and Passive) is making common distinctions at this level, indicated in Figure 8 by the assignments of D + and D −. This illustrates one of the troubles with trees: the lower the order or significance of a feature, the more dispersed will be its operation over the tree and hence the more difficult it will be to identify.

As an internal check on tree categories as discovery procedures, we decided to create an IPV tree directly from a priori feature codings. The 20 adverbs were carefully coded on the same 10 features (e.g., *firmly* was + Potent, + Supraordinate, + Deliberate and 0 on all other features). Then the code-strips of IPV/AV pairs were used to generate the "judgments" of anomalous (one or more opposed codings), apposite (no opposed and one or more same codings) and permissible (no opposed and no same codings) combinations for all 600 items. In a sense, we were testing a "native speaker" whose semantics we knew absolutely. Figure 9 presents the resulting tree. Here we can do a better job of identifying features, as would be expected: the Associative/Dissociative limbs are nearly perfectly consistent with the a priori codings of the IPV's, with the single misplacement of *Evade* again. A major subdivision of both the Associative and Dissociative limbs is into Alter-oriented/Ego-oriented branches, and all verbs are perfectly allocated, with the single exception of *Corrupt* (which is coded as Alter-oriented as contrasted with *Seduce,* for example), but we notice that an Immoral/Not Immoral feature overlaps with Alter/Ego on the Dissociative side. The Associative Alter-oriented set is further subdivided into Supraordinate/Subordinate, and without errors. Again, inspecting the terminal twigs, we find the same

165

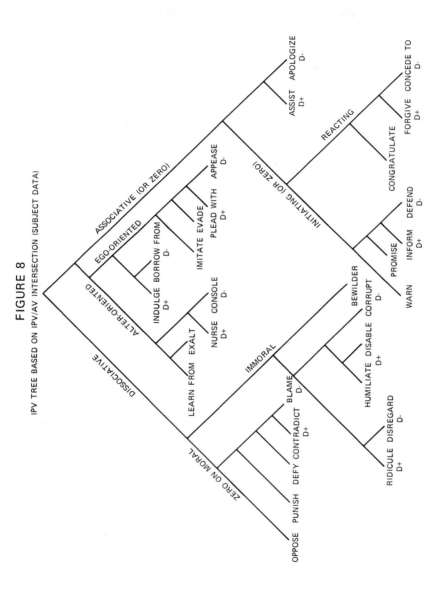

FIGURE 8

IPV TREE BASED ON IPV/AV INTERSECTION (SUBJECT DATA)

166

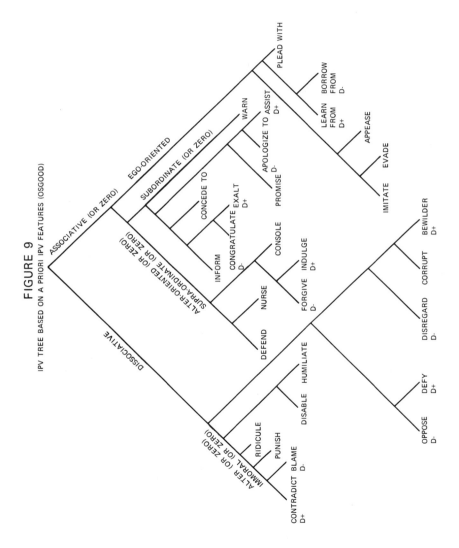

FIGURE 9

IPV TREE BASED ON A PRIORI IPV FEATURES (OSGOOD)

dispersed Dynamism feature, indicated in the figure by D + vs. D —. However, we find no clear evidence for an Initiating/Reacting feature, for a Future-oriented/Past-oriented feature, for a Terminal/Interminal feature or for a Deliberate/Impulsive feature. Of course, these latter a priori features may well be Osgoodian fictions.

What is the trouble with trees? For one thing, it seems that very slight distinctions, if they are on a higher order feature, can override many similarities. A strictly hierarchical system may not be appropriate for finer semantic features. For another, as the a priori analysis shows, the methodology of treemaking is capable of mis-assigning items (*Evade* and *Corrupt*, for example), although the reason for this is not clear. As yet another trouble, lower order but still significant features are so dispersed among the twigs that (without already knowing what they are) they get lost to view. As a fourth difficulty, branches may be co-determined by more than one feature, and if one does not know the features already, they will not be independently discoverable.

But there is a quite different and more serious trouble with trees: even though one can derive trees for both members of an intersection (here, IPV's and AV's), each based on usage with respect to the other, *there is no rigorous way we could discover to relate the categories of one to the categories of the other.* Yet our theory is based on the notion of interaction within shared features among the words in the two sets.

Before leaving them I should say something nice about trees. The fact that an empirical tree based on the judgments of real speakers (Figure 8) matches as well as it does a tree generated from a small set of a priori semantic features (Figure 9) is very encouraging. It encourages me to believe that an empirical discovery procedure is at least possible.

Factor and Feature Analysis Methods

Since factor analytic methods are generally familiar, they need not be detailed here. Either discrete (+1 = Apposite, 0 = Permissible, or — = Anomalous) or continuous (scaled) judgments are entered into a rectangular matrix, with columns defined, in our case, by IPV's and rows by AV's. Correlations among the columns indicate similarity of usage of the verbs (across the adverbs) and correlations among the rows indicate similarity of usage of the adverbs (across the verbs). Factor analysis serves to cluster together those verbs (or adverbs) which, as indicated by large factor loadings, share certain dominant characteristics of usage but not necessarily the same single semantic feature. By assigning the adverbs factor scores on the verb factors (or vice versa), verb and adverb usages can be directly (mathematically) related. The factor analytic measurement model assumes that codings on features are continuous, that the interactions of verb and adverb meanings on the features are algebraic, and that the weights on different features are cumulative or aggregate in determining each judgment. This method will be appropriate to the degree that the semantic system actually has these characteristics.

What kind of a measurement model is appropriate for the semantic theory Forster and I postulated as one possibility? It will be recalled that this theory assumed discrete coding on features, all-or-nothing resolutions within features for word combinations, and independence or segregation of effects across features. There appeared to be no familiar quantitative measurement model that would both satisfy these requirements and serve to relate IPV and AV features directly. So we tried to devise such a procedure from scratch. Since we never quite succeeded, even to our own satisfaction, my description will be appropriately brief.

The verb x adverb matrix of judgments of all combinations as being anomalous (-1), permissible (0) or apposite $(+1)$ is what we call the 'Target Matrix' — i.e., the pattern we wish to predict from the features "discovered" by our empirical procedure. This information is also the input to the Feature Analysis Program. The same program that generates "trees from the bottom up" is used to isolate a small number of IPV's that are maximally similar in usage (e.g., *Promise, Apologize to* and *Appease*), and these are automatically assigned + on the first Trial Feature; AV's judged apposite or anomalous with all of these verbs are assigned + or — respectively on this Trial Feature, and all others are assigned zero. Applying the same similarity procedure to the AV's, with the restriction that the AV sub-sets all have the same + or — coding as the IPV subset, all remaining IPV's are coded on the same hypothetical feature.[23]

The computer now uses this first Trial Feature to generate a Predicted IPV/AV Matrix, i.e., those judgments of each combination which, in theory, would have to be made if only this feature were involved. Obviously many errors are made, some being "patchable" (e.g., Predicted +, Target —) by subsequent features and others "unpatchable" (e.g., Predicted —, Target +, since the theory says that a single opposition is sufficient for anomaly). The computer "decides" on the minimum number of changes in coding which will eliminate the "unpatchable" errors. This series of linked programs now reiterates, generating a second Trial Feature and both features are now used simultaneously to produce another Predicted Matrix. This procedure is continued until some criterion (e.g., less than five percent "unpatchable" errors) is reached.

---

[23] We now believe selection of IPV and AV "pivots" in this manner to be a weakness in the method; not only may the verb and adverb subsets have more than one feature in common, but one of these shared features may determine the verb assignments and another the adverb assignments.

Intuitive vs. Empirical Features

Throughout these studies I have used myself as a preliminary guinea pig, executing exactly the same tasks that the subjects would face (but not always with the prescribed methods), and I have used my own processed data as a kind of criterion for the group results.[24]   I am certainly a dedicated and, I hope, sensitive native speaker, and, being aware of a wider variety of potential semantic features than the "ordinary" speaker, it seemed that my own computed results could serve as a guide for interpreting and evaluating the group results.

If one reads a list of those IPV's loading high and low on a given factor or feature in a computer print-out without "having a particular feature in mind," it is usually very confusing (eg.: + *Oppose, Defy, Corrupt, Warn, Promise, Nurse, Borrow from, Plead with;* − *Punish, Blame, Ridicule, Apologize, Congratulate, Console, Concede to*). The reason is that each word form is simultaneously coded on many features, only one of which is presumably being consistently contrasted in the factor or feature array. If, on the other hand, one does have a specific semantic feature in mind, the array may be sharply meaningful. (Try the feature Future-oriented/Past-oriented on the above example.) The intuitively derived solutions also serve another purpose: they provide data against which to evaluate the empirical methodology itself. I will come back to this point.

I am sure that some linguists and philosophers will ask: "Why bother with empirical tests at all? Isn't your own competence as a native speaker, coupled with your training as a scientist, a more valid instrument for making fine discriminations among the meanings of words than a casual (if not bored) college sophomore?" This *may* be true, but it is also the garden path to "scholarly schizophrenia." We already have evidence in the IPV trees for Forster and Osgood that two native speakers of the same language can have honest differences in their semantic codings of words: can this not also hold for inferred features? Furthermore, as noted earlier, the intuitions of even the most sophisticated native speaker of Language A are likely to be misleading when he wades into Language B.[25]   What we would prefer would be rigorous empirical discovery procedure that could be applied "blindly" to appropriate samples of linguistic data from any language and yield semantic features.

Some Results to Date

We may look first at a factor analysis of my own IPV/AV Target Matrix, generated deliberately with my own a priori features in mind. The question is

---

[24] I am not in this case referring to the a priori analysis of the semantic features of interpersonal verbs; the latter was done explicitly as an intuitive approach.

[25] Within any given language, there could be a fruitful "mix" of judgments of sophisticated native speakers and empirical checks − a kind of computerized lexicography.

whether or not the resulting factors correspond in any obvious way with my features. Table 3 presents the results of such a factor analysis, along with an Equimax rotation.[26] In this case, AV factors were obtained and IPV's were given factor scores on them. Table 3 lists, for each rotated factor, the highest positive and highest negative verbs along with their a priori code-strips. Factor I is most clearly the dominant Associative/Dissociative feature, with some Moral/Immoral and Subordinate/Supraordinate implications. The adverb factor loadings corroborate this interpretation (*sincerely* and *considerately* versus *unfairly*, *meanly* and *despicably*). Factor II clearly differentiates Supraordinate/Subordinate IPV's, but here there is some fusion of Supraordinateness with Alter-orientation, Dissociation and Activity (a not too surprising human pattern!). The adverb factor loadings are again consistent (*angrily*, *drastically* and *emphatically* vs. *submissively*, *reluctantly*, *guiltily* and *desperately*). Factor III simply repeats the Supraordinate/Subordinate distinction − for some unfathomable reason − but now with *firmly* as one of the defining adverbs. Factor IV seems to clearly isolate the Future-oriented/-Past-oriented a priori feature, along with Ego (Future)/Alter (Past) characteristics; the defining adverbs are *hopefully*, *successfully*, and *desperately*. Factors V and VI do not yield to any obvious interpretation for verbs; the adverbs make V look like our Deliberate/Impulsive feature (*firmly* vs. *impulsively*) and VI look like our Terminal/Interminal feature (*rapidly* and *emphatically* vs. *hopefully* and *appreciatively*). Factor VII is our Alter-Ego feature (again fused with Associative/Dissociative); contrasts between *considerately*, *sincerely*, *appreciatively* and *selfishly*, *meanly*, *unfairly* confirm this interpretation.

Before evaluating this result, let us look at the parallel analysis using the specially devised Feature Program. Table 4 presents these results in a format similar to the previous table, except that simple signs (+ or −) replace factor scores for both IPV's and AV's. Feature I appears to be some combination of Terminal-Potent-Active versus Interminal-Impotent-Passive − a rather reasonable patterning − and this is confirmed by the adverbs identified by the same feature combination (*emphatically*, *angrily*, *drastically* vs. *hopefully*, *considerately*, *submissively*). Feature II is clearly the dominant Associative/-Dissociative one. *Appreciatively* and *considerately* contrast with *meanly*, *unfairly* and *despicably* on this feature. If we close our eyes to the presence of *Corrupt* in Feature III, then it is clearly an Ego-oriented/Alter-oriented distinction − and I suppose the coding of *Corrupt* as Alter-oriented is at least debatable; distinguishing AV's are *selfishly* and *unfairly* vs. *considerately*. Feature IV is equally sharply the Supraordinate/Subordinate distinction so

────────────
    [26] I wish to express my thanks to Kenneth Forster who made all of the computer analyses of these early IPV/AV matrices after returning to Melbourne, Australia.

TABLE 3

Osgood Output and A Priori Features Compared; Factor Analysis (Equimax Rotation) of a 30 IPV/20 AV Matrix

	Factor Scores	A Moral Immoral	B Potent Impotent	C Active Passive	D Associative Dissociative	E Initiating Reacting	F Ego- Alter	G Supra Sub	H Terminal Interminal	I Future Past	J Deliberate Inpulsive
Factor I		?			*			?			
Apologize	1.18	+	−	0	+	−	0	−	+	−	+
Promise	1.16	0	0	0	+	0	0	0	+	+	0
Concede to	1.11	0	−	−	+	−	−	−	+	−	+
Defend	1.09	+	+	0	+	0	−	0	−	+	0
Disable	−1.67	−	+	+	−	0	0	+	+	+	+
Humiliate	−1.55	0	0	0	−	+	−	+	+	0	0
Ridicule	−1.47	−	0	+	−	−	−	+	+	−	+
Blame	−1.31	0	0	0	−	−	−	+	+	−	0
Factor II				?	?		?	*			
Learn from	1.85	0	0	0	0	0	+	−	0	+	+
Borrow from	1.61	0	0	0	0	+	+	−	+	+	+
Apologize	1.44	+	−	0	+	−	0	−	+	−	+
Plead with	1.38	0	0	0	0	+	+	−	0	+	0
Humiliate	−1.38	0	0	0	−	+	−	+	+	0	0
Punish	−1.27	0	+	+	−	−	0	+	+	−	0
Disable	−1.27	−	+	+	−	0	0	+	+	+	+
Ridicule	−1.22	−	0	+	−	−	−	+	+	−	−
Factor III			?		?			*			
Punish	1.76	0	+	+	−	−	−	+	+	−	0
Humiliate	1.76	0	0	0	−	+	−	+	+	0	0
Blame	1.72	0	0	0	−	−	−	+	+	−	0
Contradict	1.72	0	0	0	−	−	0	+	+	−	+

TABLE 3 (cont.)

	Factor Scores	A Moral Immoral	B Potent Impotent	C Active Passive	D Associative Dissociative	E Initiating Reacting	F Ego- Alter	G Supra Sub	H Terminal Interminal	I Future Past	J Deliberate Inpulsive
Assist	-1.26	0	-	+	+	0	-	-	0	+	+
Learn from	-1.27	0	0	0	0	0	+	-	0	+	0
Borrow from	-1.11	0	0	0	0	+	+	-	+	+	+
Apologize to	-1.10	+	-	0	+	-	0	-	+	-	+
Factor IV											
Borrow from	1.31	0	0	0	0	+	?	-	+	*	+
Appease	1.27	0	-	-	+	-	+	0	0	0	0
Learn from	1.27	0	0	0	0	0	+	-	0	+	+
Plead with	1.26	0	0	0	0	+	+	-	0	+	0
Oppose	1.00	0	+	0	-	0	+	0	-	+	0
Punish	-1.65	0	+	+	-	-	-	+	+	-	0
Contradict	-1.53	0	0	0	-	-	0	+	+	-	+
Blame	-1.53	0	0	0	-	-	-	+	+	-	0
Exalt	-1.25	+	+	+	+	+	-	-	+	-	-
Factor V											
Disable	2.03	-	+	+	-	0	?	?	+	+	?
Humiliate	2.01	0	0	0	-	+	0	+	+	0	+
Corrupt	1.71	-	0	0	-	+	-	+	-	+	+
Nurse	1.23	0	0	+	+	0	-	+	-	+	0
Imitate	-1.57	0	-	+	0	-	+	-	0	0	0
Plead with	-1.43	0	0	0	0	+	+	-	0	+	0
Promise	-1.40	0	0	0	+	0	0	0	+	+	0
Defy	-1.13	0	+	+	-	-	+	0	0	+	-

TABLE 3 (cont.)

	Factor Scores	A Moral Immoral	B Potent Impotent	C Active Passive	D Associative Dissociative	E Initiating Reacting	F Ego-Alter	G Supra Sub	H Terminal Interminal	I Future Past	J Deliberate Inpulsive
Factor VI											
Defend	1.75	?	+	0	?	0	–	0	?	+	0
Nurse	1.72	+	0	+	+	0	–	+	–	+	0
Indulge	1.60	0	0	0	+	–	–	+	0	0	–
Forgive	1.47	+	0	0	+	–	–	+	+	–	0
Ridicule	–1.29	–	0	+	–	–	–	+	+	–	–
Contradict	–1.12	0	0	0	–	–	0	+	+	–	+
Plead with	–1.12	0	0	0	0	+	+	–	0	+	0
Inform	–0.96	0	0	0	0	+	–	0	+	0	0
Factor VII											
Concede to	1.34	0	–	–	*	–	*	–	+	–	+
Congratulate	1.32	0	0	0	+	–	–	0	+	–	+
Forgive	1.30	+	0	0	+	–	–	+	+	–	0
Nurse	1.26	0	0	+	+	0	–	+	–	+	0
Defy	–1.34	0	+	+	–	–	+	0	0	+	–
Disable	–1.26	–	+	+	–	0	0	+	+	+	+
Oppose	–1.16	0	+	0	–	0	+	0	0	+	0
Evade	–1.11	0	–	+	–	–	+	0	–	0	0

TABLE 4

Osgood Output and A Priori Features Compared; Feature Analysis of a 30 IPV/20 AV Matrix

	Feature Sign	A Moral / Immoral	B Potent / Impotent ?	C Active / Passive ?	D Associative / Dissociative	E Initiating / Reacting	F Ego- / Alter	G Supra / Sub	H Terminal / Interminal ?	I Future / Past	J Deliberate / Impulsive
Feature I			?	?					?		
Punish	+	0	+	+	−	−	−	+	?	−	0
Disable	+	−	+	+	−	0	0	+	+	+	+
Contradict	+	0	0	0	−	−	0	+	+	−	+
Ridicule	+	−	0	+	−	−	−	+	+	−	−
Corrupt	−	−	0	0	−	+	−	+	−	+	+
Disregard	−	0	0	−	+	−	0	0	0	0	+
Console	−	+	−	−	+	−	−	0	0	−	−
Appease	−	0	−	−	+	−	−	0		0	0
Feature II											
Defend	+	+	+	0	*	0	−	0	−	+	0
Forgive	+	+	0	0	+	−	−	+	+	−	0
Assist	+	0	−	+	+	0	−	−	0	+	+
Nurse	+	0	0	+	+	0	−	+	−	+	0
Blame	−	0	0	0	−	−	−	+	+	−	0
Disable	−	−	+	+	−	0	0	+	+	+	+
Corrupt	−	−	0	0	−	+	−	+	−	+	+
Humiliate	−	0	0	0	−	+	−	+	+	0	0
Feature III											
Defy	+	0	+	+	?	−	*	0	0	?	−
Corrupt	+	−	0	0	−	+	+	+	−	+	+
Learn from	+	0	0	0	0	0	−	−	0	+	+
Plead with	+	0	0	0	0	+	+	−	0	+	0

TABLE 4 (cont.)

	Feature Sign	A Moral Immoral	B Potent Impotent	C Active Passive	D Associative Dissociative	E Initiating Reacting	F Ego- Alter	G Supra Sub	H Terminal Interminal	I Future Past	J Deliberate Impulsive
Defend	−	+	+	0	+	0	−	0	−	+	0
Congratulate	−	0	0	0	+	−	−	0	+	−	+
Console	−	+	0	0	+	−	−	0	0	−	−
Indulge	−	0	0	0	+	−	−	+	0	0	−
Feature IV											
Punish	+	0	+	+	−	−	−	*	+	−	0
Ridicule	+	−	0	+	−	−	−	+	+	−	−
Humiliate	+	0	0	0	−	+	−	+	+	0	0
Forgive	+	+	0	0	+	−	−	+	+	−	0
Apologize	−	+	−	0	+	−	0	−	+	−	+
Borrow from	−	0	0	0	0	+	+	−	+	+	+
Plead with	−	0	0	0	0	+	+	−	0	+	0
Concede to	−	0	−	−	+	−	−	−	+	−	+
Feature V											
Forgive	+	*	0	0	?	−	−	+	+	−	0
Concede to	+	+	−	−	+	−	−	−	+	−	+
Disable	−	−	+	+	−	0	0	+	+	+	+
Corrupt	−	−	0	0	−	+	−	+	−	+	+
Ridicule	−	−	0	+	−	−	0	+	+	−	0
Bewilder	−	0	0	+	0	0	0	+	0	0	0
Feature VI											
Indulge	+	0	0	0	+	−	−	+	0	0	*
Console	+	+	0	0	+	−	−	0	0	−	−
Forgive	+	+	0	0	+	−	−	+	+	−	0
Defy	+	0	+	+	−	−	+	0	0	+	−

TABLE 4 (cont.)

	Feature Sign	A Moral/Immoral	B Potent/Impotent	C Active/Passive	D Associative/Dissociative	E Initiating/Reacting	F Ego-/Alter	G Supra/Sub	H Terminal/Interminal	I Future/Past	J Deliberate/Impulsive
Concede to	−	0	−	−	+	−	0	−	+	−	+
Disregard	−	0	0	−	−	−	0	0	−	0	+
Disable	−	−	+	+	−	0	0	+	+	+	+
Corrupt	−	−	0	0	−	+	−	+	−	+	+
Feature VII											
Promise	+	0	0	0	+	0	0	0	?	+	0
Congratulate	+	0	0	0	+	−	−	0	+	−	+
Oppose	−	0	+	0	−	0	+	0	−	+	0
Evade	−	0	−	+	−	−	+	0	0	0	0
Console	−	+	0	0	+	−	−	0	0	−	−
Feature VIII											
Warn	+	0	0	0	0	0	−	0	+	?	0
Promise	+	0	0	0	+	0	0	0	+	+	0
Console	−	+	0	0	+	−	−	0	0	+	−
Nurse	−	0	0	+	+	0	−	+	−	−	0
Exalt	−	+	+	+	+	+	−	−	+	+	−
Feature IX											
Inform	+	0	0	0	0	+	−	?	+	?	0
Apologize	+	+	−	0	+	−	0	0	+	0	+
Congratulate	+	0	0	0	+	−	−	0	+	−	+
Exalt	+	+	+	+	+	+	−	−	+	−	−
Indulge	−	0	0	0	+	−	−	+	0	0	−
Forgive	−	+	0	0	+	−	−	+	+	−	0
Defend	−	+	+	0	+	0	−	0	−	+	0
Oppose	−	0	+	0	−	0	+	0	−	+	0

important in interpersonal relations; the AV assignment is one-sided, with only *reluctantly, guiltily* and *desperately* (yet not *submissively*) being negatively coded. Feature V neatly taps the Moral/Immoral distinction, and this shows up in the adverbial *sincerely/guiltily* contrast as well; as expected, Morality parallels the dominant Associative/Dissociative feature, adding its moral tone, so to speak. Feature VI is an equally neat specification of the Deliberate/Impulsive aspect of interpersonal behavior, with *submissively, guiltily* and *despicably* (Deliberate) contrasting with *excitedly* and *impulsively* (Impulsive). Beyond this point, nothing is clear. Feature VIII is suggested as Future-oriented/Past-oriented by the adverbs coded + on it (there are no minus codings). These are *hopefully, successfully, sincerely, considerately, desperately,* and also *guiltily.* But among the verbs shown in Table 4 only *Warn, Promise,* and *Nurse* have a priori Future codings.

What can be said of these tests of empirical discovery procedures? Both factor analysis and feature analysis yield clearly identifiable (in terms of my a priori codings) Associative/Dissociative, Supraordinate/Subordinate and Ego-oriented/Alter-oriented features, and it may well be that these are the dominant ways that humans characterize interpersonal relations. Factor analysis yields a Future/Past feature fused with one Ego/Alter factor; feature analysis yields pretty clear Moral/Immoral and Deliberate/Impulsive features as well as a fused Terminal-Dynamic/Interminal-Insipid kind of feature. Neither analysis yields the hypothesized Initiating/Reacting feature, and this may well be part of Osgoodian fantasy. Factor analysis returns five reasonably clear a priori features; feature analysis returns perhaps six. In my opinion, the feature analysis yields generally cleaner features. Most of the factors obtained show complex fusions among features, and if we didn't have a pretty good idea of what to look for from the a priori analysis, they would be hard to interpret. Of course, this is precisely what one would expect from the assumptions underlying the factor analytic approach as compared with the assumptions underlying the feature measurement model.

In general these results are encouraging. They suggest that, when a known set of semantic features generates the judgments of appositeness, permissiveness and anomaly entering the target matrix, either standard factor analysis or our new feature analysis *can* yield at least some of the original features. As to the failure of either method to yield all of my own a priori features, it must be kept in mind that some of my features may be illusions, that the features in any semantic domain are probably hierarchically ordered in significance (amount of "work" done), and that my own judgments of the 600 verb/adverb combinations are certainly fallible. But what about "ordinary" native speakers? Will identifiable semantic features — either those hypothesized or different ones — emerge when they perform in the IPV/AV task?

To obtain really ordinary native speakers of English we turned to the usual source: college sophomores taking Introductory Psychology at the University of Illinois and required to put in so many hours as subjects for experiments. (Nothing derogatory is intended here!) A somewhat modified set of 30 IPV's and an expanded set of 30 AV's were presented in all 900 possible combinations to 40 subjects,[27] along with careful instructions and examples. For each item we obtain a distribution of +, 0 and − judgments (apposite, permissible, anomalous), e.g., *Nurse rashly* (2, 15, 23), *Criticize unceasingly* (29, 11, 0), *Manipulate considerately* (5, 21, 14); although in general the modal subject judgments agreed with mine, there were some exceptions. For example, our subjects considered *Cooperate reluctantly* to be apposite (merely permissible, I would say), *Contradict unceasingly* to be apposite (I would say anomalous), *Help appreciatively* to be apposite (anomalous, I would say), and so on. A single value for each item was obtained by the following formula:

$$\frac{\text{Apposite} - \text{Anomalous}}{\text{Apposite} + \text{Permissible} + \text{Anomalous}}$$

It was either treated as a continuous variable (in factor analyses) or assigned to one of three categories (in feature analyses).

Table 5 presents the results of a Varimax rotation of the Illinois subject data; factor scores for the verbs high and low on each adverb factor are related to their a priori feature codings. Factor I is the dominant Associative/Dissociative feature; differentiated adverbs on this factor are *considerately*, *kindly* and *sincerely* versus *despicably* and *unfairly*. The second factor is hard to interpret on the basis of the Verb Factor Scores, but the adverb loadings make it look like a Dynamism feature (combination of Potency and Activity) − *emphatically, firmly, angrily* and *rashly* are opposed to *appreciately* and *warmly*. Factor III appears to tap the Alter vs. Ego-orientation feature: verbs *Congratulate, Concede to, Show Respect for* and *Forgive* and adverbs *appropriately, generously, sincerely* and *unwillingly* versus verbs *Compete with, Manipulate, Repel* and *Plead with* and adverbs *efficiently, desperately, successfully* and *hopefully*. Factor IV does not yield to any obvious a priori interpretation. Factor V is probably best identified as a version of Supraordinate/Subordinate, and the unipolar adverb factor, defined by *unwillingly, submissively, reluctantly* and *timidly*, fits this interpretation. Although the Verb Factor Scores for VI suggest the a priori Future/Past Orientation feature (*Oppose, Defy, Hinder* vs. *Congratulate, Forgive, Show Respect*), it is the adverbs of Factor VII which carry this

[27] I wish to thank Dr. Earle Davis for his help in administering this test and arranging for the data summations. Because of the length of the task, 4 groups of 40 subjects each judged 225 times.

TABLE 5

Illinois Subject and Osgood Features Compared; Varimax Solution of 30 IPV/30 Matrix

	Factor Scores	A Moral Immoral ?	B Potent Impotent	C Active Passive	D Associative Dissociative *	E Initiating Reacting	F Ego- Alter	G Supra Sub	H Terminal Interminal	I Future Past	J Deliberate Impulsive
Factor I											
Congratulate	1.34	0	0	0	+	–	–	0	+	–	+
Help	1.31	0	0	+	+	0	0	+	0	0	0
Apologize	1.30	+	–	0	+	–	–	–	+	–	+
Forgive	1.30	+	0	0	+	–	–	+	+	–	0
Nurse	1.24	0	0	+	+	0	–	+	–	+	0
Ridicule	–1.61	–	0	+	–	–	–	+	+	–	–
Defy	–1.51	0	+	+	–	0	+	0	0	+	+
Deceive	–1.34	–	0	–	–	0	0	0	0	0	+
Corrupt	–1.31	–	0	0	–	+	–	+	–	+	+
Repel	–1.29	0	+	+	–	+	+	0	+	0	0
Factor II											
Learn from	2.17	0	0	0	0	0	+	–	0	+	+
Console	1.44	+	0	0	+	–	–	0	0	–	–
Corrupt	1.39	–	0	–	–	+	–	+	–	+	+
Show Respect for	1.22	0	0	+	+	0	–	–	0	+	–
Nurse	1.09	0	0	+	+	0	–	+	–	+	0
Forgive	1.00	+	0	0	+	–	–	+	+	–	0
Oppose	–1.86	0	+	0	–	0	+	0	–	+	0
Criticize	–1.55	0	0	+	–	–	0	+	+	0	+
Cooperate	–1.43	0	0	0	+	0	0	0	+	0	+
Disregard	–1.17	0	0	–	0	–	0	0	–	0	+
Warn	–1.16	0	0	0	0	0	0	0	+	+	0
Repel	–1.07	0	+	+	–	–	+	0	+	0	0

TABLE 5 (cont.)

	Factor Scores	A Moral Immoral	B Potent Impotent	C Active Passive	D Associative Dissociative	E Initiating Reacting	F Ego- Alter	G Supra Sub	H Terminal Interminal	I Future Past	J Deliberate Impulsive
Factor III				?			*			?	
Congratulate	2.20	0	0	0	+	−	*	0	+	?	+
Concede to	2.07	0	−	−	+	−	−	−	+	−	+
Show Respect for	2.05	0	0	−	+	0	−	−	0	−	0
Forgive	1.83	+	0	0	+	−	−	+	+	−	0
Compete with	−1.47	0	+	0	0	0	+	0	−	+	0
Manipulate	−1.32	0	0	+	0	+	+	+	0	+	+
Repel	−1.23	0	+	+	−	−	+	0	+	0	0
Plead with	−1.05	0	0	0	0	+	+	+	0	+	0
Factor IV							?				
Show Respect for	2.01	0	0	−	+	0	?	−	0	−	−
Learn from	1.82	0	0	0	0	0	+	−	0	+	+
Congratulate	1.47	0	0	0	+	−	+	0	+	−	+
Console	1.35	+	0	0	+	0	−	0	0	−	−
Nurse	1.26	0	0	+	+	0	−	+	−	+	0
Plead with	−1.77	0	0	0	0	+	+	−	0	+	0
Seduce	−1.60	−	0	0	0	+	+	+	−	+	+
Defy	−1.53	0	+	+	−	−	+	0	0	+	−
Apologize	−1.08	+	−	0	+	−	0	−	+	−	+
Factor V								*			
Apologize	1.91	+	−	0	+	−	0	−	+	−	+
Cooperate	1.48	0	0	0	+	0	0	0	+	0	+
Inform	1.41	0	0	0	0	+	−	0	+	0	0
Concede to	1.25	0	−	−	+	−	−	−	+	−	+

TABLE 5 (cont.)

	Factor Scores	A Moral Immoral	B Potent Impotent	C Active Passive	D Associative Dissociative	E Initiating Reacting	F Ego- Alter	G Supra Sub	H Terminal Interminal	I Future Past	J Deliberate Impulsive
Corrupt	-1.72	–	0	0	–	+	–	+	–	+	+
Ridicule	-1.63	–	0	+	–	–	–	+	+	–	–
Seduce	-1.62	–	0	0	0	+	+	+	–	+	+
Deceive	-1.37	–	–	–	–	0	0	0	0	0	+
Factor VI											
Oppose	1.64	0	+	0	–	0	+	0	–	*	0
Deceive	1.42	–	–	–	–	0	0	0	0	+	+
Defy	1.26	0	+	+	–	–	+	0	0	+	–
Hinder	1.13	0	0	0	–	+	–	0	+	+	0
Congratulate	-2.28	0	0	0	+	–	–	0	+	–	+
Forgive	-1.72	+	0	0	+	–	–	+	+	–	0
Show Respect for	-1.47	0	0	–	+	0	–	–	0	–	–
Factor VII											
Concede to	1.96	0	?	–	+	–	–	–	+	–	*
Learn from	1.51	0	0	0	0	0	+	–	0	+	+
Seduce	1.44	–	0	0	0	+	+	+	–	+	+
Oppose	-1.61	0	+	0	–	0	+	0	–	+	0
Compete	-1.61	0	+	0	0	0	+	0	–	+	0
Plead with	-1.54	0	0	0	0	+	+	–	0	+	0

feeling (*hopefully, resolutely, excitedly* vs. *contemptuously* and *guiltily*). The verbs on Factor VII suggest our Deliberate/Impulsive feature, but there is no confirmation in the Adverb Factor Loadings.

How did the discrete feature analysis method fare with data from ordinary native speakers? The answer, in a nutshell, is *miserably*. Not only did no identifiable features appear, but it was obvious that the program was not working. For some reason, it was the adverbs which were being assigned values while nearly all of the verbs on each feature were being turned back to zero. Various adjustments were made – in the cut-off points for assigning +1, 0 and −1 to combinations in the target matrix, in the number of unpatchable errors tolerated, and so on – but nothing came of it.

It was also at about this time we were becoming disenchanted, for other reasons, with the discrete theoretical model and measurement procedure. In our work at Illinois with the intersection of emotion nouns and modifying adjectives, it was becoming clear that factor analysis, with its continuous theoretical assumptions, did a consistently better job than feature analysis. And a colleague in mathematics demonstrated conclusively that, given the number of features we were working with and their possible combinations, the number of alternative solutions of the *same* Target Matrix was – if not infinite – very large. [28]

The *coup de grace,* empirically, for the feature analysis method was delivered by Dr. Marilyn Wilkins. Using my own a priori codestrips for 40 emotion nouns and 30 adjectives, she generated that specific Target Matrix which had to be consistent with these specific features and their codings, following the discrete theory described earlier. In other words, we knew that here a unique and "correct" solution was possible. A feature analysis run through 11 iterations, to equal the number of hypothesized features, accounted for 81 percent of the Target Matrix, but the features themselves clearly did not match the a priori ones. The basic affective features (dominant in this domain) were there along with a couple of our other features and a couple of novel but interpretable ones, but the remainder were meaningless. It appears that our friend in mathematics was right.

We are left with something of a paradox. How are we to explain the fact that, when applied to my own Target Matrix (but made up of judged combinations, not generated from a priori features) for the 30 IPV/20 AV intersection, the feature analysis method did just as well as, and perhaps a bit better than, the factor analysis method (cf., Tables 3 and 4)? This may have just been coincidence, of course, the feature program yielding one of many alternative solutions that happened to match the a prior one. Or the difficulty may lie in the looseness of the procedure whereby the program determines

[28] We wish to thank Dr. Klaus Witz for the interest he has shown in our work and for the time he has put into trying to help us solve this problem.

the IPV and AV pivots to be used in assigning codings for Trial Features. We have noted that the verbs assigned to a given computed feature appear to reflect a different a priori feature than the adverbs assigned to it.

By way of summarizing the results obtained with these empirical discovery procedures, we may note, first, that there is reasonable consistency across testings in terms of which a priori features are "discovered" and which are not. Omitting the feature analysis of the Illinois subject data, which yielded nothing interpretable, we find that Associative/Dissociative, Supraordinate/-Subordinate and Ego-oriented/Alter-oriented features come through clearly in all tests — suggesting that these characteristics of interpersonal behavior are most sharply represented in the semantics of interpersonal verbs. Moral/-Immoral, Future/Past, Deliberate/Impulsive and some fusion of Potent-Active/Impotent-Passive (which I have called Dynamism) appear occasionally and less clearly. Initiating/Reacting and Terminal/Interminal never appear clearly and independently. It looks as if ordinary native speakers, when presented with interpersonal verb/adverb combinations, react primarily in terms of those features which are most salient to them in the given semantic domain. From the point of view of a performance model, this is not surprising. If, however, one wishes to determine the semantic competence of speakers, these procedures leave much to be desired.

Finally, we might ask this question: if "ordinary" speakers are given the a priori features explicitly, can they use them to differentiate the meanings of interpersonal verbs consistently among themselves and in agreement with the "expert" codings? As part of a larger study, Judith Ayer gave her subjects a scaling task, using semantic differential format but with the ten seven-step scales defined by the a priori features themselves (e.g., Initiating/Reacting, Moral/Immoral, Deliberate/Impulsive, etc.), with each of 40 IPV's to be rated by each subject on each feature-scale. Very careful instructions, definitions and examples of each a priori feature were given. This is not a discovery procedure, of course, but rather a validity test.

Our first answer comes from a factor analysis of these scaling data. As shown in Table 6, several features appear clearly and independently: Ego/Alter (Factor III), Supraordinate/Subordinate (Factor IV), Future/Past (Factor VIII) and, interestingly enough, for the first time Initiating/Reacting (Factor VII). Potency and Activity again fuse into what we have called Dynamism (Factor II). The dominant Associative/Dissociative feature appears as Factor I, but it is fused with Moral/Immoral, Impulsive/Deliberate, and, particularly, a version of Reacting/Initiating — in other words, in our subjects' semantics, Associative behaviors tend to be Moral, Impulsive and Reactive, and the converse qualities characterize Dissociative behaviors. Factors V and VI are not clear, the former apparently being some fusion of Terminal-Past-Associative features and the latter some fusion of Supraordinate-Past-Dissociative features.

TABLE 6

Factor Analysis of Feature Scaling Data

	Loading	A Moral Immoral	B Potent Impotent	C Active Passive	D Associative Dissociative	E Initiating Reacting	F Ego Alter	G Supra Sub	H Terminal Interminal	I Future Past	J Deliberate Impulsive
Factor I											
Molest	.82	?	+	+	*	*	0	+	0	0	?
Ambush	.82	−	0	0	−	+	+	0	+	0	0
Betray	.75	−	0	0	−	+	0	0	+	−	+
Cheat	.74	−	0	0	−	+	+	0	0	0	+
Seduce	.64	−	+	+	0	+	+	+	0	+	+
Bully	.62	−	0	+	−	+	0	+	0	0	0
Embarrass	.60	0	0	0	−	+	−	+	0	+	0
Reassure	−.25	0	+	0	+	−	−	+	+	−	0
Accept	−.25	0	0	−	+	−	0	0	0	0	0
Console	−.23	+	0	0	+	−	−	0	0	−	−
Share with	−.25	0	0	0	+	0	0	0	−	0	0
Factor II											
Resist	.82	0	*	*	?	−	+	0	−	+	0
Defy	.71	0	0	+	−	0	+	0	0	+	−
Compete with	.67	0	0	+	−	0	+	+	−	+	0
Hold Contempt for	.64	0	+	0	0	−	−	+	−	−	0
Spurn	.58	0	+	+	0	−	0	+	+	0	0
Refute	.56	0	+	0	−	−	0	+	+	−	0
Share with	−.16	0	0	0	+	0	0	0	−	0	0
Confide in	−.16	0	−	0	+	+	+	0	+	−	0
Be Submissive to	−.14	0	−	−	0	−	−	−	−	0	0

TABLE 6 (cont.)

	Loading	A Moral/Immoral	B Potent/Impotent	C Active/Passive	D Associative/Dissociative	E Initiating/Reacting	F Ego/Alter	G Supra/Sub	H Terminal/Interminal	I Future/Past	J Deliberate/Impulsive
Factor III											
Advise	.79	0	0	0	0	+	*	0	0	+	+
Console	.71	+	0	0	+	–	–	0	0	+	–
Reform	.70	+	0	0	0	+	–	+	+	0	+
Reassure	.70	0	+	0	+	–	–	+	+	–	0
Convert	.64	0	0	0	0	+	–	+	+	+	0
Train	.62	0	0	0	0	+	–	+	–	+	+
Share with	.60	0	0	0	+	0	0	0	–	0	0
Cheat	-.24	–	0	0	–	+	+	0	0	0	+
Confess to	-.17	+	0	0	0	0	0	–	+	–	0
Evade	-.14	0	–	+	–	–	+	0	0	0	0
Factor IV											
Pay Attention to	.71	0	?	0	0	–	0	*	0	0	+
Be Submissive to	.69	0	0	–	0	–	–	0	–	0	0
Obey	.59	0	–	0	0	0	0	–	0	0	0
Serve	.53	0	0	0	+	–	–	–	0	0	0
Evade	.50	0	–	+	–	+	+	0	0	+	0
Plead with	.36	0	0	0	0	+	+	–	0	+	0
Bully	-.32	–	+	+	–	+	0	+	0	0	0
Seduce	-.32	–	0	0	0	+	+	+	0	+	+
Embarrass	-.24	0	0	0	–	+	–	+	0	–	0
Distress	-.21	0	0	0	–	+	–	0	0	0	0
Spurn	-.21	0	+	+	–	–	0	+	+	0	–

TABLE 6 (cont.)

	Loading	A Moral Immoral	B Potent Impotent	C Active Passive	D Associative Dissociative	E Initiating Reacting	F Ego Alter	G Supra Sub	H Terminal Interminal	I Future Past	J Deliberate Impulsive
Factor V											
Confess to	.77	+	0	0	?	0	0	−	?	?	0
Confide in	.67	0	−	0	0	+	+	0	+	−	0
Accept	.52	+	0	−	+	−	0	0	+	0	0
Console	.39	+	0	0	+	−	−	0	0	0	−
Share with	.35	0	0	0	+	0	0	0	−	0	0
Reform	−.28	+	0	0	0	+	−	+	0	0	+
Train	−.33	0	+	0	0	+	−	+	−	+	+
Harrass	−.27	−	+	+	−	+	0	0	−	0	0
Bully	−.23	−	+	+	−	+	−	+	0	0	0
Convert	−.21	0	0	0	0	+	−	+	+	+	0
Factor VI											
Disregard	.64	0	0	−	?	−	0	?	−	?	+
Exclude	.40	0	0	−	−	0	0	0	0	0	0
Hold Contempt for	.30	0	+	0	0	−	0	+	−	−	0
Depreciate	.26	0	0	0	−	0	0	+	0	−	+
Plead with	−.60	0	0	0	0	+	+	−	0	+	0
Serve	−.50	0	0	0	+	0	−	−	0	0	0
Court	−.31	0	0	+	+	+	+	0	−	+	0
Obey	−.25	0	−	0	0	−	0	−	0	0	0

TABLE 6 (cont.)

	Loading	A Moral Immoral	B Potent Impotent	C Active Passive	D Associative Dissociative	E Initiating Reacting	F Ego Alter	G Supra Sub	H Terminal Interminal	I Future Past	J Deliberate Impulsive
Factor VII											
Confuse	.77	0	0	0	0	*	−	0	0	0	0
Distress	.57	0	0	0	−	+	−	0	0	0	0
Embarrass	.41	0	0	0	−	+	−	+	0	−	0
Depreciate	.41	0	0	0	−	0	0	+	0	−	+
Appease	-.32	0	−	−	+	−	0	0	0	0	0
Refute	-.25	0	+	0	−	−	0	+	+	0	0
Serve	-.18	0	0	0	+	0	−	−	0	0	0
Factor VIII											
Court	.67	0	0	+	+	+	+	0	−	*	0
Promise	.60	0	0	0	+	0	0	0	+	+	0
Seduce	.38	−	0	0	0	+	+	+	0	+	+
Refute	-.42	0	+	0	−	−	0	+	+	−	0
Argue with	-.33	0	0	+	−	0	0	0	0	0	0
Depreciate	-.24	0	0	0	−	0	0	+	0	−	+

More impressive were contingency analyses of the relations between a priori and subject scalings. Where the distributions of subject mean judgments into plus 3 and plus 2 on the scale (coded +), plus 1, zero and minus 1 (coded 0), and minus 3 and minus 2 (coded −) were sufficiently balanced, these absolute judgments were used for contingency analyses; where they were highly skewed, the subjects' ratings were divided into upper, middle and lower thirds. Table 7 summarizes these analyses, reporting numbers of words in corresponding cells (perfect agreements in direction of coding), numbers of

TABLE 7
Significance Tests for Contingency Tables Relating
A Priori Codings to Subject Feature Scaling

FEATURE	WORDS IN ++ and −− CELLS	WORDS IN +− and −+ CELLS	SIGNIFICANCE LEVEL
Moral/Immoral	10	0	*
Potent/Impotent	10	0	.05
Active/Passive	11	0	*
Associative/Dissociative	24	0	.001
Initiating/Reacting	22	0	.001
Ego/Alter Orientation	21	0	.001
Supraordinate/Subordinate	22	1	.001
Terminal/Interminal	14	0	.05
Future/Past Orientation	16	0	.001
Deliberate/Impulsive	14	3	.30 (ns.)

* Coefficients have not been computed because a priori codings were too skewed for a legitimate test.

words in diametrically opposed cells (a priori judgments coded one sign, subjects chose the opposed sign), and significance levels. The features on which we would expect agreement − Associative/Dissociative, Ego/Alter, and Supraordinate/Subordinate − show agreement at the .001 level (i.e., one chance in a thousand of such agreement occurring by chance); but now to this group are added Initiating/Reacting and Future/Past. Two features reach only the .05 level of significance − Potent/Impotent and Terminal/Interminal − and one feature clearly does not show a significant relationship between a priori and subject coding − Deliberate/Impulsive. It should be noted that, with the exception of Deliberate/Impulsive, radical disagreements in a priori and subject codings almost never occur; there is only one exception, on Supraordinate/Subordinate: *Defy* is considered Subordinate by the author but Supraordinate by the subjects, and I still think I'm right!

This highly significant correspondence between a priori codings and subject scalings may, at first blush, seem rather trivial since, after all, we told them what the features were and gave them good examples. If these semantic features were explicitly tagged in word-forms (like the singular vs. plural of nouns), then, of course, this would be trivial. But such is not the case. Something about the meaning of the interpersonal verbs must be operating. If these interpersonal verb word-forms produced no semantic reactions which differentiate them in ways corresponding to the a priori features, then no amount of instruction and example would enable native speakers to make such fine and agreed-upon distinctions — if, for example, we asked them to apply a feature such as "being closer to or further from Paris than Boston." As for Deliberate/Impulsive, either IPV's are not coded discriminatively in such terms or our instructions and examples were inadequate. We take these results in general, then, as strong evidence for the psycholinguistic reality of most of the a priori features or close correlates of them.

SOME CROSS-CULTURAL AND CROSS-LINGUISTIC COMPARISONS

One of the goals of our research program, it will be recalled, has been to determine the degree of generality of semantic features across human groups differing in language and culture. From the viewpoint of psycholinguistic theory, demonstration of shared features would contribute to our understanding of language universals; from a more practical viewpoint, it could provide a set of constants against which to measure cultural differences in norms of interpersonal behavior. Even though discovery and validation procedures have not yet been worked out satisfactorily for American English, by any means, a number of cross-cultural studies have been made in an exploratory fashion. As might be expected, problems have mutliplied — particularly problems associated with translation and the interpretation of observed differences.

Japanese Japanese vs. American English Speakers[29]

The same 30 verbs and 30 adverbs that had been used in the IPV/AV intersection test with Illinois student subjects were translated into Japanese by Dr. Agnes Niyekawa, along with the instructions, and the "same" test was then given to a group of 40 monolingual college students in Japan. As a first step in analysis of these data, a 30 verb x 30 adverb table was used to record all IPV/AV combinations on which the modal[30] judgments of appositeness, permissiveness and anomaly by Japanese and American subjects differed. Of the 900 total items, 68 percent had identical modal judgments for Japanese and Americans, 24 percent disagreed by a half step (i.e., + 0, 0 —, etc., one culture considering apposite or anomalous what the other considered merely permissible), and only 8 percent disagreed completely (one group judging

---

[29] This comparative study was undertaken in cooperation with Drs. Agnes Niyekawa (University of Hawaii at that time) and Kenneth Forster.

[30] If 25/40 subjects judged an item merely permissible, it was scored 0; for all other items, ratios of apposite to anomalous greater than 3-to-1 were scored +, ratios of anomalous to apposite greater than 2-to-1 were scored —, and the remainder scored 0 also. There was a slight positive bias in both sets of data.

apposite what the other judged anomalous). These overall percentages indicate reasonable agreement. Furthermore, it will be recalled that I expressed some doubts about the reliability of the Illinois data taken from subjects in a "pool" serving as a course requirement; as a matter of fact, I agreed with the Japanese judgments in a considerable number of cases.[31] If the items on which I agreed with the Japanese (6 percent) were added to the total percent agreement, it would rise to 74 percent.

What about *sets* of items where Americans (including myself) disagree with the Japanese judgments consistently? The Japanese consider it fitting to *Learn from submissively, desperately* and *timidly* (not Americans); Japanese say one can't *Forgive sincerely, warmly* or *impulsively* (Americans say one can); Japanese judge it fitting to *Congratulate successfully* and *drastically* but anomalous to *Congratulate appropriately* (Americans just the reverse). As for adverbs, the Japanese find it fitting to *Imitate, Console, Cooperate, Nurse,* and *Contradict desperately* (for Americans these are merely permissive combinations); and whereas for Japanese almost all interpersonal verbs are anomalous when done *appropriately*, for Americans the same verbs are all apposite when done *appropriately*!

How is one to interpret such differences? The first possibility is that they are due to translation failures — the referent (interpersonal behavior or actor state) of the Japanese translation differs from that of the English verb or adverb. If translation fidelity can be assumed, then a second possiblity is that differences are due to semantics — the features being used may vary, or, if they are the same, then codings of translation-equivalent terms upon the features may differ. The third possibility is strictly cultural — norms of interpersonal behavior may render inappropriate the modes of human relationship implied by adequately translated and semantically acceptable combinations.

For example, to *Compete quietly* is judged apposite by Americans and anomalous by Japanese. This may be due to one of at least three possibilities: (1) The adverb *quietly* may have been translated into a Japanese form which would actually back-translate as English *contemplatively,* which Americans would also judge anomalous when combined with *Compete.* (2) Translations may be adequate, but *Compete* (in Japanese) may be coded + rather than 0 on the Activity feature and hence be anomalous with *quietly*. [32]

---

[31] Some examples are the following: *Nurse excitedly* (A 0, J −); *Display Affection for selfishly* (A +, J 0); *Compete, Cooperate, Help, Manipulate* and *Disregard emphatically* (A +, J −); *Console* and *Plead with efficiently* (A +, J −); *Plead with* and *Manipulate angrily* (A 0, J −); *Confide in rashly* (A −, J 0).

[32] One could argue that this is also a translation failure; although *Compete* is the "best" translation of the Japanese form (and vice versa), it is not a "perfect" translation, since its features are not identical, and in many if not most translations this will be the case. Translation "failure" is used here in cases where a better translation was demonstrably available.

(3) Although the translation is adequate and there is no semantic anomaly it may be simply a cultural fact about Japanese society that competition is expected to be an overt, "noisy" business (this is merely an example, of course!).

Before one can attempt to discriminate between semantic and cultural determinants of differences, it is necessary to eliminate translation failures as far as possible. Accordingly, Agnes Niyekawa arranged for six reasonably coordinate English/Japanese bilinguals[33] to translate her Japanese translations of the 30 verbs and 30 adverbs back into English. Column 4 in Table 8 gives the dominant back translations (*S* means same as original English and *none* means no dominant translation). Although some of the non-identical back-translations are near synonyms (e.g., *Inform/Tell* and *Selfishly/- Egotistically*), many are not (e.g., *Defy/Oppose, Repel/Refuse, successfully/- well*, and *drastically/fiercely*).

There are difficulties with back-translation as a procedure. To use an example given me by Agnes Niyekawa, let us suppose that English verb *play* (which itself has some 68 different uses according to Webster's *International Dictionary*) is translated into Japanese *asobu; asobu* also has various senses, one of which is translatable as English *loaf*; now if, in back-translation, *loaf* comes out rather than *play,* this does not mean that *asobu* was an inadequate translation to begin with. This is particularly the case when words are translated out of context. To counteract this difficulty, we ran a subsequent scaling test, using seven bilinguals. Sets of three English translation alternatives of each of Niyekawa's Japanese words — the original or "correct" English word, the dominant back-translation (if other than the original), and another word offered in the back-translation task — were rated comparatively on a seven-step scale ranging from 'excellent' to 'poor.' We assume that the set of three words serves to restrict the senses of the individual terms to that common to all of them, e.g., the senses of *To Nurse* as "to hold" (as a grudge) or as "to feed at the breast" are eliminated by combining *Nurse, Look After* and *Take Care of*. Column 5 in Table 8 gives the preferred (most excellent) translations for each of the Japanese verbs and adverbs.

Column 6 in Table 8 gives my own decisions as to the adequacy of our translations. Where both tests yield something other than the original English term (e.g., *Defy* to *Oppose, Criticize* to *Blame* and *Accuse, drastically* to *fiercely*), I call it a translation failure (marked *X*). In some of these cases, the alternatives are quasi-synonyms (like *Disregard* to *Ignore* and *submissively* to *obediently*) and probably would not affect interpretation of the data. Where a failure in back-translation is followed by a success in the preference test, I consider the translation adequate on the assumption that the correct English

---

[33] We wish to thank particularly Miho Steinberg and her brother, Peter Tanaka, for their careful work on this task.

TABLE 8
Translation Analysis for American/Japanese Disagreements

Verbs	Total A/J Disagree	CEO Agrees w.J.	Significant Disagreements	Dominant Back Translation	Preferred Alternate Translation	Decision	N "Translation Based" Disagreements	N "Real" Disagreements
	(1)	(2)	(3)	(4)	(5)	(6)	(7)	(8)
Defy	7	1	2	Oppose	Oppose	X	1	6
Imitate	8	1	3	S	S	++	2	6
Display Affection	6	2	3	S	S	++	1	5
Ridicule	10	4	2	Laugh at	S	++	4	6
Console	6	2	3	S	S	++	1	5
Corrupt	8	2	4	S	Make Degenerate	+	2	6
Cooperate	7	1	2	S	S	++	2	5
Plead with	6	3	3	S	S	++	2	4
Deceive	6	3	3	Cheat	S	+	2	4
Criticize	9	3	4	Blame	Accuse	X	3	6
Confide in	6	1	2	Disclose	S	+	3	3
Protect	4	1	1	S	S	++	1	3
Hinder	5	2	1	Interfere with	S	++	1	4
Show Respect for	4	1	1	S	S	++	2	2
Concede	4	2	1	Compromise	Yield	X	1	3
Repel	6	2	3	Refuse	Reject	X	1	5
Compete with	12	4	3	S	S	++	4	8
Help	10	3	2	S	S	++	3	7
Manipulate	9	4	2	S	S	++	1	8
Nurse	4	2	2	S	S	++	1	3
Contradict	9	3	5	Oppose	S	+	2	7
Disregard	5	3	0	Ignore	Ignore	X	1	4
Inform	4	0	4	Tell	S	+	2	2
Congratulate	8	0	5	(None)	Show Delight	X	4	4
Forgive	13	6	5	S	Pardon	X	4	9
Learn from	8	1	5	S	S	++	2	6
Oppose	6	2	2	S	S	++	2	4

				Announce Tempt	Give Notice Tempt			
Apologize	7	0	4	S	S	++	2	5
Warn	7	3	3			X	2	5
Seduce	9	3	1			X	2	7
Adverbs								
Firmly	6	0	5	S	Strongly	+	1	5
Unfairly	8	3	1	Dishonestly	Unjustly	X	2	6
Excitedly	8	3	2	S	S	++	1	7
Hopefully	8	2	4	S	S	++	3	5
Selfishly	5	2	1	Excitedly	Skillfully	X	0	5
Successfully	9	1	4	Well	S	++	3	6
Emphatically	9	5	1			X	4	5
Submissively	4	3	0	Obediently	Obediently	++	1	3
Sincerely	6	1	4	S	S	++	3	3
Efficiently	14	8	4	S	S	X	4	10
Reluctantly	2	1	0	Unwillingly	S	++	2	0
Warmly	6	2	3	(None)	Heartily	++	3	3
Angrily	7	5	1	S	S	X	2	5
Guiltily	2	0	0	S	S	++	0	2
Contemptuously	7	3	0	S	S	++	4	3
Appreciatively	4	2	0	Thankfully	Gratefully	X	2	2
Despicably	8	3	3	Cowardly	S	+	2	6
Drastically	7	3	2	Fiercely	Fiercely	X	3	4
Kindly	9	6	2	S	S	++	4	5
Rashly	8	2	5	(None)	S	+	2	6
Quietly	7	0	3	S	S	++	1	6
Resolutely	5	2	2	Firmly	S	++	3	2
Impulsively	9	3	4	Unexpectedly	S	++	5	4
Generously	4	0	2	S	S	+	1	3
Desperately	10	0	8	S	S	++	1	9
Appropriately	21	0	13	Suitably	(None)	X	5	16
Unceasingly	5	2	0	Continuously	S	++	2	3
Timidly	4	1	2	(None)	S	+	1	3
Unwillingly	6	0	3	S	Reluctantly	+	2	4
Considerately	5	3	1	Thoughtfully	S	+	1	4

word is one of the legitimate senses of the Japanese term. When the preference test fails where the back-translation test had succeeded, I call the translation adequate if the preferred word is near-synonymous with the correct word (e.g., *Corrupt* to *Make Degenerate, unwillingly* to *reluctantly*) but deem it a failure if correct and preferred words are clearly not synonymous (e.g., *Forgive* to *Pardon*).[34] We end up with nine verbs and seven adverbs inadequately translated. When I say "inadequately translated" it must be realized that there may simply not *be* any Japanese word that differs from the Japanese translation the way the correct English word differs from the preferred English word semantically. There may not be any Japanese verb that includes the features of Impulsiveness and Subordinateness by which *Defy* differs from *Oppose,* for example.

Columns 1, 2 and 3, respectively, give the total number of American/-Japanese disagreements in modal judgment, the number of cases where I would agree with the Japanese subjects, and the number of what I consider to be potentially significant disagreements (for semantic or cultural interpretation). Column 7 gives the number of disagreements which could be accounted for on the grounds of inadequate translation — i.e., for each verb the number of inadequately translated adverbs with which it displayed disagreements and vice versa for each adverb. And, finally, column 8 gives the number of "real" disagreements between American and Japanese subjects open to semantic or cultural interpretation (which is simply column 1 minus column 7, since I do not here subtract the items where I happened to agree with the Japanese).

Before attempting to distinguish between semantic and cultural bases of the remaining disagreements (if indeed such a distinction can be made at all), it will be necessary to see to what extent Japanese use the same semantic features as Americans. Table 9 presents the results of a Varimax rotation of the first six factors for adverbs in the Japanese intersection data.[35] The first factor is clearly the familiar Associative/Dissociative feature (*considerately, warmly, sincerely, appropriately, kindly, appreciatively* as opposed to *despicably, unfairly, angrily*). The second factor appears to be a Dynamism feature (combination of Potency and Activity), characterized by the contrast between *drastically, excitedly, firmly* and *kindly, generously.* Factor III is a uniquely Japanese factor which might be called "Subordinate Striving" (*efficiently, reluctantly, unwillingly, hopefully, desperately*) vs. "Supra-ordinate Complacency" (*contemptuously* and *firmly*). Factor IV appears to be a "Social Deliberateness" feature (*appropriately, efficiently, unceasingly* and *warmly* as opposed to *rashly, contemptuously, resolutely, impulsively*

---

[34] The one exception to these rules is *firmly* to *strongly,* where our two best bilinguals did prefer *firmly* in the second test.

[35] This analysis was done by Forster in Melbourne. It will be noted that it analyzes adverb rather than verb relations, as previously reported; the choice is, in a sense, arbitrary.

TABLE 9

Japanese Subject Data: Varimax Rotation of First
Six Principal Axes Factors

	I	II	III	IV	V	VI
Angrily	-.53	-.61	.05	-.43	.17	-.04
Appreciatively	.79	.13	.36	.08	-.02	.29
Appropriately	.80	-.17	.14	.24	-.08	.10
Considerately	.87	.07	.16	-.15	-.18	-.22
Contemptuously	-.34	-.28	-.36	-.62	-.01	-.07
Desperately	.12	-.47	.56	.09	-.47	-.06
Despicably	-.87	-.26	-.08	-.23	-.16	.06
Drastically	-.20	-.92	-.12	-.01	.12	.06
Efficiently	.13	.07	.81	.22	-.22	-.21
Emphatically	.27	-.40	-.03	-.17	-.21	.76
Excitedly	-.33	-.72	.17	-.19	.07	.38
Firmly	.19	-.71	-.23	-.28	-.04	.29
Generously	.67	.30	.42	-.29	.01	.13
Guiltily	-.50	-.01	.25	-.24	-.61	.35
Hopefully	.64	-.05	.65	.19	.02	.02
Impulsively	.30	-.12	.21	-.47	-.56	.21
Kindly	.79	.33	.33	-.05	-.12	-.10
Quietly	.69	-.16	.27	.00	-.03	.35
Rashly	-.19	-.18	.13	-.66	-.01	.43
Reluctantly	.12	-.08	.81	-.20	-.21	.14
Resolutely	-.08	-.67	.28	-.59	.10	.05
Selfishly	-.18	-.69	-.03	-.12	-.38	-.14
Sincerely	.85	-.02	.44	.01	.03	.18
Submissively	.62	.16	.46	.05	-.14	.46
Successfully	.15	.02	.29	.17	-.78	.06
Timidly	.30	-.17	.54	-.18	-.27	.51
Unceasingly	.24	-.63	.28	.30	-.36	.23
Unfairly	-.62	-.34	.38	-.08	.11	-.14
Unwillingly	.30	.14	.74	-.15	-.14	.27
Warmly	.89	-.06	-.18	.21	-.15	.05

and *angrily*). Factor V is a reasonably clear (although unipolar) "Ego-oriented" feature, defined by *successfully, guiltily, impulsively* and *desperately.* Factor VI is "Supraordinate/Subordinate" clearly enough, but the nature of it is strange indeed, with *emphatically, timidly, submissively* and *rashly* on one side and *considerately* and *efficiently* on the other. The total pattern has all the appearances of a transitional society, with traditional values and status markers in sharp conflict (among Japanese college students) with modern realities.

How similar is the Japanese adverb structure to the American? Forster used the PROCRUSTES factor-matching program (Hurley and Cattell, 1962) to find an answer. PROCRUSTES generates the best "fit" of one set of data (here, the Japanese judgments of IPV/AV combinations) to another set of data (here the Illinois subject-pool judgments of same combinations). Table 10 gives the results of this analysis. It can be seen that the first factor is

TABLE 10
Best Match Via PROCRUSTES of Japanese Data to Illinois Subjects Factors

	I		II		III		IV		V		VI		VII	
	I	J	I	J	I	J	I	J	I	J	I	J	I	J
Angrily	.70	.69	-.59	-.52										-.40
Appreciatively	-.80	-.88												
Appropriately	-.44	-.71							.45					
Considerately	-.68	-.64							.62					
Contemptuously	.74	.51	-.53	-.53								.44		-.71
Desperately					-.45	-.79	-.52	-.38						
Despicably	.85	.87						-.46						-.72
Drastically	.74	.45		-.52										
Efficiently					-.91	-.50								
Emphatically	-.86		-.61	-.61										
Excitedly	-.58	.41		-.55									-.40	-.53
Firmly	-.77			-.72										-.46
Generously	-.89	-.76								.67				
Guiltily		.46					-.88	-.86						
Hopefully	-.58	-.69			-.42					.54			-.41	-.39
Impulsively	-.80		-.80					-.47						
Kindly	-.85	-.75							.47	.42				
Quietly	-.71	-.59								.53				
Rashly	.69		-.60	-.62						.44				
Reluctantly									.80	.53				
Resolutely	-.40		-.40	-.74										
Selfishly		.44									.67		-.75	-.55
Sincerely	-.81	-.81							.57			.61		-.57
Submissively	-.55	-.77								.59				
Successfully				-.41	-.89	-.61	-.63	-.42						
Timidly	-.54	-.32							.69	.56				
Unceasingly		.53												
Unfairly	.75												-.77	-.74
Unwillingly									.88	.64				
Warmly	-.92	-.71												

clearly Associative/Dissociative — *appreciatively, generously, kindly, sincerely,* and *warmly* vs. *despicably, unfairly, contemptuously* and *angrily* — but the Japanese would add *guiltily, excitedly* and *selfishly* to the list of Dissociative motives. Factor II is again a Dynamism feature (unipolar), with *emphatically, impulsively, rashly, excitedly,* and *firmly* (the last a bit strange to Americans) heading the list. The Japanese would add *selfishly, drastically,* and *timidly* to Dynamism, again suggestive of upward mobile members of a transitional society. Factor III transforms the American "Future-oriented" factor into the Japanese "Subordinate Striving" factor — characterized by *desperately, successfully,* and *efficiently.* Factor IV seems to be a "Social Volatility vs. Deliberateness" kind of feature, with *successfully, guiltily, impulsively, despicably* (and *timidly*) opposed to *appropriately.* Factor V, on the American side, looks like Subordinateness, but on the Japanese side it takes on an "Alter-oriented and Moral" flavor (*sincerely, appreciatively,* and *generously*). Factor VI defies interpretation. Factor VII seems to be an attempt of PROCRUSTES to wed an American "Terminal/Interminal" factor (*unceasingly, resolutely*) with an "Ego-oriented" Japanese factor (*unceasingly, desperately, drastically, selfishly*).

Is it possible to distinguish purely semantic bases of disagreement between Americans and Japanese from cultural differences in their norms of interpersonal behavior? In the following interpretive analysis I have eliminated disagreements attributable to translation failures (as defined earlier by back-translation and preference tests), and I have been skeptical about disagreements where I happen to agree with the Japanese subjects. If a *set* of disagreements can be related to a clear-cut difference in the factor analyses, then I attribute them to semantic coding. If not, I attribute them to culture, buttressing this attribution with occasional commentary by Dr. Agnes Niyekawa.[36] Since it is the adverbs for which we have direct factor loadings, we begin with them.

Disagreements on the usage of *efficiently* seem to be cultural, there being perfect agreement with Niyekawa's translation and yet ten unresolved items. According to Niyekawa, the Japanese word is restricted in usage to verbs related to productivity *in work,* having been introduced with industrialization. Thus one cannot *Corrupt* or *Criticize efficiently* in Japanese. Americans seem to be able to do just about anything *efficiently*! The fact that *desperately* and *unwillingly* are considered apposite combinations with *Imitate, Console,* and *Learn from* is also interpreted as cultural by Dr. Niyekawa, and this she relates to a syntactical device found in Japanese but not English — the Causative Passive, in which the deep structure Actor is

---

[36] From personal correspondence.

being forced into his actions by persons or conditions beyond his control. However, these same adverbs, along with *efficiently, hopefully* and *reluctantly,* define what I called the 'Subordinate Striving' factor, so again the distinction between what is semantic and what is cultural is not clear. Disagreements on *firmly* suggest that it was a translation failure after all; if one substitutes *strongly* (the preferred back-translation for the majority of the bilinguals) for *firmly,* then all of the strange items for Americans become acceptable, e.g., judgments of fitting for *Display Affection, Plead with,* and *Show Respect firmly.* [37]

Apparently "semantic" are the following: The adverb *excitedly* is identified as Dissociative on PROCRUSTES, which would explain why the Japanese find *Protect excitedly* and *Cooperate excitedly* anomalous. Unlike English usage, *sincerely* is shown in PROCRUSTES to have definite Subordinate coding, hence the Japanese cannot *Contradict sincerely* but they can *Learn from sincerely.* On the Varimax Factor IV, both *contemptuously* and *resolutely* fall on the Impulsive side, which would explain why the Japanese subjects cannot *Imitate, Corrupt* or *Seduce* (all rather deliberate behaviors) *contemptuously,* whereas they find it fitting to *Defy resolutely.* The adverb *kindly* is shown to be both non-Dynamic and Subordinate in the Japanese analyses, and we note that *Learn from kindly* is an apposite combination for them but anomalous for Americans. From Varimax Factor VI we discover that, strangely enough for Americans, both *rashly* and *emphatically* go along with *timidly* and *submissively* as Subordinate. Appropriately enough, Japanese cannot *Ridicule rashly* or *emphatically,* yet they can *Apologize* both *rashly* and *emphatically.* On PROCRUSTES V *quietly* is coded both Alter-oriented and Moral, and our Japanese subjects consider it anomalous to *Imitate, Corrupt, Deceive* or *Compete quietly.* Finally, *considerately* falls on the Supraordinate side of Varimax VI, and the Japanese subjects can *Protect* and *Nurse considerately* but they cannot *Congratulate* or *Apologize considerately.*

In interpreting the verb disagreements, I have eliminated those already accounted for by the semantic codings of the adverbs with which they were combined as well as those attributable to translation failures. Very few sharp differences remain. It would appear that for Japanese *Repel, Contradict* and *Oppose* are all Immoral as well as being Dissociative (rather than being coded 0 in Morality, as they were by Americans). For example, to *Repel, Contradict* and *Oppose despicably* are all apposite combinations for Japanese but merely permissable for Americans. Similarly, *Imitate* and *Compete* appear to be Immoral as well as Ego-oriented; Japanese cannot do either of these things

---

[37] Ideally, we should give a new IPV/AV intersection test to American subjects, but with the preferred back-translations substituted, and see to what extent this eliminates disagreements — but this remains to be done.

quietly (a + Moral AV), for example. *Confide in* probably should have been considered a translation failure (the dominant back-translation was *Disclose to*, cf., Table 8); the Japanese subjects consider *Confide in unwillingly* to be an apposite combination. We are left with a few puzzling items: why do the Japanese consider it anomalous to *Display Affection for, Concede to,* and *Help generously*? Why can't they *Deceive hopefully*?

By way of summarizing this exploratory comparison of American and Japanese interpersonal verb usage, we may first note the evidence for common semantic features. On nearly three fourths of the IPV/AV combinations, students from the two cultures give identical modal judgments, and on only eight percent are they flatly opposed (apposites for one being anomalies for the other). Both the Varimax and PROCRUSTES rotations provide evidence for sharing of Associative/Dissociative, Dynamism, Supraordinate/Subordinate and Ego/Alter-Oriented features and these, it will be remembered, regularly come through most clearly in our data for American subjects. But within these overall similarities some striking cultural differences appear. For one thing, the Japanese college subjects fuse a Future-Striving feature (which Americans also have) with a varient of Subordinateness; they also fuse a Deliberate/Impulsive feature (which Americans also have) with what looks like a Social/Asocial feature; indeed, the entire Japanese description of Subordinateness (with *efficiently* and *hopefully* on Varimax IV and *emphatically* and *rashly* on Varimax VI) is quite strange to the American mind.

Is "Subordinate Striving" and an identification of "Impulsiveness" with "Asocial" behaviors as opposed to "Deliberate and Conforming" behaviors a valid characterization of major differences in the norms of interpersonal relations for Japanese versus American college students? I find some confirming evidence of this in a study by Kenneth Berrien (1966) in which Japanese and American college students were compared in terms of 15 social needs (The Edwards Personality Preference Schedule). Japanese scored significantly lower on Deference (not accepting leadership of those they admire, not conforming to customs) and on Dominance (not accepting leadership positions themselves, not defending their own point of view when attacked) than Americans, yet they scored significantly higher than Americans simultaneously on Abasement (accepting blame when things go wrong, feeling inferior to others) and on Endurance (working hard, avoiding interruptions in their work). Both "Subordinate Striving" and conflict over "Conforming" seem to be evident here.

Although only 8 percent of the IPV/AV pairs display extreme disagreement, this is still about 72 items. However, if disagreements attributable to translation failure and/or Illinois subject failure (those where I agree with the Japanese) are discounted, then only 22 maximal disagreements remain — all of which were discussed above. Since nearly all of these "real" disagreements are based on adverbs marked on the uniquely Japanese features (factors), and since these are probably best interpreted as *cultural* differences between Americans and Japanese, it would appear that one cannot really distinguish between "semantic" and "cultural" bases of disagreement. And this conclusion — considering that language is, after all, a part of culture — would seem to be in order.

A Semantic Feature Analysis of Thai Pronouns

Although not strictly a comparative analysis, a study of Thai pronoun usage by W. Wichiarajote and Marilyn Wilkins does have implications for the universality of semantic features. Unlike English, where pronouns are distinguished mainly in terms of person, number, and sex, in Thai pronouns are also distinguished in a complex way on the basis of status relations between addresser and addressee. There are about 20 first-person pronouns translatable as 'I' and an equal number translatable as 'you,' and when one Thai speaks with another he must keep in mind the relationship of himself to the other if he is to maintain social protocol. As a matter of fact, two Thai will avoid the use of personal pronouns by circumlocution until they have enough information about each other to permit proper pronoun selection. Mr. Wichiarajote decided to apply the procedures described in this paper to an analysis of the semantic features of Thai first-person pronouns. Since usage of these pronouns depends upon the role relations between speaker and hearer, rather than upon the linguistic context *per se*, the "intersection" was between 14 fairly common pronouns and 60 role-pairs (e.g., **father** *speaking to* **son, official** *to* **citizen, pupil** *to* **teacher**, and so on). Role-pairs were selected to sample a wide variety of role relations.

Based on Wichiarajote's familiarity with Thai culture and language, 11 a priori features were intuited: Sex (male/female), Age (old/young), Status (high/low), Formality (formal/informal), Urbanity (urban/rural), Social Distance (close/distant), Politeness (polite/impolite), Nobility (noble/common), Potency (potent/impotent), Kinship (relative/non-relative), and Titleship (title/non-title). The 14 pronouns and 60 role-pairs were individually and independently coded (+, 0, −) on these 11 features, always in terms of the speaker (left-hand member of the role-pairs). Then the code-strip of each pronoun was matched with the code-strip of each role-pair and the programmed rules of the discrete model were used to predict the judgment of each pronoun/role-pair combination (opposed signs on any feature yielding anomaly, etc.; cf. page 152 here). This process yielded a 14 (pronoun) x 60 (role-pair) Predicted Matrix. This matrix is actually the "hypothesis" being tested in the study. Empirical data were collected from 53 native Thai subjects (undergraduate students in the United States), by having them assign a plus (fitting), zero (permissible) or minus (anomalous) sign to each pronoun/role-pair combination in the usual fashion. The 14 x 60 matrix (averages across subjects) generated in this manner constitutes the data or Target Matrix.

An interesting innovation in this study was the use of all a priori features simultaneously, as they determine the Predicted Matrix, as if this were the final stage of application of the Forster Feature Analysis Program. Thus, this is not a "discovery" procedure, but rather a "test" procedure for intuited features. Matching of the Target Matrix and Predicted Matrix yields a Residual Matrix, which can be checked for percentage of correct and unpatchable cells. The first run yielded 65 percent correct and 14 percent unpatchable. A few modifications in coding and changes in the cut-off points for assigning discrete signs to the Target Matrix were undertaken twice (three cycles through the analysis procedures). The third Residual Matrix yielded 84 percent correctly predicted cells and only 9 percent unpatchable errors.

A principal axis factor analysis and Varimax rotation was applied to the raw subject data, the correlations being taken between role-pairs across pronouns. Only six factors accounted for 94 percent of the total variance. By inspecting the role-pairs having the highest loadings on each factor, it was possible to make assignments of Wichiarajote's a priori features to the six factors (that is, in terms of the sharing of particular features by the high-loading role-pairs). Table 11 summarizes these results. The first factor, called Potency by the investigators, shows highest loadings for **officer** *to* **private, official** *to* **farmer, prime minister** *to* **official, lad** *to* **lass, doctor** *to* **patient, educated** *to* **uneducated, official** *to* **citizen**, and **noble boss** *to* **commons**. I would be inclined to relate this feature to the Supraordinate/ Subordinate feature of our interpersonal verb analyses. Factor II, labeled "Deference," displays highest loadings for **layman** *to* **monk, official** *to* **prime minister, junior official** *to* **senior official, employee** *to* **employer** and **pauper** *to* **millionaire**. It is identified with a priori Politeness in the pronoun system, and seems to represent the other pole of the Supraordinate/Subordinate verb feature. Factor III, labeled Kinship, loads highest for **father** *to* **son, father** *to* **daughter, elder brother** *to* **younger brother**, and **father-in-law** *to* **son-in-law** – clearly Kinship, but also including Supraordinateness. Factor IV, termed Sex, shows highest loadings for **woman** *to* **man, lass** *to* **lad**, and **wife** *to* **husband**. Again, it appears that *male* is Supraordinate. Factor V, Age, loads highest for **daughter** *to* **father, daughter-in-law** *to* **mother-in-law, pupil** *to* **teacher** and **child** *to* **adult**, again exhibiting a combination of Subordinateness with a specific social feature, Age. Finally, Factor VI, labeled Social Distance (or Hostility) by the investigators, shows highest loadings for **Mr. A**

TABLE 11

Role-pair Factor Analysis and Varimax Rotation
Related to A Priori Thai Pronoun Features

FACTOR	PROPOSED SOCIAL TRAIT	PERCENT VARIANCE	CORRESPONDING A PRIORI FEATURES
I	Potency	40	Potency, Status, Nobility, Titleship, Urbanity
II	Deference	22	Politeness
III	Kinship	11	Kinship
IV	Sex	10	Sex
V	Age	5	Age
VI	Social Distance	6	Social Distance, Formality

to opponent, hoodlum *to* hoodlum, Angry man *to* Mr. A and Chinese *to* Thai (!). Clearly this is our Associative/Dissociative interpersonal verb feature without Supraordinateness.

Several aspects of this study are of special interest. There is, first, the obvious utilization of semantic features that also occur in American English, although they are used in form-classes other than pronouns (except for Sex). The two dominant features operating appear to be Supraordinateness and Associativeness. This testifies to the universality of these semantic features. Second, there is the fusion of the underlying Supraordinate/Subordinate feature — which, of course, reflects the traditional Thai concern with status relations — with features representing various specific social role differentia. Potency and Deference directly reflect the underlying status feature, but Supraordinateness fuses with Kinship (**father** *to* **daughter**), Sex (**lad** *to* **lass**) and Age (**adult** *to* **child**) as well.

In other words, in Thai we have an explicit elaboration, reflected in semantics, of the universal Supraordinate/Subordinate feature. We may note also the convergence of a priori pronoun features — Potency, Status, Nobility, Titleship, and Urbanity (**urbans** speaking to **rurals** and vice versa) — upon a single factor, here called Potency but interpretable as Supraordinateness.

Mr. Wichiarajote tells us that the traditional pronoun distinctions within these categories are breaking down in modern times, with the relevant pronouns being used interchangeably and a few dominant ones becoming more so. This would appear to be a very intriguing instance of mediated generalization among a set of very similar mediation processes, when the environmental supports for their discrimination break down.

Finally, there is evidence for a hierarchical structuring of the Thai pronoun features. When the 11 a priori features are ordered according to their

FIGURE 10

HIERARCHICAL STRUCTURE OF THAI A PRIORI PRONOUN FEATURES

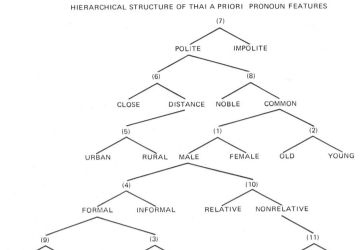

differentiating power,[38] contingencies among the features in terms of codings across roles indicate a high degree of "nesting" of lower-order features within higher-order features. For example, only when role relations are coded (+) on Politeness (with a few exceptions) do any of the other features become relevant; it is when roles are already coded (−) on Kinship (non-relative) that Titleship becomes relevant; and so on. This ordered "nesting" was sufficiently transitive for Wilkins to be able to construct the "nesting tree" shown in Figure 10. Of the 28 nestings predicted in this tree, 24 were confirmed in the feature-contingency data. One can imagine a rapid scanning process in which (going down the tree) the Thai speaker first determines if his relation to the listener is Polite, then if not-Noble, then if Male, then if the relation is Formal and then (given all of these conditions) he determines his relative status to the listener — all before choosing the appropriate pronoun. Although this hierarchical nesting system is by no means perfect for Thai pronoun semantics, it is much clearer than in the case of interpersonal verbs in English.

Cross-cultural Test of a Role Differential

A practical purpose behind our studies of the semantics of interpersonal verbs was to develop instruments for comparing norms of interpersonal behavior across cultures and languages. It was expected that people in

---

[38] $D.P. = \dfrac{\text{number of coded roles}}{\text{total number of roles}}$ x 100, i.e., the importance of a feature in discriminating among role-pairs.

different language-culture communities would share the same underlying feature system, but would differ in the weights given to features, in the codings of translation-equivalent verbs and roles, and particularly in the prescribed appropriateness of certain intentions for certain role relations. Although we had not demonstrated the universality of the IPV semantic features at the time, Hawaii seemed an ideal location in which to initiate a comparative study of role differentiation. Japanese college students in Tokyo, English-speaking college students of Japanese ancestry in Hawaii, and English-speaking college students in Illinois would serve as subjects. All possible 800 combinations of 20 IPV's and 40 role-pairs (drawn from a set of 100 used by Triandis and his associates at Illinois) would be rated. The interpersonal verbs used are listed in Table 12 and the role-pairs in Table 13.

Since 800 items constituted too long a task, eight groups of 20 subjects each rated subsets of 100 items, role-pairs and verbs being rotated against each other through the entire 800 items so that repetitions of either were maximally separated. Each item appeared as follows:

father *to defy* **son**

never   seldom   sometimes   depends   often   usually   always

The subject was instructed to circle the appropriate quantifier. In the instructions, *never* was specified as "practically zero percent of the time," *seldom* as "from 1 to 20 percent of the time," *sometimes* as "from 20 to 40 percent," *depends* as from "40 to 60 percent." Quantifiers were valued equivalently on the other side of the scale. After some discussion, it was decided to use an "actual" (how people *actually* behave toward each other) rather than an "appropriate" (how people ought to behave)[39] criterion, in the thought that ideal cultures might be overly polarized and obscure differences.

With the exception of two IPV's (*Keep at a Distance* and *Attract the Attention of*), all verbs were among those translated by Agnes Niyekawa and tested in the previously described study. In the present instance, we would expect translation difficulties to show up in consistent differences between Illinois-Hawaiian means (same language) and Japanese means. The greatest apparent offender is *Show Respect for*, with Japanese subjects attributing less of it to 30 of the 40 role relations; since this verb was successfully translated, by both tests, we assume this is characteristic of Japanese (college student) culture — and it is consistent with Berrien's observations cited earlier. For

---

[39]A subsequent comparison of the two types of instructions by Marilyn Wilkins, using Illinois subjects and only Form A (first one hundred items), suggests that this was a wise decision. The "appropriate" criterion produced greater, not lesser, item variance than the "actual" criterion, and the item means were pushed outward toward *never* or *always,* depending on the Social Desirability of the interpersonal behaviors involved.

verbs which were considered to be translation failures (*Defy* better translated as *Oppose, Criticize* better as *Blame* or *Accuse*,*Confide in* perhaps better as *Disclose to*, and *Concede to* perhaps better as *Compromise* or *Yield*), only *Confide in* yields consistent Illinois-Hawaiian versus Japanese differences (12/40 role-pairs) and should be considered a translation failure for present purposes. It would appear that the semantic shifts involved in *Defy* to *Oppose, Criticize* to *Blame*, and *Concede to* to *Yield* have little effect upon appropriateness judgments in role relations, even though they may influence acceptability judgments of IPV/AV combinations.

To obtain an overview of the role differential data, factor analyses for both behaviors-across-roles and roles-across-behaviors were run separately for each language/culture community. Factor-matching of the first four rotated factors across cultures proved to be simple in both cases, testifying to the underlying similarities. Table 12 gives the results for interpersonal behaviors. Those IPV's having large and consistent loadings for all three cultures may be used as identifiers of the factors, and inspection of those role relations having the most extreme ratings on these IPV's — again consistently across cultures — helps to clarify the semantic quality of the factors.

Verb Factor I has its highest negative loadings on *Cooperate with,* and *Show Respect for* and its highest positive loadings on *Defy, Ridicule, Criticize* and *Hinder*; it would thus appear to be some variant of Associative/ Dissociative. Factor II has its highest positive loadings on *Display Affection for, Console, Protect* and *Help* with its only high negative loading on *Keep at a Distance*; it would thus appear to be some other variant of Associative/ Dissociative. However, the verbs in Factor I suggest Formal Associative relations, and the extremely rated role-pairs confirm this inference. **Patient** *to* **doctor, sales person** *to* **customer, host** *to* **guest, guest** *to* **host** and **teacher** *to* **student** are Formally Associative while **stranger** *to* **local person, old person** *to* **young person** and, interestingly enough, **man** *to* **woman** are Formally Dissociative. The verbs in Factor II suggest Intimate Associative vs. Remote Dissociative and again the extremely rated roles confirm the inference. **Husband** *to* **wife, wife** *to* **husband** and **girl friend** *to* **girl friend** are distinctively Intimate while **local person** *to* **stranger, citizen** *to* **political leader** and, interestingly, **boy friend** *to* **boy friend** are consistently Remote. Most parental relations (**father** *to* **daughter** and vice versa, **mother** *to* **son** and vice versa, but *not* **father** *to* **son**) are rated high on both Formal and Intimate Associativeness, whereas **person** *to* **his opponent** is rated extremely negative on both factors. Appropriately enough, **employee** *to* **employer** is simultaneously Formally Associative but Remote.

Verb Factor III is clearly Supraordinate/Subordinate across all groups, although it is unipolar. *Plead with* and *Concede to* have the highest positive loadings (Subordinate) and, except for the Japanese, *Manipulate* represents

TABLE 12

Rotated Factors and Variances for Interpersonal Verbs for Illinois (I), Hawaiian (H) and Japanese (J) Subjects

	I			II			III			IV		
	I (17%)	H (28%)	J (25%)	I (27%)	H (21%)	J (25%)	I (14%)	H (14%)	J (20%)	I (19%)	H (10%)	J (7%)
1. Defy	74	86	90	-06	-15	-13	08	14	-12	-49	-10	03
2. Imitate	-08	27	03	-09	-12	-18	46	59	83	-59	02	-36
3. Display Affection for	13	13	-03	88	73	83	21	18	16	-02	-28	09
4. Ridicule	72	87	72	-17	-10	-47	-05	07	02	-51	22	-16
5. Console	04	04	08	90	91	82	-25	-20	-11	-08	-11	-25
6. Corrupt	20	67	79	08	-01	07	-26	07	02	-80	-52	-23
7. Cooperate with	-60	-48	-11	48	30	75	35	51	46	14	-23	11
8. Deceive	35	55	64	-19	-38	15	41	24	02	-70	-56	-39
9. Plead with	40	26	02	53	44	-05	65	62	90	08	28	02
10. Criticize	82	76	80	-04	10	-34	-10	-15	03	-04	04	08
11. Confide in	-17	04	07	61	49	34	56	71	66	-31	-34	-52
12. Protect	-11	-29	-11	86	85	89	-11	01	-12	23	22	08
13. Hinder	50	78	68	-28	-29	-35	-12	-07	-21	-64	-20	-38
14. Show Respect for	-37	-54	-11	66	41	14	44	55	92	14	-07	06
15. Concede	-12	-20	-05	-01	-27	07	92	80	87	01	-20	19
16. Keep at a Distance	51	52	55	-77	-65	-63	-06	-11	-15	-13	17	-02
17. Compete with	17	76	51	05	-01	-17	-04	11	00	-92	-31	-70
18. Help	-46	-51	-05	79	72	89	-19	-01	01	19	07	04
19. Manipulate	21	40	66	37	26	52	-48	-43	-12	-39	-31	-08
20. Attract Attention of	-17	01	61	46	20	39	22	10	25	-29	-83	04

the other direction. The extremely rated role-pairs confirm this identification: **father** *to* **son** and *to* **daughter, employer** *to* **employee, doctor** *to* **patient, teacher** *to* **student** and **political leader** *to* **citizen** are all highly Supraordinate while all of their opposite role relations (e.g., **son** *to* **father, student** *to* **teacher**) are highly Subordinate. The fourth verb factor shows the least scale consistency. The only common theme seems to be Immorality: *Corrupt, Deceive, Hinder* and *Compete with* for Illinois; *Corrupt, Deceive* and *Attract the Attention of* for Hawaii; *Compete with, Confide in* (translated as *Disclose to), Deceive* and *Imitate* for Japan. The role-pairs consistently differentiated by these verbs are interesting, cross-sex parental and nurturent professional being what might be called Morally Alter-oriented (**mother** *to* **son, father** *to* **daughter, son** *to* **mother, daughter** *to* **father, doctor** *to* **patient, patient** *to* **doctor,** and **teacher** *to* **student,** but *not* **student** *to* **teacher**) and various remote relations (permitting immoral behavior?) being what might be called Immorally Ego-oriented (**person** *to* **opponent, light-skinned person** *to* **light-skinned person** and **light-skinned person** *to* **dark-skinned person** – but *not* **dark-skinned person** *to* **dark-skinned person**).

Some sharp differences in verb loadings are worth noting: *Corrupt* is less Dissociative but more Immoral for Illinoians; *Cooperate with* is less Formally Associative and more Intimately Associative for Japanese; *Hinder* is more Immoral for Americans; *Show Respect for* is less Intimately Associative for Japanese but much more Subordinate; *Compete with* is more Dissociative and much less Immoral for Hawaiians, but *Attract Attention of* is distinctly Immoral for the Hawaiians as compared with the others; *Help* is less Formally Associative for the Japanese than the other groups. If one assumes that the four verb factors are shared (based on the sets of verbs with consistent loadings), then these differences can be interpreted as differences in semantic coding for the three cultures involved.

Commonness of interpersonal verb factors was expected and, indeed, hoped for; what was not expected, and not exactly hoped for in the interest of cross-cultural comparisons, was the extraordinarily high correspondence of role-pair factors taken across the IPV's, as evident in Table 13. Since these factors tend to be unipolar, I will report only the highest loading role-pairs in each case. Role Factor I identifies itself as what might be called Nurturence (Supraordinate Associativeness); culture-common role relations loading high are **father** *to* **son, mother** *to* **son, employer** *to* **employee, doctor** *to* **patient, policeman** *to* **citizen, teacher** *to* **student** and **father** *to* **daughter,** and the lowest loading roles are **stranger** *to* **local person** and **person** *to* **opponent.** Role Factor II identifies itself as what might be called Dependence (Subordinate Associativeness); culture-common role relations are **employee** *to* **employer, patient** *to* **doctor, citizen** *to* **policeman,** and **student** *to* **teacher.** It is notable that the children to parents relations are *not* highly loaded, Factor II thus not

208

TABLE 13
Rotated Factors and Variances for Interpersonal Role-pairs
for Illinois (I), Hawaiian (H), and Japanese (J) Subjects

	I			II		
	I (28%)	H (39%)	J (36%)	I (18%)	H (20%)	J (27%)
1. Father-Son	.91	.89	.94	.03	.15	.11
2. Employee-Employer	.11	.36	.20	.88	.84	.90
3. Old-Young	.85	.88	.40	-.18	-.16	.04
4. Light Skinned-Another	.11	.40	.62	-.04	-.04	.22
5. Patient-Doctor	.19	.21	-.05	.72	.84	.90
6. Host-Guest	.55	.73	.72	.30	.43	.61
7. Wife-Husband	.64	.74	.66	.22	.27	.56
8. Person-Opponent	-.28	-.36	-.38	-.00	.02	-.31
9. Mother-Son	.87	.90	.85	.11	.19	.31
10. Citizen-Policeman	.01	.17	.17	.87	.83	.78
11. Man-Woman	.75	.78	.90	-.05	-.01	.10
12. One Sister-Another	.46	.72	.89	.04	.19	.14
13. Student-Teacher	.04	.26	-.09	.95	.85	.94
14. Brother-Sister	.70	.78	.76	.02	.31	.38
15. Stranger-Local	-.32	-.23	-.10	.77	.52	.51
16. One Neighbor-Another	.41	.61	.44	.28	.39	.46
17. Sales Person-Customer	.35	.50	.46	.44	.55	.67
18. Daughter-Father	.62	.65	.50	.37	.55	.76
19. Dark-Skinned-Light-Skinned	-.14	.00	-.17	.36	.55	.47
20. Girl-Girl Friend	.26	.57	.32	.01	.20	.19
21. Son-Father	.33	.46	.40	.53	.56	.72
22. Employer-Employee	.72	.76	.85	.35	.39	-.13
23. Young-Old	.39	.57	.73	.54	.58	.44
24. One Dark Skinned-Another	.37	.59	.66	.02	.20	.48
25. Doctor-Patient	.77	.90	.94	.10	.18	.18
26. Guest-Host	.46	.57	.10	.53	.57	.83
27. Husband-Wife	.65	.77	.83	.07	.19	.28
28. Boy-Boy Friend	.16	.48	.45	.15	.42	.30
29. Son-Mother	.70	.76	.65	.39	.47	.65
30. Policeman-Citizen	.74	.80	.84	.20	.30	.31
31. Woman-Man	.42	.37	.32	.08	.14	.57
32. Worker-Co-Worker	.43	.54	.57	.09	.19	.73
33. Teacher-Student	.78	.85	.90	.32	.31	.06
34. Sister-Brother	.67	.81	.55	.28	.33	.66
35. Local-Stranger	.25	.32	.12	.36	.34	.17
36. One Brother-Another	.30	.59	.87	.11	.32	.03
37. Customer-Sales Person	.21	-.02	.15	.76	.72	-.23
38. Father-Daughter	.88	.93	.95	.14	.22	.18
39. Light-Skinned-Dark Skinned	.06	.18	-.18	.20	.06	-.38
40. Citizen-His Political Leader	.27	.54	.19	.65	.74	.77

TABLE 13 (cont.)

	III			IV		
	I (11%)	J (8%)	H (10%)	I (27%)	J (17%)	H (9%)
1. Father-Son	.03	-.07	-.04	.33	.24	.13
2. Employee-Employer	-.15	.00	0.17	.31	.31	.05
3. Old-Young	-.10	-.15	-.58	.08	.19	-.16
4. Light Skinned-Another	.14	.14	.26	.83	.82	.53
5. Patient-Doctor	.31	.30	.25	.38	.25	.10
6. Host-Guest	.14	.12	.08	.63	.42	.00
7. Wife-Husband	.44	.22	.33	.53	.46	.32
8. Person-Opponent	-.71	-.71	-.78	-.32	-.06	-.12
9. Mother-Son	.25	.09	.19	.31	.25	.23
10. Citizen-Policeman	-.10	-.30	.10	-.06	-.12	.08
11. Man-Woman	.19	-.00	.05	.47	.47	.00
12. One Sister-Another	.23	.26	.03	.78	.48	.33
13. Student-Teacher	-.06	.02	-.11	-.05	.27	.07
14. Brother-Sister	.00	.02	-.04	.51	.10	.30
15. Stranger-Local	-.23	-.16	-.36	.05	.70	-.45
16. One Neighbor-Another	-.14	.12	.42	.82	.57	.50
17. Sales Person-Customer	-.01	-.14	.13	.42	.28	.09
18. Daughter-Father	.51	.34	.06	.31	.30	.21
19. Dark-Skinned-Light-Skinned	-.78	-.19	-.63	.11	.61	.10
20. Girl-Girl Friend	.06	.18	-.12	.93	.62	.83
21. Son-Father	.30	.39	.12	.60	.39	.29
22. Employer-Employee	-.42	-.26	-.14	.09	.04	-.14
23. Young-Old	.33	.30	-.14	.52	.33	.29
24. One Dark Skinned-Another	.33	.23	-.06	.80	.70	.40
25. Doctor-Patient	.12	.02	-.00	.46	.28	.16
26. Guest-Host	.09	.05	.26	.63	.49	.24
27. Husband-Wife	.30	.17	.20	.64	.47	.30
28. Boy-Boy Friend	-.09	.13	.04	.84	.43	.62
29. Son-Mother	.38	.25	.15	.31	.20	.15
30. Policeman-Citizen	-.30	-.09	-.17	.38	.18	.01
31. Woman-Man	.26	-.05	.10	.50	.58	.17
32. Worker-Co-Worker	-.12	-.06	.16	.83	.73	.19
33. Teacher-Student	-.28	-.26	-.25	-.28	.07	.17
34. Sister-Brother	.11	.08	.00	.54	.30	.42
35. Local-Stranger	-.80	-.72	-.80	.15	.23	.05
36. One Brother-Another	.03	-.24	-.09	.90	.52	.38
37. Customer-Sales Person	-.28	-.37	-.80	-.07	.06	.28
38. Father-Daughter	.17	.06	-.01	.29	.11	.13
39. Light-Skinned-Dark-Skinned	-.81	-.91	-.68	-.41	-.16	-.42
40. Citizen-His Political Leader	-.23	-.05	-.19	.14	.07	-.15

210 CHARLES E. OSGOOD

being a mirror image of Factor I. Factor III identifies itself neatly as an Intimacy/Remoteness dimension, and it is more bipolar; relatively Intimate relations for all cultures are **patient** *to* **doctor, wife** *to* **husband, husband** *to* **wife, son** *to* **mother** and (excepting Japanese) **daughter** *to* **father**, but *not* **father** *to* **daughter** or **son** nor **mother** *to* **son**. The very Remote relations are **person** *to* **opponent, local person** *to* **stranger** (but not reverse) and **light-skinned person** *to* **dark-skinned person**. Role Factor IV identifies itself with equal clarity as what I shall call Egalitarianism, the high loading relations are **light-skinned person** *to* **another, one neighbor** *to* **another, girl** *to* **girl friend, boy** *to* **boy friend** and **one dark-skinned person** *to* **another** while the lowest loading relations are, most interestingly, **light-skinned person** *to* **dark-skinned person** and **person** *to* **opponent**, the former being more extreme than the latter.

Within this overall pattern of similarity, there are differences that are both consistent and intriguing. On Nurturence (Factor I) the Japanese students see **old** *to* **young** relations as less so and **young** *to* **old** as more so. **Man** *to* **woman, husband** *to* **wife** and **brother** *to* **another** are also seen as more Nurturent (protective?) by the Japanese. The Illinois subjects attribute much less Nurturence to **sister, brother** and **boy friend** relations than the other groups, as well as to **young** toward **old** and **light-skinned** toward **dark**; only in **sister** to **brother** and **citizen** toward **political leader** do Hawaiians see more Nurturence. As to Dependence (II) differences are all on the Japanese side — **wives** more on **husbands, women** more on **men, dark-skinned** more on **each other, hosts** more on **guests** and **workers** more on **co-workers**; for both **daughter** *to* **father** and **son** *to* **father** relations, a trend of increasing Dependence is noticeable from Illinoians through Hawaiians to Japanese; and whereas **customers** are highly dependent upon **sales persons** for both groups of Americans, they are decidely not so for Japanese. On the Intimacy/ Remoteness dimension (III), **customers** are extremely Remote from **sales persons** for Japanese, as are **old** from **young** and vice versa, as compared with the American groups. Illinoians see **employers** as more Remote from **employees** while Hawaiians, appropriately enough, see much less Remoteness between **dark-skinned** and **light-skinned** persons. The **daughter** toward **father** (but *not* **son** toward **father**) relations are progressively less Intimate from Illinoians through Hawaiians of Japanese ancestry to native Japanese.

Finally, on Egalitarianism (Factor IV) we observe a remarkably consistent trend on many role relations for Illinoians to be most Egalitarian, Hawaiians to be in the middle and Japanese to be least Egalitarian — in family relations (**wife** *to* **husband** and reverse, **one sister** *to* **another, son** *to* **father**) as well as social and professional relations (**guest** *to* **host** and reverse, **young** *to* **old, sales person** *to* **customer, policeman** *to* **citizen, worker** *to* **co-worker** and **doctor** *to* **patient** and reverse). The Hawaiian students stand out in seeing **light-skinned** *to* **dark-skinned** and the reverse as relatively *more* Egalitarian and **brother** *to* **sister** and the reverse as relatively *less* Egalitarian. In fact they stand at opposite poles from the Japanese in this respect as far as relations between **strangers** and **local persons**. The Japanese differ sharply from both American groups in attributing less Egalitarianism to the relation between **man** and **woman** — in both directions.

Do the a priori semantic features of interpersonal verbs display any consistent relations to the norms of interperson behavior, as inferred from the role differential? Several severe limitations of the present data must be emphasized as cautions against over-interpretation. First, the a priori features apply to American English at best, the hypothesis of universality remaining to be demonstrated. The IPV factor analyses given in Table 12 provide evidence for two types of Associativeness (Formal and Intimate), for a common Supraordinate/Subordinate feature, and perhaps for some combination of Moral and Ego/Alter features, but there is no evidence for other features. Second, the over-all similarities in the patterning of judgments about role relations across these cultures, evident in Table 13, will certainly reduce the likelihood of discovering fine differences in semantic feature assignments. And there remain, of course, questions as to the validity of some of the a priori features and the coding of IPV's on all of them.

One must also question the notion of "semantic anomaly" when applied to assertions relating role-pairs and interpersonal verbs. Since all IPV's by definition, so to speak, share higher-order codings on Transitiveness, Concreteness, Animateness and Humanness, any role subject or any role object should be semantically acceptable with any IPV. Thus **fathers** *Imitate* **successful people** but not ***Pebbles** *Imitate* **successful people** and **sons** *often Defy* **fathers** but not ***Sons** *often Defy* **pebbles**. Therefore it is not *semantically* anomalous for any role-pair to accept any IPV, and one can certainly imagine some human societies in which the assertion **fathers** *Imitate* **sons** would be entirely appropriate. Nevertheless, in most human societies it is *culturally* "anomalous" for **fathers** *To Imitate* **sons**, and so it would appear that "cultural features" corresponding to the semantic features of interpersonal verbs have been assigned or attributed to Actor-Object role-pairs. If such is the case, then one should be able to infer the cultural features of role-pairs from the shared semantic features of the IPV's that are considered appropriate or inappropriate in association with them.

As a first step in inferring such "cultural features," all role-pairs for each culture having mean appropriateness values on verbs greater than 5.0 (i.e., judged "usually" or "always") were assigned the feature code-strips for those IPV's. They were then assigned the inverse code-strips (signs reversed) for those IPV's on which they had appropriateness values less than 3.0 (i.e., judged "seldom" or "never"). In the summation over all IPV's meeting these criteria, a ratio of 4-to-1 plus-over-minus, or the reverse, was required for assigning that coding to the role-pair on a given feature.

As could have been predicted from the factor analyses of roles, the "cultural features" of role-pairs proved to be very similar for Illinoians, Hawaiians and Japanese. A few marked differences do appear, however: **employee** *to* **employer** is + Moral for H (Hawaiian) and J (Japanese), but zero for I (Illinois); **old** *to* **young** is Alter-oriented for I and J but zero for H, for whom, however, it is Impulsive; **person** *to* **opponent** is + Potent for I and H, but zero for J; **citizen** *to* **policeman** is Passive for H and J but zero for I. **Student** *to* **teacher** is Impotent, Passive and Past-oriented for J, but zero on these features for H and I; **stranger** *to* **local person** is Dissociative for I, but zero for H and J; **neighbor** *to* **neighbor** is coded Moral, Associative and Subordinate for H, but zero on these features for I and J; **daughter** *to* **father** is Initiating for I and not for H and J, but Subordinate for H and J and not for I; both **daughter** *to* **father** and **son** *to* **father** are coded Past-oriented by J, but zero by H and I; and, finally, **worker** *to* **co-worker** is not Active and Future-oriented for J, as it is for I and H, but it is Subordinate for J.

General culture differences between Illinoians, Hawaiians of Japanese ancestry and native Japanese have already been noted in connection with the verb and role factor analyses. If we think of the Hawaiians as a group in transition between two cultures, Japanese and American, we may now ask in terms of particular role-behavior norms about some of the details of this process of culture change. All 800 tri-culture sets of role-pair/verb appropriateness means were inspected; any item displaying a difference equal to or larger than 0.9 scale units for any pair of cultures was assigned to one of four categories:

(I) $I = H > J$ Hawaiians and Illinoians more alike and differing from Japanese

(II) $I > H = J$ Hawaiians and Japanese more alike and differing from Illinoians

(III) $I > H > J$ progression from Illinoians to Hawaiians to Japanese

(IV) $H > I = J$ Hawaiians differing from both American and Japanese cultures

Items in Category I presumably reflect American norms which have been largely adopted by Hawaiians of Japanese ancestry, and this constitutes the largest group of differences (150 of 800 items, or 19 percent). Items in Category II presumably reflect Japanese norms which have tended to be preserved (42 items, or 5 percent) and those in Category III reflect retardation in culture change (17 items, or 2 percent). Items in Category IV presumably reflect either "overshooting" of the American norms or norms unique to the multi-racial Hawaiian situation (35 items, 4 percent).

Clearly, the over-all picture is one of adaptation to American norms, but can we identify the regions of relatively complete and relatively retarded adaption, as well as those which appear to be uniquely Hawaiian? Table 14 lists the items falling in the four categories simultaneously according to role-pairs and interpersonal verbs involved. The differences for particular role-pairs are worthy of inspection.[40] For example: Hawaiians of Japanese ancestry are like other Americans in seeing **daughters** as *Confiding in* and *Protecting* but also as *Conceding to, not Competing with* and *not Imitating* **fathers** (generally Associative, alter-oriented behaviors); Hawaiians are more like Japanese in seeing **daughters** as *not Defying, not Pleading with, not Manipulating* and *not Displaying Affection toward* **fathers** (generally negative on Initiating, Future-oriented and Ego-oriented behaviors). (Note that we say *not* in this case because Column 2 is oriented in terms of I being "greater than" H and J.) Another example: Hawaiians are more like Illinoians in seeing **students** as both *Cooperating with* and *Manipulating* **teachers**, but they are more like Japanese in *Protecting* and *not Ridiculing* **teachers** (Column 2) as well as tending toward the Japanese in *not Deceiving, not Criticizing*, and *not Attracting the Attention of* **teachers** (Column 3). And a third example: Hawaiians are like Illinoians in seeing **neighbors** as *Cooperating with, Confiding in* and *Helping* **each other**; they are like the Japanese in seeing **neighbors** as *not Manipulating* and *not Competing with* **each other** the way most Americans do!

Can we generalize about IPV usage across roles and see what features seem to be operating? The verbs which tend to appear in Column 1 but not in Columns 2 and 3 (i.e., behaviors shared by Illinoians and Hawaiians as against Japanese) are *Console, Cooperate with, Protect, Show Respect for* and *Help*; in terms of the a priori features, these verbs would be characterized as dominantly Moral, Associative, and Alter-oriented. Verbs having the reverse pattern of appearance (i.e., behaviors tending to be shared by the Hawaiians and Japanese as against the Illinoians) are *Ridicule, Criticize, Manipulate* and *Attract Attention*; these verbs would be characterized as sharing Active, Deliberate, Terminal and Supraordinate features. In other words, these behaviors would seem to be aspects of American culture which the Hawaiians of Japanese ancestry have *resisted* taking over. Verbs which appear most frequently in Column 4 (i.e., behaviors perhaps most uniquely characterizing the Hawaiian culture) are *Console, not Imitate, not Corrupt, not Deceive, not*

---

[40] A little guidance in interpreting Table 14 may be helpful here. First, all "values" are relative; the table says that Illinoians see **fathers** as *ridiculing* **sons** more than either Hawaiians or Japanese — but even for Illinoians the median judgment is only "sometimes." Second, because each column is labeled to indicate all mean values of one group which were greater than (>) those of the others, the IPV's on which the group's mean values were *not* greater, but lesser, have been prefixed by *not*. For example, we say "**Father** *not Display Affection for* **son**" in Column 1 because Column 1 is oriented in terms of I and H being greater than J, and on this IPV, J had a significantly greater, not lesser, mean value than I and H.

TABLE 14

Interpersonal Verbs Differentiating Role Relations Cross-culturally

	I = H > J*	I > H = J	I > H > J	H > I = J
FA/SON	not Display Affection Protect	Ridicule Manipulate	Criticize	not Compete with
SON/FA	not Display Affection Protect Help	Deceive	Attract Attention	
FA/DAU	not Imitate	Plead with	Ridicule	not Display Affection
DAU/FA	not Imitate Confide in Protect Concede to not Compete with	Defy Display Affection Plead with Manipulate		
MO/SON	not Imitate	Criticize		not Manipulate
SON/MO	not Imitate	Defy Attract Attention		not Deceive
SIS/SIS	Imitate Confide in	Criticize Compete with		not Deceive
BRO/BRO	Imitate not Display Affection not Console Plead with Confide in			not Deceive
SIS/BRO	Plead with Criticize Protect Manipulate	Defy Attract Attention		not Imitate not Help
BRO/SIS	Defy Ridicule Console Criticize Confide in	Compete with Manipulate	Attract Attention	

WIF/HUS	not Imitate not Corrupt		Criticize	Console not Plead with	not Imitate not Corrupt
HUS/WIF	Confide in Attract Attention of				
WO/MAN	not Imitate Cooperate with Confide in Compete with Manipulate	Display Affection Ridicule	Help Attract Attention		
MAN/WO	not Imitate Console Confide in		Display Affection	not Concede to	
OLD/YG	Console Protect not Keep Distance Help	Corrupt	Display Affection		
YG/OLD	not Console Plead with Confide in Compete with	Criticize			
TCH/STU	Manipulate	Criticize			
STU/TCH	Cooperate with Manipulate	Ridicule not Protect	Deceive Criticize Attract Attention	Console not Plead with	
DR/PAT	not Display Affection not Cooperate with not Deceive Confide in			not Ridicule	
PAT/DR	not Imitate Deceive not Plead with Confide in Concede to Help				
EMP/EE	not Display Affection	Criticize	not Console		not Defy not Compete with

TABLE 14 (cont.)

EE/EMP	not Plead with	not Help	not Imitate
POL/CIT	not Display Affection Console not Concede to Keep at a Distance Manipulate	Criticize	Imitate
CIT/POL	Deceive Hinder Concede to Keep at a Distance	not Cooperate with Criticize Attract Attention	
GIRL/GF	Help		
BOY/BF			not Criticize not Compete with
HOST/GST	not Plead with Help	Cooperate with Compete with	
GST/HOST	Cooperate with not Plead with Protect Help	not Imitate	
LOC/STR	Cooperate with Criticize Compete with Manipulate		Help
STR/LOC	Defy Imitate Concede to Compete with Attract Attention		Confide in
NBR/NBR	Cooperate with Confide in Help	Compete with Manipulate	Console
WK/COWK	Console Compete with Manipulate		Ridicule

SP/CUST	not Display Affection Deceive not Plead with not Protect not Compete with Help		Hinder Manipulate	not Imitate
CUST/SP	Cooperate with not Protect Concede to not Compete with Attract Attention			Criticize Confide in
CIT/LEAD	not Plead with	not Deceive		not Imitate not Corrupt not Attract Attention
L-SK/L-SK	Defy Display Affection Attract Attention	Imitate		not Manipulate
D-SK/D-SK	Display Affection Console Confide in Protect	Corrupt Attract Attention	Compete with	
L-SK/D-SK	not Attract Attention			not Defy not Criticize
D-SK/L-SK	Protect Attract Attention	Defy not Display Affection Ridicule		
PER/OPP	Defy Hinder Compete with not Help Manipulate		Deceive	not Keep Distance

*Column 1 does not include 29 cases of I = H J on *To Show Respect for*, J displaying less for all roles except EE/EMP, PAT/DOC, WIF/HUS, CIT/POL, STU/TCH, DAU/FA, D-SK/L-SK, SON/MO, WK/COWK, L-SK/D-SK, and CIT/LEAD.

Criticize and *not Compete with;* the shared semantic features of this set are interesting — Morally Associative and Alter-oriented, like other behaviors Hawaiians share with Illinoians, more Passive like the Japanese, and distinctively Impulsive (rather than Deliberate).

The only role-pairs for which there are more differentiating verbs in Columns 2 and 3 (Hawaiian/Japanese affinites) than in Column 1 (Hawaiian/ Illinoian affinities) are **father** *to* **son, father** *to* **daughter, son** *to* **mother, student** *to* **teacher, employer** *to* **employee** and **dark-skinned person** *to* **light-skinned person.** In general, there are not enough differentiating verbs in the different categories for particular role-pairs to warrant interpretation. However, it is possible to collapse the role relations into certain components: Sex, Age, Status and Egalitarianism. The feature codings of the IPV's associated with each role-pair displaying a given component (e.g., **man** *to* **woman,** +Sex) under each category (e.g., I = H > J) were tabulated and inspected for points of gross cultural difference.

Sex component. The +Sex role-pairs consisted of **father** *to* **daughter, son** *to* **mother, brother** *to* **sister, husband** *to* **wife** and **man** *to* **woman.** Illinois (I) and Hawaiian (H) subjects agree, and differ from the Japanese (J), in the attribution of behaviors to males which are Supraordinate and Past-oriented; H and J agree, and differ from I, in having Males more often display Alter-oriented behaviors; I subjects depart from both H and J in having more Male behaviors that are simultaneously Ego and Future Oriented toward Females *(Pleading, Defying, Competing, Manipulating).* The —Sex role-pairs are the reverse of the above, of course (**daughter** *to* **father, mother** *to* **son** etc.). Americans (H and I) differ from Japanese in having Females behave more Associatively but also more Supraordinately and Deliberately toward Males; H and J differ from I in having Females behave more Passively and Reactively toward Males.

Age component. The +Age role-pairs are **father** *to* **son, father** *to* **daughter, mother** *to* **son, old** *to* **young** and **teacher** *to* **student.** Americans (I and H) differ from Japanese in seeing the Old as being more Potently and Supraordinately Alter-oriented toward the Young, whereas Illinoians differ from both H and J in the tendency to attribute behaviors to the Old which are more Actively Supraordinate (e.g., *Ridiculing, Criticizing, Corrupting*). Again, it should be kept in mind that these are all *relative* differences. For the —Age role-pairs (opposites of above), Americans see the Young as being more Initiating and Deliberate toward the Old, whereas H and J agree in seeing the Young as being more Impulsive and Interminal in their relations with the Old.

Status component. The +Status role-pairs include both professional and social relations: **teacher** *to* **student, doctor** *to* **patient, employer** *to* **employee, policeman** *to* **citizen, customer** *to* **sales person** and (things being as they are) **light-skinned person** *to* **dark-skinned person.** The only marked difference here is that Illinoians see High Status persons as being less Associative in their behaviors toward Low Status persons than the other cultures. This contrast is even more marked for the —Status role-pairs, with Illinoians tending to attribute behaviors to Low Status persons which are not only less Associative but also relatively more Active, Terminal and Supraordinate. Both American groups agree, and differ from the Japanese, in seeing Low Status people as behaving more Deliberately (calculatedly?) with respect to High Status people.

Egalitarianism. This is treated as a uni-polar component. The role-pairs considered logically Egalitarian are **sister** *to* **sister, brother** *to* **brother, girl** *to* **girl friend, boy** *to* **boy friend, neighbor** *to* **neighbor, worker** *to* **co-worker, light-skinned person** *to* **light-skinned person** and **dark-skinned person** *to* **dark-skinned person.** We have already noted in the role factor analysis that Americans generally tend to attribute the most Egalitarianism to these parallel roles and Japanese the least. What about differences in the (English) a priori features of the verbs which distinguish the cultures for these role relations? Americans (I and H) differ from Japanese in seeing these role relations as more Moral, Active, Initiating and Ego-oriented (a more competitive Egalitarianism?); H and J agree on behaviors which are more Passive and Alter-oriented (a more cooperative Egalitarianism?); and Hawaiians stand out in attributing Morality (even more than their agreement with Illinoians), Associativeness and particularly Impulsiveness to these Egalitarian relations (*not Deceive, not Criticize, not Compete with, not Manipulate,* but *Console*).

This exploratory study with a Role Differential was our first attempt to fuse semantic feature analysis with cross-cultural research on interpersonal norms. It was premature, in that we have still to validate and stabilize our analysis procedures and demonstrate generality of the features derived. It is probably best construed as a methodological demonstration of what *might* be done cross-culturally with better materials. Even within these limitations, I find the results very encouraging. The verb factors — including Formal Associative/Dissociative, Intimate/Remote, Supraordinate/Subordinate and some fusion of Morality and Ego/Alter Orientation — are very similar to those reported in related research by Triandis and his associates with American, Indian and Japanese cultures (Triandis, Shanmugam and Tanaka, 1966) and with American and Greek cultures (Triandis, Vassiliou and Nassiakou, 1968). These investigators have developed what they call a Behavioral Differential; it differs from the Role Differential, as used here, in that (a) many of the IPV's refer to observable behaviors (e.g., *throw rocks at, go to movies with*) rather than more abstract intentions and (b) there is no explicit selection of IPV's in terms of previously analysed semantic features.

Does analysis in terms of differences in semantic and "cultural" feature coding contribute in any way? Within the limitations noted earlier, many of the distinctions drawn are consistent with my own observations during a year in Hawaii and several visits to Japan. To cite examples: the greater and more competitive Egalitarianism (Active, Initiating and Ego-oriented) of the American culture as compared with the Japanese, including the American perception of low status individuals as more Dissociatively and Actively Supraordinate in their behavior toward High status individuals; the uniquely Hawaiian stress on Impulsive and Moral Associativeness among people, among equals as well as among unequals; the more Actively Supraordinate behaviors of older Americans toward younger, along with general acceptance by Americans (but not Hawaiians and Japanese) of more overtly aggressive behaviors toward others (e.g., *Criticizing, Ridiculing, Manipulating* and the like); the greater Ego-orientation, Deliberateness and Supraordinateness of the American female toward the male — this showing up particularly in **daughter** *to* **father** relations — coupled with the American male's greater competitiveness with the female (Ego and Future-oriented); the more Passive, Impotent and Subordinate role of the Japanese student with respect to his teacher as compared with the more competitive American student.

Of course, since casual observations on "national character" have an ink-blottish and projective nature, apparent consistency of these data with my own observations does not constitute very strong evidence. On the other hand, Triandis, Shanmugam and Tanaka (1966) also report on the relatively greater supraordinateness of the Japanese male and the American female, on the "greater importance of subordination and respect in the Japanese than in the American Behavioral Differential," and on the fact that "older people may not be liked, but they are respected" by the Japanese. The potential value of linking comparative studies of interpersonal norms to the (hopefully universal) semantics of interpersonal verbs is that this can provide a standardized, stable and reasonably rigorous basis for the comparisons.

CRITICAL SUMMARY

As I observed early in this paper, the appropriate method of analysis of a semantic domain depends upon how that domain is "in truth" organized. One of the difficulties of research in this area is that we do not know on a priori grounds how particular domains are arranged — and worse, we have good reasons to suspect that different domains are quite differently and even inconsistently arranged. To get an idea of at least some of the possibilities, observe the five "types" of possible semantic systems described in Figure 11. Only three variables are treated here: *nested* vs. *replicated* features, *ordered* vs. *unordered* features, and *independent* vs. *dependent* (or *contingent*) features. Many other variables could have been considered: unipolar vs. bipolar feature systems (items being marked or unmarked rather than + or —), binary vs. trinary vs. continuous feature systems, and so forth.

The Type I system (nested, ordered, independent) is called a "taxonomic

FIGURE 11

Some Types of Semantic Systems

I Nested, Ordered, Independent Feature Hierarchy

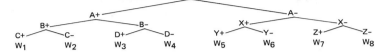

II Replicated, Ordered, Independent Feature Hierarchy

III Replicated, Ordered, Dependent Feature Hierarchy

IV Replicated, Unordered, Independent Feature Matrix

	W_1	W_2	W_3	W_4	W_5	W_6	W_7	W_8
FA	+	+	+	+	–	–	–	–
FB	+	–	+	–	+	–	+	–
FC	+	+	–	–	+	+	–	–

V Replicated, Unordered, Dependent Feature Matrix

	W_1	W_2	W_3	W_4	W_5	W_6	W_7	W_8
FA	+	+	+	0	0	–	–	–
FB	+	+	0	+	–	0	–	–
FC	+	0	–	+	–	+	0	–

hierarchy," I believe. It is the only nested system given, for nesting presupposes both hierarchical ordering and independence of features (because either B+ or B– can only occur when A is +, B cannot be correlated with A). This is the most constrained system. Only when the higher-order feature has been determined does it make sense to ask about any lower-order feature; only when a term is marked as Concrete (rather than Abstract) does it make sense to ask if it is Animate or Inanimate, only when it has been marked Animate does it make sense to ask if it is Animal or Vegetable, and so forth down the nested hierarchy. Furthermore, each distinguishing feature appears only once in the system, e.g., Animal/Vegetable cannot appear anywhere under the nodes marked Abstract or Inanimate. It is also characteristic of such systems that all supraordinate categories must be marked 0 on all of the features of its nested subordinate categories; Animal must be marked 0 on Vertebrate/Invertebrate, Human/Non-human, Male/Female and so forth, even though it is reasonable to ask if an animal is Vertebrate or Invertebrate, etc.

In elaborating and testing a theory of sorting, George Miller (1968) concluded that his free-sorting discovery procedure (cf., pp. 159-161 here) was ideally suited to semantic systems of this nesting type, but that multi-dimensional scaling procedures were more appropriate for what he called "paradigmatic" organizations (Type IV here). His free sorting procedure proved to be reasonably successful with nouns but not with verbs. The system for Thai pronouns also seems to approximate this arrangement (see Figure 10 here). However, even within the taxonomic system for nouns used as an example above, inconsistencies appear below the node marked Human (vs. Non-Human): although a Married/Single feature is nested within Mature (as opposed to Immature), Mature/Immature can be asked sensibly about either Male or Female and vice versa, so both nesting and hierarchical ordering principles are violated.

In Type II systems (replicated, ordered, independent) each semantic feature is applicable to all terms (W_1 through W_8 in the diagrams), but the *order* in which decisions are made must be maintained. In the pure or ideal case, it would be absurd to ask if a word was B+ or B− before deciding whether it was A+ or A−. In a sensitive intuitive analysis, Vendler (1967, Ch. 4) derives a two-feature system of this type for English verbs with respect to the time dimension. The supraordinate feature is Action vs. State: one can say significantly *I am pushing it* (Action verb), but it is strange to say *I am knowing it* (State verb); conversely, one can answer the question *Do you know ..?* sensibly by saying *I do*, but there seems to be no sensible answer to the question *Do you push ..?* The subordinate feature is Terminal vs. Interminal (my terms, not Vendler's): one can reasonably ask *How long did it take to dress?* (Terminal Action verb) but not really *For how long did you dress?* The situation is the reverse for *push* (an Interminal Action verb). Similarly, one can ask *At what time did you meet the girl?* (Terminal State verb) but not really *For how long did you meet the girl?* The situation is likewise the reverse for *know* (an Interminal State verb). Although there are some verbs with fuzzy edges (by virtue of having several senses), as Vendler acknowledges, these features seem necessary, if not sufficient, for the semantic characterization of verbs-in-general.[41] Vendler refers to the four verb categories established by these features as "Activities" (Interminal Actions), "Accomplishments" (Terminal Actions), "Achievements" (Terminal States) and "States" (Interminal States). Note that one cannot decide on the appropriate Terminal/Interminal questions until he has answered the Action/State question — hence the ordered, hierarchical nature of the system.

---

[41] In asking these questions of a sample of 40 of our interpersonal verbs, I find a nearly perfect correlation of Vendler's Action vs. State with our Active/Passive feature and of his Definite (*the* time stretch or instant) vs. Indefinite (*a* or *any* time stretch) with our Terminal/Interminal feature.

In "pure" systems of Types I and II, the basis of ordering is logical inclusion. However, there may also be ordering on the basis of psychological salience, and the latter clearly plays some role in the semantics of interpersonal verbs. Throughout the analyses reported in this chapter the Associative/Dissociative feature has been the dominant mode for characterizing interpersonal verbs, this typically being followed by Supraordinate/ Subordinate and Ego-orientation/Alter-orientation. The other features, to the extent that they appear at all — Morality, Dynamism, Terminality, Time-orientation and the like — seem to merely refine the basic semantic categories already established. What is not clear is the performance implications of psychological salience as compared with logical inclusion. Whereas "inclusion" would definitely imply temporal ordering of decisions, "salience" could merely imply differences in the weights or generalities of features.

The Type III semantic system shown in Figure 11 (replicated, ordered, dependent) differs from Type II in that the features are not independent of each other. To illustrate the situation as diagrammed, an interpersonal verb must be Associative (+A) if it is to be Subordinate (−B) and Dissociative (−A) if it is to be Supraordinate (+B), and it must be both Associative and Subordinate (+A, −B) if it is to be Moral (+C) or both Dissociative and Supraordinate (−A, +B) if it is to be Immoral (−C). This situation is approximated by our data, but only approximated; for example, IPV *Seduce* is Supraordinate and Immoral but not Dissociative and IPV *Defy* is clearly Dissociative but neither Supraordinate nor Immoral. Note that this kind of system, in its extreme form, resembles the nested hierarchy, but that the "limbs" of subordinate features are bifurcated, and separated within the tree. Any correlational discovery procedure will tend to fuse such dependent features into single factors — in the present case, an Associative-Subordinate-Moral vs. Dissociative-Supraordinate-Immoral factor. Yet, logically speaking, three distinct features are operating, the lower ones in the hierarchy serving to further distinguish terms already grossly distinguished by the higher features.

If a semantic system is unordered, then any "tree" diagram is both arbitrary and misleading. The unordered system instead must be represented by a Feature-By-Term Matrix or, equivalently, by an N-Dimensional Spatial Model, in which the features are dimensions and the terms are locations. In the Type IV semantic system (replicated, unordered, independent), the features are uncorrelated and the dimensions are orthogonal; in the Type V system (replicated, unordered, dependent), the features are correlated and the dimensions are oblique with respect to each other. For simplicity of exposition, in the diagrams in Figure 11 I have assumed discreteness in coding, although I am sure this is not the general situation in semantics. Such discreteness gives a simplistic system toward which behavioral principles may tend, but only occasionally reach. It should be noted that my own representational mediation theory of meaning (in which the meaning of a sign is that simultaneous "bundle" of distinctive mediating reaction components elicited by the sign, termed its r_m) implies an unordered system although it does not rule out differences in salience and does not make any assumptions about discrete vs. continuous coding.

Pure Type IV systems (features independent) seem to be rare in semantics — at least I cannot think of any. I believe the Turkish vowel phonemic system is of this type; three distinctive phonetic features (tongue high/tongue low, tongue front/tongue back, lips rounded/lips flat) generate a complete eight-phoneme system, neatly representable as the corners of a cube. Our affective E-P-A (Evaluation, Potency, Activity) system approximates this, but E has much more weight than P and A. Kinship systems ("paradigmatic" according to Miller, 1968) approximate Type IV, but again usually imperfectly. The American English kinship system, for example, is unordered in the sense that questions about Sex (Male/Female) seem to have no logical priority over questions about Generation (+Ego, 0 Ego, −Ego) or Consanguinity (Blood-related/Blood-non-related). Furthermore, it is replicated, in the sense that one may ask about the Sex of any Generationally defined member (and vice versa), about the Generation of any Consanguinally defined member (and vice versa), and so on. But questions about Lineality ("Is X in my lineage or not? My *mother* is but my *aunt* is not.") only make sense when Consanguinity has already been determined to be positive. Therefore this kinship system is partially nested, and hence neither perfectly unordered nor perfectly replicated.

The Type V system (features to various degrees dependent or correlated) probably holds for many semantic systems, and it greatly complicates empirical discovery procedures. Features A and B, as distributed in Figure 11 (V), are highly correlated, as are features B and C; features A and C, on the other hand, are independent (zero correlation). Only an oblique factor analysis (or feature analysis) would "discover" the three underlying features, and oblique analyses are difficult to interpret in my experience. The results of all of our studies suggest this Type V system, with "fused" rather than independent features, but nothing readily interpretable has emerged from oblique factor analyses. However, the data also clearly imply a system partially ordered in terms of the psychological salience of the features.

In sum, it would appear that the semantic system for interpersonal verbs (1) is not nested, (2) is partially replicated (features applying to all terms only when zero codings are allowed), (3) is partially ordered (but in terms of psychological salience rather than logical inclusion), and (4) is partially dependent (with features correlated in usage to various degrees). This is obviously not the neatest kind of system to study.

Not only is a particular empirical discovery procedure appropriate to a semantic domain of a particular type, but when it is applied to a domain of a *different* type it will tend to force the data toward correspondence with the system for which it is appropriate. Fortunately, our intuitions as native speakers enable us to note the absurdities which must result. Thus when Miller's free sorting procedure was applied to verbs it presumably yielded a "nested" system, but not apparently an intuitively satisfying one. Miller did not present these results because, as he said (1967), "I do not yet understand them." And thus when our factor and feature analytic procedures, which are most appropriate for a pure Type IV paradigmatic system, are applied, they do yield independent factors, but when these factors are compared with the a priori features it becomes clear that the semantic system of interpersonal verbs is not of this straightforward type either.

The resolution is at once obvious and complicated: *restrict the semantic domain under study to a pure type of system and then apply the appropriate discovery procedure.* If the domain is even partially ordered by logical inclusion (Types I, II, and III), then one must ask first questions first a la Vendler and thereby divide the domain into subdomains, all of which are at the same hierarchical level and each of which contains terms with the same supraordinate features. If these subdomains do include more than one term and they are not synonymous (which seems most likely for the major form classes), then multivariate procedures of the sort we have employed should be appropriate for the discovery of finer semantic feature distinctions. In part, this is what we did by restricting our domain to interpersonal verbs − a subdomain of verbs defined by the sharing of certain higher-order features.

Working in the domain of adjectives, and applying the three-mode factoring method developed by Ledyard Tucker (1966), John Limber[42] has made such a serial approach explicit. The three modes were sentence frames (N = 10), nouns (N = 10) and adjectives (N = 50). The sentence frames were deliberately selected to differentiate the major types of adjectives in terms of syntactic derivation, e.g.:

(1) The N that they did it was A.
(2) It was A of the N to do it.
(3) The N was A about something.

The nouns were deliberately selected to represent major semantic categories, e.g., *man, horse, team, tree, computer, pebble, fact.* Simple acceptability judgments of each of the 5,000 possible combinations (*The fact that they did it was obvious; The computer that they did it was happy,* and so forth) and their latencies were obtained. Three frame factors account for a large share of

---

[42] Semantic Categorization of English Adjectives in Terms of Usage. Doctoral dissertation, University of Illinois, August, 1968.

the variance, and these do seem to tap higher-order semantic features. Frames 2 and 3 above, for example, both load on a factor requiring Animate subjects; for most speakers, it was absurd to say *It was A of the (tree, fact, gravity —* but not *computer) to do it,* but frame 3 accepts mental state adjectives (like *happy*) whereas frame 2 does not. However, *within* frames which accept particular nouns (with certain adjectives) and particular adjectives (with certain nouns), it is apparent that semantic interactions *between* these nouns and adjectives serve to further differentiate them. *The horse was happy about something* and *The man was strict about something* are both acceptable, but *The horse was strict about something* is clearly absurd. By analysis of usage distributions within the sub-domains defined by such sentence frames it would seem possible to get at lower-level semantic features. The problem of course, is to select those frames ("questions") which reliably differentiate higher-order features and have complete generality of application across the domain in question. Limber was guided in his selections by a great deal of prior linguistic spade-work.

Similar spade-work is required in the domain of interpersonal verbs. Much of it already has been done for verbs-in-general by linguists and philosophers of ordinary language, as exemplified by Vendler (1967) and Fillmore (1967). The features distinguished obviously relate to what is now referred to as the "deep" structure of the syntactic component, and I wonder how long it will be before the deep structure of the syntactic component and the semantic component become identified as the same thing. Fillmore seems to be thinking along similar lines when he includes among his closing words the following statement (p. 110): "If it is possible to discover a semantically justified universal syntactic theory along the lines I have been suggesting; if it is possible by rules, beginning, possibly, with those which assign sequential order to the underlying representations, to map these 'semantic deep structures' into the surface forms[43] of sentences; then it is likely that the 'syntactic deep structure' of the type that has been made familiar from the work of Chomsky and others is going to go the way of the phoneme." There is also a question as to whether the universals we have been discovering — certainly in the domain of affect and apparently as well in the domain of interpersonal behavior as reflected in language — are properly to be considered a part of semantics or a part of pragmatics. But questions like these go far beyond the scope of this paper, intended to be primarily methodological in nature.

---

[43] Precisely such a sequentially ordered scanning of a hierarchically ordered semantic system has been suggested by James E. Martin as an explanation of pre-nominal adjective ordering in the surface structure of English in his doctoral dissertation; A Study of the Determinants of Preferred Adjective order in English. University of Illinois, July, 1968.

REFERENCES

Amster, Harriet, 1964. Semantic Satiation and Generation: Learning? Adaptation? *Psychol. Bull.*, *62*, 273-286.
Berrien, F. K., 1966. Japanese Values and the Democratic Process. *J. Soc. Psychol.*, *68*, 129-138.
Chomsky, N., 1965. *Aspects of the Theory of Syntax*. Cambridge, Mass.: The M.I.T. Press.
Fillmore, C. J., 1967. *The Case for Case*. Ohio State University (Austin, Texas, April 13).
Harris, Z. S., 1954. Distributional Structure. *Word*, *10*, 146-162.
Hurley, J. R. and Cattell, R. B., 1962. The Procrustes Program: Producing Direct Rotation to Test a Hypothesized Factor Structure. *Behav. Sci.*, *7*, 258-262.
Jakobovits, L. A. and Lambert, W. E., 1967. A Note on the Measurement of Semantic Satiation. *J. Verb. Learn. Verb. Behav.*, *6*, 954-957.
Jakobson, R., 1959. Boas' View of Grammatical Meaning. *Amer. Anthropol.*, *61*, 139-145.
Jakobson, R. and Halle, M., 1956. *Fundamentals of Language*. 'sGravenhage (The Hague), Netherlands: Mouton.
Johnson, S. C., 1967. Hierarchical Clustering Schemes. *Psychometrika*, *32*, 241-254.
Kaiser, H., 1960. Relating Factors between Studies Based Upon Different Individuals. Unpubl. manuscript, University of Illinois.
Katz, Evelyn W., 1964. A Content-Analytic Method for Studying Interpersonal Behavior. Communication, Cooperation and Negotiation in Culturally Heterogeneous Groups, Tech. Report No. 19.
Lambert, W. E. and Jakobovits, L. A., 1963. The Case for Semantic Satiation. Department of Psychology, McGill University. (Mimeographed)
Miller, G. A., 1967. Psycholinguistic Approaches to the Study of Communication. In *Journeys in Science: Small Steps – Giant Strides*, ed D. L. Arm. Albuquerque, New Mexico: University of New Mexico Press.
Miller, G. A., 1968. A Psychological Method to Investigate Semantic Relations. Prepublication draft, The Rockefeller University, pp. 39.
Osgood, C. E., 1957. Motivational Dynamics of Language Behavior. In *The Nebraska Symposium on Motivation*, ed. M. R. Jones. Lincoln, Nebraska: University of Nebraska Press.
Osgood, C. E., 1964. Semantic Differential Technique in the Comparative Study of Cultures. *Amer. Anthropol.*, *66*, 171-200.
Osgood, C. E., 1968. Speculation on the Structure of Interpersonal Intentions. *Behav. Sci.*

Osgood, C. E., Suci, G. J., and Tannenbaum, P. H., 1957. The Measurement of Meaning. Urbana, Illinois: University of Illinois Press.

Osgood, C. E. and Tannenbaum, P. H., 1955. The Principle of Congruity in the Prediction of Attitude Change. *Psychol. Rev., 62,* 42-55.

Ryle, G., 1938. Categories. *Proc. Aristotelian Soc., 38,* 189-206.

Triandis, H. C., Shanmugam, A. V., and Tanaka, Y., 1966. Interpersonal Attitudes among American, Indian and Japanese Students. *Internat. J. Psychol., 1,* 177-206.

Triandis, H. C., Vassiliou, V., and Nassiakou, M., 1968. Three Cross-cultural Studies of Subjective Culture, *J. Person. Soc. Psychol., 1968, Monogr. Suppl., 8,* No. 4, Part 2, p. 42.

Tucker, L. R., 1966. Some Mathematical Notes on Three-Mode Factor Analysis. *Psychometrika, 31,* 279-311.

Vendler, Z., 1967. *Linguistics in Philosophy.* Ithica, N.Y.: Cornell University Press.